DRESSING UP

DRESSING UP

THE WOMEN WHO INFLUENCED FRENCH FASHION

ELIZABETH L. BLOCK

THE MIT PRESS
CAMBRIDGE, MASSACHUSETTS
LONDON, ENGLAND

The MIT Press would like to thank the anonymous peer reviewers who provided comments on drafts of this book. The generous work of academic experts is essential for establishing the authority and quality of our publications. We acknowledge with gratitude the contributions of these otherwise uncredited readers.

This book was set in Arnhem Pro and Frank New by Westchester Publishing Services. Printed and bound in the United States of America.

Library of Congress Cataloging-in-Publication Data

Names: Block, Elizabeth L., author.
Title: Dressing up : the women who influenced French fashion / Elizabeth L. Block.
Description: Cambridge, Massachusetts : The MIT Press, [2021] | Includes bibliographical references and index.
Identifiers: LCCN 2020036772 | ISBN 9780262045841 (hardcover)
Subjects: LCSH: Fashion—United States—History—19th century. | Fashion—France—History—19th century. | Women's clothing industry—France—History—19th century. | Women consumers—United States—History—19th century. | Affluent consumers—United States—History—19th century. | United States—Social life and customs—1865–1918.
Classification: LCC GT610 .B56 2021 | DDC 391.00973—dc23
LC record available at https://lccn.loc.gov/2020036772

10   9   8   7   6   5   4   3   2   1

For Judith M. Block, Dr. Michael J. Block, Seth R. Friedman,
Abbott Ruthson Block Friedman, Jennifer Block Martin, and Dr. Eric M. Block

CONTENTS

POWER DRESSING

1

INTRODUCTION

Dressing Up

French fashion of the late nineteenth century is known for its allure, its inimitable chic. For Parisian couturiers and their U.S. customers, it was also serious business. *Dressing Up: The Women Who Influenced French Fashion* examines the influential and discerning clientele of elite women who bolstered the French fashion industry through a steady stream of orders from the United States. The book engages the consumer perspective: it repositions wealthy U.S. women buyers as active participants in the large, transnational fashion system while looking critically at the cultural impulse toward all things French.

Consistent with their preferences in interior decoration and furniture, U.S. women favored French historical references in costumes for fancy dress balls, often presenting themselves in fashions associated with monarchs who met their ends at the guillotine. The choice of dressing in a couture outfit as Marie Antoinette is all the more bewildering when considered against the political and economic climate in the United States in the second half of the nineteenth century. In the midst of continuous labor strikes and periodic nationwide depressions, the wealthiest citizens were hosting extravagant social events while wearing costly outfits that recalled the ancien régime of France and its overthrow.

The enthusiasm for wearing monarchal attire in homes built to resemble French Renaissance châteaux is only one of the trends of the period. Women were navigating the change from buying mostly domestically manufactured clothing, along with some British and French imports, to having access through international networks to fashions that they considered to be of the finest design and production.

The rootedness in familiar local practices had produced an entrenched frugality that was not relinquished quickly and resulted in some wealthy women bargaining prices with French couturiers or bringing extra French fabric to a local dressmaker to produce supplementary pieces. And while they traveled to and placed orders with premier French couturiers, they also shopped at their city's department stores, the hallmarks of democratic marketplaces.

Underlying the women's choices and decisions was an extensive knowledge of fabric and dressmaking—what may be termed the culture's "high textile I.Q." Since the colonial period, women had been taught to sew and mend clothing and to clean and maintain various fabrics. This knowledge, passed through the generations, resulted in a respect for the attributes and particularities of textiles and informed the shopping practices of the wealthy and middle classes alike. They applied both visual and haptic skills to their decision making within the retail environment—viewing and handling fabrics, trimmings, and accessories to judge their quality and suitability.

The work of many researchers—sociologists Yuniya Kawamura and Joanne Entwistle, fashion theorist Elizabeth Wilson, design and fashion theorist Ulrich Lehmann, and fashion historian Alexandra Palmer—has laid the foundation for the present type of interdisciplinary study. Kawamura defines fashion as an institutionalized system in which groups of individuals collectively determine how dress functions to express certain aspects of the wearer's social, economic, or political standing at a given time.[1] *Dressing Up* does not perpetuate the concept of the couturier as a genius who directed all aspects of a brand's success, nor does it scrutinize the details of how garments were made. Rather, it explores how the lives of couture garments enrich our understanding of the French-U.S. fashion industry in the late nineteenth century. As in Lehmann's formulation, the emphasis here is on the seriousness of how fashion functions and contributes to the development of culture.[2] At several points, while appreciating Nancy J. Troy's formidable *Couture Culture: A Study in Modern Art and Fashion* and its probing of couture's inherent theatricality, the present text steers away from the method of demonstrating how one couturier crafted an image as an artist and connoisseur to maneuver the placement of his designs in the market.[3] Rather, the guiding principal is to "follow the dresses," a tack that opens onto an analysis of labor, gender, space, and performance and the ways in which they relate to fashion. The focus on women's consumerism necessitates that men's fashion, itself a rich topic, be set aside.

Engaging with insights by Heidi Brevik-Zender, Louise Crewe, and John Potvin on the geographies and spaces of fashion, the study radiates outward from the conviction that fashion is transnational and transcultural and must be considered from multiple vantage points that obviate borders.[4] Further, by bringing the decision-making and spending power of patrons to the center of the inquiry (hence the title Power Dressing for part I of the book), *Dressing Up* redoubles Entwistle's and Wilson's emphasis on the quotidian life of garments.[5] In this regard, too, Crewe's and Palmer's attention to patterns of consumption and the biographies of clothes is called on.[6] Employing this formulation, the book disrupts the conception of major couturiers of the period as unparalleled geniuses, in line with Kawamura's view of the couturier as just one of the participants in the broader system.[7] As the power of the other forces within the fashion system—the hairdressers and milliners, the actresses and wealthy U.S. patrons—comes into focus, the individual couturiers are seen in proper perspective.

France first emerged as a center of fashion in the mid- to late seventeenth century, when the finance minister to Louis XIV, Jean-Baptiste Colbert, sought to grow the nation's industries so they could compete with and eventually supersede its neighbors.[8] Textile manufacturing, especially when it came to fine cloths, was a competitive arena, and tariffs were imposed on foreign silk.[9] Fashion became a vital aspect of court life, and information about it was disseminated to the public in such early periodicals as *Le Mercure galant*, which Mary E. Davis and Justine de Young have identified as a pioneering effort, as early as the 1670s, to include fashion plates along with music criticism and create an aura of a desirable lifestyle.[10] In the late eighteenth century, the circulation of dressed dolls and new periodicals escalated the transmission of fashion styles. From 1830 onward, fashion magazines rapidly expanded, reaching growing audiences in France, England, Germany, and the United States. The luxury periodical *Le Moniteur de la mode*, for instance, began publication in 1843, and the less expensive *La Mode illustrée* launched in 1860. French fashions were reproduced in middle-class magazines like *Lady's Book* (founded in 1830 and retitled *Godey's Lady's Book* in about 1840) in the United States and the *Englishwoman's Domestic Magazine* (1852) in England.[11] By 1847, the garment trade was the predominant employer of Paris workers.[12] The fashion industry in Paris had grown so large that it required a united organization, and the Chambre syndicale de la confection et de la couture pour dames et fillettes was founded in 1868.[13] It represented both *confection* (ready-made garments) and couture (the creation of prefabricated designs that were later custom-fit to each client), which were not yet fully distinguished from one another.[14] The syndicate looked after the interests of its members' businesses and organized collective action when necessary.[15] After the dissolution of that organization in December 1910 because of divergent interests among couturiers, *confectioners*, and women's tailors, the Chambre syndicale de la couture parisienne was begun in 1911, representing only the newly elevated couture business.[16]

Since Paris took the lead of high fashion in the late eighteenth century, its grip has rarely faltered, including in its influence on U.S. taste. In the mid-eighteenth century, colonial elites in the larger cities of Boston, New York, Philadelphia, and Charleston were positioned to emulate English dress, as Britain was the main source of textile imports. The British government had set in place Navigation Acts that outlawed direct trade between continental Europe and America, so imports into America were required to pass through ports in Britain.[17] As a result, British wools and Indian cottons and Chinese silks arriving via the British East India Company became the most prevalent textiles in the North American colony; French silk was scarce.[18] The style to follow was that of the British aristocracy, as seen in colonial-era portraiture by John Singleton Copley. Copley exerted great effort to meet his clients' desire to be portrayed in this vein and looked to prints of British portraits as models.[19] The style is exemplified in the English silks worn by sisters Mary and Elizabeth Royall, daughters of a wealthy merchant, for their double portrait of about 1758.[20]

After gaining independence, the United States continued to import European textiles to make clothing and also ordered, either directly or through agents, finished garments from London.[21] Doing so made more economic sense than using local linen, cotton, and wool, which was often in short supply and thus expensive although indispensable during periods of embargo.[22] Only the wealthiest citizens traveled abroad and had the opportunity to purchase clothing in Europe. Katharine Greene Amory of Boston was one of them and wrote in her diary of the late 1770s about her appreciation for the quality of goods she was able to obtain in London and Paris.[23]

By the early to mid-nineteenth century, when Britain looked to Paris for refined textiles and design innovation, and despite several travel and trade embargoes, the U.S. gaze shifted there as well.[24] As explained in chapter 2, Midcentury Tastemakers, women in the United States came to French fashion on their own terms. Many of them participated in the French couture market while still buying locally manufactured items. While visiting and placing orders from high-end couturiers in Paris, they also engaged U.S. dressmakers and shopped in department stores. The multifaceted nature of elite shopping was informed by a deep knowledge of textiles and a familiarity with the quality of French goods that had been imported by local dressmakers, dry goods stores, and early department stores since the middle of the century. By tracing the availability of French garments and fancy articles in the United States from the 1840s to early 1870s, the enthusiasm for French dresses later in the century may be viewed as a continuum of interest rather than a sudden phenomenon.

By the 1880s, Parisian couture from Worth, Doucet, Félix, and Laferrière, to name a few of the renowned fashion houses, had become a transnational industry. Wealthy women from principal cities in the United States traveled annually, sometimes biannually, to Paris to see the latest designs and order customized, seasonal gowns.[25] Their selections and the ways they wore them were reported by journalists for the newly founded society columns in the national and local press. In turn, French gowns became the preferred choice in society portraiture by the most prestigious painters, many of whom were French and traveled internationally for commissions. Choosing an ensemble in which to be painted was a significant decision, often made jointly by sitter and artist. Some women purchased dresses from couturiers, especially the House of Worth, founded by Charles Frederick Worth, with later portraits in mind. This practice followed in the vein of royal portraiture by artists like Franz Xaver Winterhalter. As Aileen Ribeiro has shown, Winterhalter's depictions of sitters, including Queen Victoria, chart fashionable dress over the course of several decades.[26]

Charles Carolus-Duran and John Singer Sargent are two of the best-known society portraitists who gave great importance to their sitters' fashion, sometimes specifying which dresses from a patron's closet would be most suitable.[27] Carolus-Duran even went on public record naming the top beauties in the United States, France, and England with whom he had worked. The criteria centered on the women's sense of fashion and the beauty of their complexions. In 1898, his U.S. selection was Nannie Leiter, one of the daughters of Levi Leiter, who in 1865 cofounded the store that eventually became Marshall Field.[28] In the numerous monumental portraits of social leaders by Carolus-Duran, Sargent, Alexandre Cabanel, Benjamin Curtis Porter, and more, in which the dresses can claim nearly three quarters of the composition, the identities of the dresses' makers have been lost. The best-documented dresses that appear in portraits are by the House of Worth, impeccably exemplified by the red velvet gown worn by actress-turned-socialite Edith Kingdon Gould in her portrait by Théobald Chartran (figs. 1.1 and 1.2).

Part II of the book, Paris as the Center of Haute Couture and Coiffure, reconstructs the vastness of the fashion industry in Paris in the late nineteenth century,

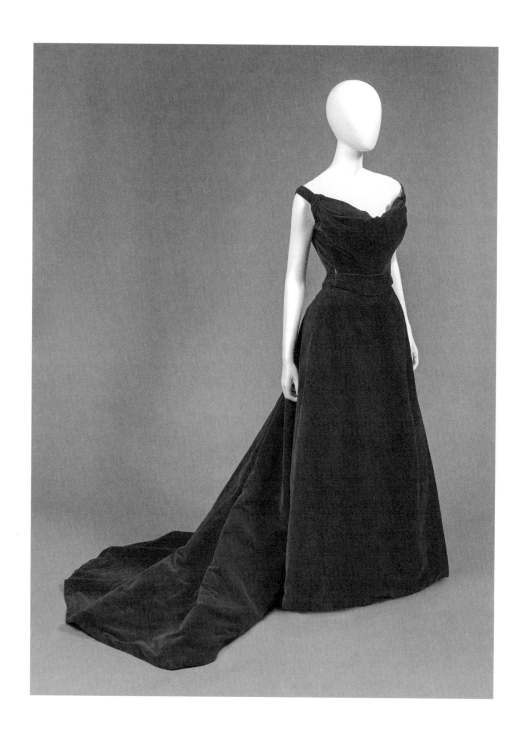

underscoring the interconnection between couture and coiffure. Hairdressing is intentionally reinserted into the story of fashion rather than considered a marginal service or an accessory. The international and diverse workforce that created, produced, distributed, and reported on gowns and hairstyles—from couturiers, coiffeurs, and portrait painters to socialites and stage actresses—is the focus.

In the literature to date, the conception of the scope of French brands worn by U.S. women in the period has been distorted by the scarcity of archives. The unusually thorough set of garments, sketches, and business records for the House of Worth, dutifully safeguarded by family descendants and now preserved in the Victoria and Albert Museum, has steered the scholarship. Relatively large numbers of garments by Worth are kept in museums throughout Europe and the United States because they specialized in ball gowns, which were more likely to be passed down within families, often royal or noble. The work of other couture houses, which may have produced more day and evening wear or whose businesses lasted years rather than decades, has survived in lesser quantities, and archival material is often completely lost. Worth was undeniably the leader, but the broader picture of how other players contributed to the vibrant scene has been obscured. In the present study, documents from international expositions, publicity, photographs, and women's personal archives and letters bring forth the breadth of options in the market. Félix, Worth, Doucet, and Paquin are well represented, while Lipman, Rodrigues, Pascaud, and others are integrated into the discussion, giving a sense of the enormity and diversity of the network.

Chapter 3, Connections among Coiffeurs, Couturiers, Milliners, and Perfumers, examines the industries in Paris from a fruitful new angle: the partnerships and rivalries between couturiers and hairdressers. The two professions, along with those of milliners and perfumers, were mutually dependent and to an extent inbred. Several couturiers began business as milliners, expanding from hats to gowns only after their names had been established. Maison Félix started with hairdressing: the founder was coiffeur to Empress Eugénie. Eugénie's personal investment in luxury and French fashion was encouraged by her husband, Napoléon III, on

1.1

House of Worth (French, 1858–1956).
Evening dress, ca. 1898. Worn by Edith
Kingdon Gould in portrait by Théobald
Chartran (fig. 1.2). Private family collection.

behalf of the nation, and she became an influential leader of taste. The house later offered couture, on the demand of its clients, but retained hairdressing services at its salon. Similarly, the coiffeur Guillaume Louis Lenthéric became best known as a *parfumier*, his brand continuing well into the 1940s with international distribution. The fluidity between the professions is evident in business directories, where a house might be listed for different specialties from one year to the next. Lenthéric's registration alternated between *cheveux* and *parfumerie*, or both, and at times supplemented by *savon* or *fleurs*. The mutual reliance of the professions, however, could create friction and was likely the impetus for some firms' broad portfolio of specialties. The hairdressers maligned the milliners if they made hats that covered too much of the coiffure, and the milliners needed to align their output with the styles and fabrics brought forth by the couturiers each season. *Parfumiers* needed to work with coiffeurs and couturiers to devise the best placement of scent in the hair and in the linings of dresses. By evaluating the interdependence of the specialties, each profession comes into view as an indispensable gear of the fashion engine.

Chapter 4, Couturiers and International Expositions, investigates the fallibility of the leaders of fashion houses. Universal expositions were massive, global productions that served the nationalistic interests of the contributing countries. The French government encouraged the participation of couturiers and coiffeurs to highlight the country's industrial power. The impact on individual business owners and their brands was mixed, however. Using the framework of risk and benefit, the text analyzes the apparently detrimental effect of the Exposition universelle in Paris in 1900 on maison Félix, contrasting it to the successes of its competitors Paquin and Worth. The chapter builds on the literature on fashion at world expositions but shifts the focus toward the complex business decisions that the exhibitions necessitated.

As discussed in chapter 5, International Clientele, the circulation of couturiers, artists, patrons, and celebrities at the Exposition universelle in 1900 reflected the diversity and internationalism of fashion culture. International royalty, society

1.2

Théobald Chartran (French, 1849–1907). *Edith Kingdon Gould*, 1898. Oil on canvas. Private family collection. Photograph by Bruce M. White © 2016. Image: courtesy Lyndhurst.

women, and stage actresses inspired and patronized the preeminent couturiers and coiffeurs in Paris. Couturiers like Doucet, Félix, and Worth kept lengthy rosters of customers from diverse and intersecting worlds, all of whom were integral to the success of the business. Worth's and Félix's celebrity clients included actresses Sarah Bernhardt, Sophie Croizette, and Lillie Langtry.[29] Opera singers Emma Eames, Nellie Melba, Lillian Nordica, and Adelina Patti also frequented the top Parisian houses. Wearing the gowns on stage, performers became live models advertising the latest designs, and audience members and journalists took close note.[30] Formerly disdained for their reputedly low moral standards, actresses were now style leaders and helped accelerate the pace of fashion trends.[31] Courtesans, too, participated in the couture market, a matter that obscured clear-cut divisions between classes and complicated the assignment of "good taste" to a distinct group. This configuration follows sociologist Pierre Bourdieu's interpretation of taste as socially constructed and of consumers' impulses to make aesthetic choices that would uphold their desired rank.[32] However, it is also necessary to account for the pliability of class demarcations that became especially apparent when U.S. women entered the market. Hundreds of strategic marriages between women from the United States and titled Europeans created a new, wealthy subclass of clients that used couture as a powerful diplomatic tool.

Part III, The U.S. Market for French Fashion, evaluates the crucial role of U.S. women as consumers, delving into the ways wealthy clients obtained and used French fashion. The complexities of their practices, which ran the spectrum between extensive transatlantic travel and quick trips downtown, are called out. Women in the main centers of consumption—New York, Newport, Philadelphia, Washington, DC, and Chicago—are the focus, but "following the dresses" takes the discussion to the West Coast as well. Economists have determined using the 1890 census that 71 percent of private wealth in the United States belonged to 9 percent of the population, but not all of it was in New York, a fact that often goes amiss in studies of the so-called Gilded Age but is beginning to be corrected by scholars.[33] The Glessners and McCormicks of Chicago entertained at their mansions in a manner comparable to the Astors and Vanderbilts in New York, hosting parties that commanded hundreds of guests. These patrons thus wielded the power to influence the success or failure of the couture houses in ways that were similar to those of European royalty. The fashion choices of actresses like Edith Kingdon Gould, who later married a financier and joined high society, provide insights into the activities of a "crossover" customer. A look at garment theft (Gould was a famous victim) and counterfeit further emphasizes the value of French fashion as U.S. cultural capital, to use Bourdieu's term.

Chapter 6, Maison Félix and Its U.S. Clients, uses this successful house as a lens through which to view the transnationality of the couture system. The work and recognition of maison Félix is threaded through the book, but here the house is reestablished in full as a significant contributor to the French-U.S. fashion industry. Maison Félix is believed to have designed the slender black dress worn by Virginie Amélie Avegno Gautreau, subject of John Singer Sargent's infamous painting *Madame X* (1883–1884, Metropolitan Museum of Art, New York). The New Orleans–born socialite living in Paris was but one of the firm's influential clients. Material evidence and continuous coverage in the U.S. press reveal a long register of patrons from Massachusetts to California and confirm Félix as a top choice for elite clientele. The chapter establishes the significant presence of French couture in the U.S. market of the 1880s and 1890s, a period in which the privileged set lavishly spent its riches, either inherited or newly gained in the booming industries of transportation, steel production, engineering, and communications. A close look at shopping practices demonstrates the substantial amount of power that women held in the market. Their frequent orders and seemingly unlimited funds for dresses, capes, coats, lingerie, undergarments, and accessories like muffs, gloves, and parasols influenced the fortunes and failures of French couture firms.

Fancy dress balls, held regularly by society leaders in their conspicuous homes, were one of the main stimuli for couture orders. In chapter 7, Gowns and Mansions: French Fashion in U.S. Homes, the soirées are viewed as staged events that were activated by the fashions worn by the hosts and guests. The chapter considers previous studies on fancy dress balls but resituates the events within the literature of material culture and interior design history. The aim is to consider the houses as stages for daily life by connecting the historical references in both the architecture and the costume parties through the medium of fashion employed by the wearers. The chapter extends Kevin D. Murphy's positing of the often perplexing choices by the homeowners to emulate royal French architecture and dress.[34] Here, theories of conspicuous consumption by the late-nineteenth-century economist Thorstein Veblen and the twentieth-century sociologist Pierre Bourdieu elucidate the behavior.

Having established the cultural value of fashion in U.S. homes and society, the book takes on the topic of investment in fashion. Chapter 8, Rising Prices: The Impact of U.S. Tariffs, analyzes the ways in which the U.S. government's implementation of heavy protectionist measures affected the French fashion industry, applying studies on tariffs to the French-U.S. fashion economy. In particular, the Tariff of 1890 (also known as the McKinley Tariff) and the Tariff of 1897 (the Dingley Tariff) curbed the flow of high-end garments. The latter led to a backlash in the press against one of the doyennes of New York society, Cornelia Bradley-Martin, who held a colossal, lavish costume party in the middle of the efforts to discourage foreign buying. The French couture houses were greatly impacted by the changes in tariff laws, and the businesses were forced to confront the specter of reduced income.

Continuing the interpretational framework of value and investment, and adding the consideration of loss, chapter 9, The Underworld and Afterlife of French Couture in the United States, explores the outgrowth of smuggling, theft, and illicit copying of French fashions in the U.S. market. Middle-class emulation of upper-class preferences for French fashion strengthened sales of unauthorized copies on the secondary market in the United States, which benefited local economies. Many wealthy buyers had a vested stake through the business interests of their husbands and extended families. A type of triple chain of influence stretched between the French market, U.S. elite women buyers in the center, and the secondary market. The chapter examines how these dynamics impacted the immense marketplace for ready-to-wear and knockoff garments. It builds on the effect of the pervasive tariff laws discussed in the previous chapter and sheds light on the underside of consumer desire. As department stores in New York, Chicago, and other major cities in the United States began carrying increasing quantities of authentic, imported clothing, as well as licensed and unlicensed copies of French designs at affordable prices, brand recognition and customer aspirations led to criminal activity. A scandal involving two French gowns purchased by Caroline Astor that were held up at the United States Custom House in New York crystallizes the personal and public implications of government intervention when it collides with elite women's purchasing power. The chapter adds these episodes and the motivations behind them to the growing literature on the secondary use of fashion.

Taken together, the larger concerns of this volume shift the traditional terms of engagement with French fashion of the late nineteenth century. After destabilizing the standard view of the couturier as all-powerful creative genius the text reestablishes the elite women of the United States who sought and used couture for their own purposes as influencers within the system. In all, the book seeks to change our conception of the power sources within the complex, transnational fashion industry.

2

MIDCENTURY TASTEMAKERS

In spring 1837, Mademoiselle J. Houdbert, milliner and dressmaker from Paris, ran advertisements in the *New York Herald* for her establishment at 39 John Street in downtown Manhattan.[1] She informed potential customers that she "receives constantly from Paris, the latest fashions." As with most early purveyors of French textiles in the United States, Houdbert carried smaller finished goods and trimmings, including hats, ribbons, embroideries, and handkerchiefs. These items augmented the complete, more complex garments that women or their staff sewed in the home, as women's ready-to-wear clothing would not become commonplace until about the turn of the century.[2] Houdbert likely would have assisted her patrons when they had difficulties with patterns and sewing and perhaps also sold her own designs.[3]

In addition to milliners and dressmakers, there were providers of specialized skills within the industry. For instance, two advertisements below that of Houdbert, Madame Jamme from Paris promoted her cleaning and repair services for lace, tulle, embroideries, and other fabrics at her place about three blocks north of Houdbert's on William Street.[4] Scores of others followed suit, with French names and terms interspersed, from Madame Behrman's Magazin [*sic*] des Robes on Canal Street (1840s) to Taylor's Emporium of Paris Fashions at 407 Broadway (1850s). Others stocked Parisian false hair, hair flowers, and ornaments.[5]

Whether or not they actually hailed from Paris, the business owners were aware of the cachet that French goods carried, and together with larger import firms, publishers of fashion plates, and authors of etiquette books, they served as tastemakers in the middle of the century. Dry goods stores and early department stores picked up the momentum, with A. T. Stewart and Lord and Taylor, among others, selling an array of French fabrics and goods.[6] In Bourdieuian terms, this set of influencers made goods available to the leaders in society who made aesthetic choices to maintain their elevated positions in society.[7]

This chapter takes into consideration the significant presence of French garments and fancy articles in urban centers in the United States from the 1840s to early 1870s. By establishing the consistent and growing availability of these goods in the middle of the century, the shopping practices of the 1880s and 1890s will later come into view as part of a continuum rather than a sudden flashpoint. In this formulation, the varied choices of shopping abroad while also frequenting local dressmakers and department stores may be regarded as cultural attitudes that developed throughout several decades. By the final two decades of the century, women had become thoroughly conversant in French designs and quality and made highly informed decisions about which items to purchase overseas and which to buy or have made near home. This knowledge became all the more valuable as it was needed to navigate the explosion of French offerings when couture came into its own, aided by technological developments in communication and travel that internationalized the business and would bring it into the twentieth century.

Who were the various tastemakers who brought in and promoted French garments and accessories in the United States in the middle of the century? Independent milliners and dressmakers like Houdbert made up a substantial category, comprising those for hire on a per-job basis and those who established premises and employed a staff. Emigrés from France and elsewhere in Europe would have brought styles and a knowledge of French goods with them, as well as a predilection for which periodicals to heed. Enterprising dressmakers in the United States followed suit, and whereas at first city business directories and newspapers show listings and advertisements for women's fashions from London and Paris, the ones for Paris begin to outnumber the former as the decades progress, a shift that is seen in parallel in the fashion coverage of magazines like *Godey's Lady's Book* and *The Casket* (precursor to *Graham's Magazine*). Downtown Manhattan was dotted with dressmakers proclaiming their skills and competence with Paris styles. *Doggett's New-York City Directory* for 1845 lists Madame Charles Glatz, a dressmaker and corsetmaker from Paris, at 394 Broadway, and Alexander Unsworth, importer of Paris fancy goods, at 42 John Street.[8] A single page of advertisements from the *New York Herald* on March 23, 1854, for instance, includes fifteen listings for Paris millinery, corsets, fancy articles, and dressmaking.[9] The names of the business owners are Anglo-Saxon, French, and Italian, but the sell is Paris, Paris, Paris.

In the mid-1850s, if a provider was not French herself, she might claim an association with the New York Crystal Palace as a sales hook. The building, on 6th Avenue between 40th and 42nd Streets, was the site of the Exhibition of the Industry of All Nations in July 1853 to October 1854. The fair was inspired by London's Great Exhibition of 1851 and carried an association of industrial advancement and worldliness. When attempting to grow her own practice and seek additional dressmakers and apprentices, dressmaker Josephine Gibbons cited her operation of a French dress-cutting machine at the exhibition.[10] It is difficult to determine to which machine she may have been referring, but the catalog for the event indicates the substantial presence of the garment and textile industries from France and the United States. France's manufacturing of and finished goods in wool, silk, velvet, flax, hemp, leathers, fur, and animal skins were well represented. The products began to appear in U.S. dry goods stores: shawls, handkerchiefs, gloves, corsets, ribbons, trimmings for hats, and silk buttons.[11] At the Crystal Palace, the U.S. textile industry, too, promoted a number of new sewing machines and looms, as well as fabrics, embroideries, shawls, hats, and some finished garments for men and women.[12]

Gibbons may have been striving to expand from a single practitioner to a larger establishment with its own storefront. Such premises may or may not have been in the same building as the principal's home. Some owners, like Mrs. Kahn on Division Street, had multiple rooms and sold her own designs in addition to Parisian imports.[13] As did others, she also sent patterns to merchants outside the city, thereby spreading the latest trends beyond the urban centers. In turn, store owners from rural towns would travel to the cities to obtain Parisian styles.[14] One of the most successful enterprises was L. P. Hollander & Co., which provided dressmaking and children's wear services and sold its creations as well as imports from Paris and London.[15] In business from 1848 until about 1932, the firm was run by Maria Theresa Baldwin Hollander with her sons after her husband died, starting in Boston and eventually opening branches in New York, Newport, Palm Beach, as well as in Cape Cod, Massachusetts, Maine, and California.[16] The firm was well represented at both the 1853 Crystal Palace in New York and at the World's Columbian Exhibition in Chicago in 1893.[17]

A well-known dressmaker who imported French garments and also created her own was Olympe Boisse (1831–1909; known as Madame Olympe), who was active in

New Orleans. Alva Erskine Smith Vanderbilt recalled that her mother, Phoebe Desha Smith, then in Mobile, Alabama, ordered French clothing for herself, Alva, and her sister twice a year from Madame Olympe.[18] She wrote about her great anticipation of unboxing the packages when they arrived. Significantly, she says that her mother wanted only clothing crafted by European dressmakers and, when not traveling overseas, was willing to order it via an importer in Louisiana. Boisse was born in Canada and after establishing her shop in New Orleans, traveled to Paris regularly to buy clothes and observe styles, which she then adapted and made available for her clients. She began labeling her dresses as early as the mid-1860s, only a few years after Worth et Bobergh pioneered the practice (figs. 2.1 and 2.2).

In addition to dressmakers who imported French goods, there were also dedicated import businesses, such as Gaynor's in downtown New York, which brought in both French and British goods but specialized in French corsets and other undergarments. When her husband passed away, Charlotte Gaynor took over the operation and by 1869 had expanded to two locations in Manhattan.[19] Similarly, in 1869, the Colby Skirt Depot on East 10th Street advertised "Paris in New York," with "French hand made undergarments imported direct from the leading houses of Paris."[20] By 1879, Joaquin et Cie, importers of Parisian bonnets and French millinery goods, had locations in Paris, Boston, Philadelphia, New York, and Brooklyn.[21] Mary A. Connelly seems to have taken over her late husband's millinery and dressmaking business in the late 1860s. In November 1877, she gained notoriety for designing the wedding gown for Florence Adele Vanderbilt Twombley (a daughter of William H. Vanderbilt), which the *New York Times* proclaimed the "most costly dress ever worn on this continent."[22] She had also designed the trousseau for Nellie Grant, daughter of the president, who had gotten married in the White House in 1874.[23] By 1879, Connelly was advertising in *Trow's New York City Directory* her imported "robes

2.1

Olympe Boisse (Canadian, 1831–1909; known as Madame Olympe). Evening dress, ca. 1865. Silk, mother-of-pearl. Brooklyn Museum Costume Collection at The Metropolitan Museum of Art, New York, Gift of the Brooklyn Museum, 2009; Gift of Mrs. H. E. Rifflard, 1932 (2009.300.3009a–d). Image: © The Metropolitan Museum of Art.

2.2

Charles Frederick Worth (French [b. England],
1825–1895) for Worth et Bobergh (French,
1857–1870). Ensemble, 1862–1865. Silk.
The Metropolitan Museum of Art, New York,
Brooklyn Museum Costume Collection at
The Metropolitan Museum of Art, Gift of
the Brooklyn Museum, 2009; Designated
Purchase Fund, 1987 (2009.300.1372a–d).
Image: © The Metropolitan Museum of Art.

et modes" at 7 East 16th Street, and at locations in Saratoga Springs, Newport, and Long Branch, New Jersey, and at 21, rue Bergère in Paris.[24]

Importers like Gaynor's, Colby Skirt Depot, Joaquin et Cie, Connelly, and a certain Peter Roberts, who sold lace goods that he proudly handpicked at an exhibition in Paris, might have storefronts but also sold to the trade, which in the middle of the century comprised dry goods stores and early department stores.[25] The former were traditional mercantile houses that sold a variety of goods (many, including textiles, needed to be kept dry to not be ruined) (fig. 2.3).[26] In its early iterations in the 1840s and 1850s, R. H. Macy's operated as a dry goods store and prominently advertised ribbons and artificial flowers from Paris.[27] Lord and Taylor started as a dry goods store in 1826 at Broadway and 9th Street, had at least three locations in 1859, and moved to the Ladies' Mile in the 1870s, the famous stretch of stores along Broadway and 6th Avenue (fig. 2.4). Bloomingdale Brothers was founded as a ladies' notions shop in 1861 and moved to 938 3rd Avenue in 1872. The stores would have obtained goods directly or through importers or agents like Mrs. S. P. Lovett and George A. Hearn, both of whom advertised in the *New York Herald*.[28] Similar arrangements between dry goods stores and importers of French goods were in place in urban centers throughout the country. Finally, trade periodicals like the *Millinery Fashion Magazine*, published in Baltimore, informed business owners of the array of fabrics available by purveyors. The firms were mostly from the United States, but the January 1886 volume featured a new brand of silk velvets by the well-established Giron Frères of Lyon.[29]

Department stores, larger enterprises that separated goods into sections, took hold by the 1870s, as they had in Europe, but the term was not commonly used until about 1888, an indication of the somewhat fluid definitions and gradual transitions between types of stores.[30] Many establishments were still referred to as "dry goods stores," even after they had divided products into departments, as at Darlington, Runk, and Co. in Philadelphia. The grand emporiums installed electric lighting, plate-glass windows, and modernized displays that welcomed browsers and buyers alike. Browsing in shops and handling goods before making a purchase or deciding otherwise had been common practice in the eighteenth century but had fallen out of favor in the early nineteenth century there and in the United States when store owners firmly required a purchase.[31] Department stores reversed the practice once again, encouraging customers to explore displays on multiple floors while they socialized, dined, and were entertained. Further, cash register machines and pneumatic tubes revolutionized these businesses that ran on cash instead of traditional

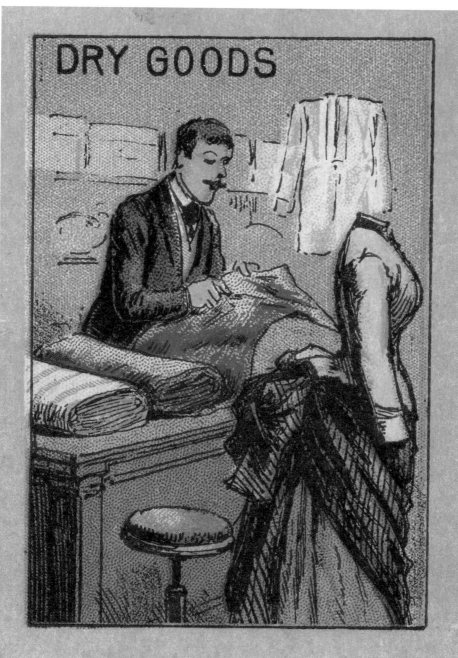

2.3

Dry goods store picture card, nineteenth century. Courtesy of Historic New England.

2.4

Opening Day at Lord and Taylor's Store, Broadway and 20th Street. *Frank Leslie's Illustrated Newspaper*, January 11, 1873. Image: Library of Congress.

2.5

Jules Chéret (French, 1836–1932).
Grands magasins de la paix, Paris, 1879.
Bibliothèque nationale de France, Paris
(VA-236 [E]-FOL). Image: Bibliothèque
nationale de France, Paris.

forms of credit, implemented fixed pricing rather than bargaining, allowed returns, and offered delivery. Salespeople, mostly men, stood behind glass display counters and assisted customers. Women worked in sales in dry goods stores beginning in the mid-1860s, in relatively small numbers, but by 1870, a contingent in New York had gathered enough support to organize for improved work conditions.[32]

The department stores regularly sent buyers, eventually both women and men, to Paris to obtain the latest fashions.[33] They visited the smaller mercantile houses and later the Parisian department stores (*grand magasins*) like Le Bon Marché, founded in 1838 and transformed in 1852 into the bohemoth for which it is still known, and the Grands magasins de la paix, opened in 1869 (fig. 2.5). Émile Zola famously used Le Bon Marché as inspiration for his 1883 novel *Au bonheur des dames*, a commentary on Paris's changing social order.[34] The extensive literature on the effect of department stores on modern society will not be recounted here, but rather the concern is how the earliest ones fit into the tastemaking network for French goods in the middle of the century.[35] For instance, in 1870, A. T. Stewart opened a new six-story location on Broadway at 9th and 10th Streets that boasted five steam elevators. The branch was one of several established over decades of business and continued the evolution of what was founded as a small dry goods store in 1823 by this Irish immigrant. It had set up a foreign purchasing department in Paris as early as 1845 and began promoting fabrics from Paris in U.S. newspapers in the 1850s.[36] As did many early department stores, Stewart's 1870 iron and glass palace retained manufacturing facilities on its uppermost floors, including women's wear, and held its retail sales on the first few floors.[37] It kept warehouses in England, Ireland, Scotland, and France and a Paris bureau to handle its European transactions. By 1872, Chicago's Marshall Field department store, which had been founded in 1865, also opened an office in Paris, where it had been purchasing goods for several years.[38] Throughout the country, department stores like these—from Memphis's Leubrie Brothers, eagerly promoting French fabrics and Paris millinery, to Columbus, Ohio's Bain and Son with its Parisian mantillas—made French goods available and familiar to shoppers.[39]

As tastemakers, the dressmakers, importers, agents, and owners of and buyers for dry goods and department stores worked in tandem with the publishers of women's periodicals and authors of etiquette books. Magazines from the United States began including French fashion early in the century—*Boston Weekly Magazine* reported on Parisian bonnet styles in 1817.[40] By 1838, Massachusetts politician Charles Sumner declared in a letter home: "Go to Paris, you will see art in its most various forms; you will see taste in the dress of everybody."[41] Twenty years later, he knew to stay at the Hotel de la paix, "at the corner of Rue de la Paix and the Boulevards, where I have a beautiful apartment from which I can see all the movements of Paris."[42] In the 1840s, U.S. journalist Margaret Fuller wrote how she enjoyed observing the fine art of French women's dress while in Paris, remarking on how wardrobe and an overall air of vivacity could improve even the "ugly ones."[43]

Readers of newspapers and magazines became well informed prior to traveling abroad. The letters of influential mapmaker and educator Emma Hart Willard explain that when she and her son arrived in Paris in 1830 for a visit, she came equipped with a working knowledge of French women's dressing customs, but she made many further observations while there and wrote home about them, thus spreading the information. She found French women to dress fairly casually in the morning, especially when they needed to contend with muddy streets while shopping, and more restrained overall than they were made out to be by U.S. commenters.[44] In one letter, she records almost in real time how U.S. visitors embraced French clothing and transmitted the styles back home. She wrote:

Although I did not intend when I came to Paris, to change much the fashion of my dresses, yet as I find real improvements, I am pleased to adopt them, for the sake of utility and health, and besides, I find myself in a manner obliged, in the circle in which I am, to conform in a degree to the modes here. . . . I go through all the shops where various articles of dress are made, and when I see something new, which is promising, buy a specimen to carry home.[45]

Fully embedding herself within French society for the months she was visiting, Willard hired a French seamstress whose work she respected and who could help her practice her language skills.[46] She also employed a French hairdresser for house calls.[47] A certain episode is especially helpful in showing how firsthand exposure could intervene in images transmitted through periodicals. One evening, she and friends noticed a fashion print from *Journal des modes* on a table in the salon of the house where they were staying. They laughed at the engraved model's stiff posture, and Willard remarked to herself, "These are the very patterns by which my young and lovely country-women are making themselves up;—the idols to which they sometimes sacrifice decency and propriety."[48] Willard's observation attests to how effectively the magazines could persuade U.S. women to revamp their fashion taste.

One of the most influential women's magazines was *Godey's Lady's Book* (begun in 1830 with the title *The Lady's Book*), published in Philadelphia, which related fashions from both London and Paris. It carried accounts of royal events and masked balls, as well as articles describing historic French costume. In 1852, it started to take mail orders from readers for patterns, and in 1853, it commenced printing patterns on its pages.[49] In the 1850s through 1870s, the reporting of French fashion increased, as did the magazine's readership, reaching an impressive 150,000 in the early 1860s. Many of the hand-colored fashion plates were taken directly from French periodicals.[50] *Peterson's Magazine* and *Frank Leslie's Magazine* (fig. 2.6) provided similar coverage, with the latter putting out several volumes of *Frank Leslie's Ladies Gazette of Paris, London & New York Fashions* in 1854 and 1855, an indication of when the "big three" cities had become ensconced in the U.S. fashion consciousness. Coverage increased as well in the 1850s and 1860s, when publisher S. T. Taylor in New York issued English versions of several French periodicals: *Dress-Maker and Milliner's Guide*, *Le Petite Messager*, and *Le Bon Ton*.[51] Clippings from the latter are included in a remarkable scrapbook of fashions kept by Ann Minshall Walter (between 1830 and 1848) and her granddaughter Elise Boardman Richards (between 1848 and 1881) of Boston. The scrapbook is preserved in the collection of Historic New England and is too fragile to photograph, but in addition to pages from *Le Bon Ton*, archivists also have documented the inclusion of plates from *Frank Leslie's Lady's Magazine* and *Ladies' National Magazine*, most of which show clothing styles from Paris.[52] The compilation records the continuous appeal of French fashion to women of two different generations of Boston's high society.

Periodicals like the ones recorded in the Walter-Richards scrapbook also reported on international fairs like the Centennial Exposition in Philadelphia in 1876, which featured textiles throughout various buildings representing participating countries. In the massive Machinery Hall, five looms from Lyall's in New York demonstrated the latest machinery for weaving large widths of fabrics with considerably less human labor than was required with hand looms.[53] France showed silk weaving looms from Lyon and weaving machines and looms from Paris. Among the French finished goods was a cabinet display of corsets by the Parisian firms Farcy and Oppenheim and P. Lenoir (fig. 2.7).[54] In advance of the 1878 Exposition universelle in Paris, periodicals like *Mme Demorest's Semi-Annual What to Wear and How to Make It* provided guidance on trunks that would fit the berth in particular steamships, the types of garments and fabrics best suited for sea air, and reminders to pack an oiled silk bag to hold soiled clothes and other essential items.[55] For the hair, simple braids were recommended, given the difficulties of maintaining a formal coiffure at sea.

The Only Authority on Fashions!
FRANK LESLIE'S

Specimens of Colored Fashion Plates in Each Number of Frank Leslie's Lady's Magazine.

Lady's Magazine *and* Gazette *of* Fashions

Contains more styles than all other Magazines combined.---Made in Paris expressly for this Work---Published monthly.---$3.50 per annum.

SUBSCRIPTIONS RECEIVED HERE.

Readers of periodicals also consulted etiquette books, a large subset of the publishing industry by the late 1870s. French fashion customs were fully incorporated into these prescriptive volumes. Sarah Josepha Hale, respected editor of *Godey's Lady's Book* (and the first female editor of a U.S. magazine), advised in her 1868 book that U.S. women should dress "entirely French" when they traveled so as not to be conspicuous.[56] Her fellow Philadelphian Claire Jessup Moore wrote with similar reverence for Parisian taste in *Sensible Etiquette of the Best Society, Customs, Manners, Morals, and Home Culture*, published ten years later (and reprinted in multiple editions) and attests to the prevalence of French exports (dresses, gloves, wines, and plays, in that order) in the United States.[57] Countless other etiquette volumes would follow.

Having employed dressmakers, shopped in dry goods and department stores, visited international expositions, and read magazines and etiquette books, wealthy U.S. women who had the opportunity to shop in Paris at midcentury were sophisticated customers. In 1858, Anna Sears Amory of Boston wrote about her time-consuming and exhausting shopping trips in Paris: "we are out every day from 10 to five."[58] Fulfilling the orders that her family and hometown friends had sent with her (now referred to as "proxy shopping") was another part of the challenge because she found their expectations of pricing to be unrealistic.[59] Amory names couturière Madame Roger at 25, rue Louis-le-Grand (since at least 1850) as the owner of one of the businesses where she shopped and with whom she was eager to settle a bill.[60]

About a decade later, Frances Willard, who would found the World Woman's Christian Temperance Union and became a dress reformer, was a decidedly reluctant customer in Paris. Despite her general displeasure with shopping, however, her journals from the period when she was in her late twenties and on hiatus from teaching evince a keen discernment of fabrics, style, and costs. A conservative dresser, she wrote of her preference for a serge walking suit rather than the velvets,

2.6

Advertisement for *Frank Leslie's Lady's Magazine and Gazette of Fashions*, 1870. Image: American Antiquarian Society.

2.7

Centennial Photographic Company. Display
of corsets by Farcy and Oppenheim and
P. Lenoir at the Centennial Exposition,
Philadelphia, 1876. Silver albumen print.
Image: Free Library of Philadelphia
(c020859).

furs, and satins that were on display throughout Paris.[61] One day, she and her friend Kate, whose fluency in French aided their shopping trips, "purchased four elegant silks at the rate of three" at the textile shop Sauvage Frères, its showroom illuminated with gas lights to simulate evening.[62] She describes the delicate green fabric as having been made to order for the House of Worth, indicating that Sauvage Frères was one of the house's many suppliers. By contrast, she was thoroughly disgusted when a street vendor attempted to sell Kate "a pepper & salt mixture in heavy cloth," an "ugly fabric."[63] Although she often felt "outside the ring" shopping in Paris[64] and referred to Le Bon Marché as "the great mongrel," she resigned that "Paris is indeed 'the consummate flower' of taste & wealth and fashion."[65] Notably, Willard does not mention a male escort accompanying her and Kate on their outing, a point of fact that supports scholars like Justine de Young's observations that women in fashion plates of the period are increasingly shown acting independently in public settings, like shopping, buying drapery, or waiting to board a train (see fig. 5.3).[66] The anonymous female U.S. author of an 1878 travel diary, wrote on May 24 from Paris: "Shopped at the Bon Marché again alone and went to bed early."[67]

Women like Amory and Willard were decidedly well versed in French textiles, garments, and trimmings. By the time their daughters, either directly or via their maids, were entering the market for bridal trousseaus and ball gowns in the late 1870s and 1880s, they came with a substantial knowledge base of which imported items could be purchased locally and which were better sought from the source. Specific fabrics as well as French dressmaking terms were familiar from visual sources like store advertisements, magazine articles, and department store catalogs but also from hands-on touching. Willard judged the hawker's fabric as undesirable, using a visual term ("ugly") and also a haptic term ("heavy"). Although Willard did not handle the fabric on the spot, she made her judgment based on prior familiarity with weightier fabrics as opposed to those that were lighter, more delicate and refined. One representative advertisement for Wanamaker's department store in Philadelphia indicates the extent to which women like Willard would have known about a range of fabrics, including plain silk grenadines, figured grenadines, black lace bunting, flannel, and nainsook with hemstitch plaid. The store also offered Paris novelties that were selected by the firm's buyer in France.[68] Furthermore, the prolific Baedeker's *Paris and Its Environs* guides saw fit to send U.S. travelers to department stores Le Bon Marché and Grands Magasins du Louvre, to *magasins de nouveautés* for fabric and trimmings, and to the couturiers.[69] With this knowledge of the range of providers coupled with their intelligence about textiles came a certain practicality, even frugality, on the part of elite shoppers that continued through the end of century. On their travels, some women bought extra bolts of fabric for use by their local dressmaker (fig. 2.8).[70] When purchasing a floral silk dress at Worth, Mary Swift Thoms of Cincinnati brought home fabric so that her dressmaker could construct a separate evening bodice for the dress at a lower cost than in Paris.[71] Similarly, even after she became vicereine of India, the Chicago-born Mary Leiter Curzon made an effort to reduce her expenses when ordering from the House of Worth, providing her own material and remaining steadfast when setting limitations.[72] Although the dualities may seem paradoxical, we may appreciate from the women's writings that it was a negotiation that they were navigating.

Women of midcentury were also managing other complexities that affected their shopping practices and that they would pass to the next generation. Not least of these were how they obtained their money and how it was made. Alva Vanderbilt Belmont—who divorced William Kissam Vanderbilt in 1895, married the wealthy banker Oliver Hazard Perry Belmont, and became an ardent suffragist after Belmont's death in 1908—later stated in her memoir that regretfully, women had no claim to capital after they married.[73] She further noted with dismay that the funds she inherited through a trust became her husband's property, as was also the case for women's dowries. She wrote about how important it was to her to have ownership of the Newport home, Marble House, in her name, lamenting that the one at 660 5th Avenue in Manhattan was listed only under her former husband's name.[74]

In fashion, as in real estate, Alva Vanderbilt Belmont was no victim and exercised a significant amount of agency when buying couture, but it is worth considering the various circumstances of other women so that we can understand the forces that helped determine their shopping practices. Many wealthy women did the majority of their spending when newly engaged to be married, when they used their father's funds for a trousseau and wedding dress, and then as new brides, they spent their husband's money on hostess outfits for their first entertainments

2.8

Adèle Anaïs Colin-Toudouze (French, 1822–1899). *Toilettes de Mme Bréant-Castel, La Mode illustrée*, 1883. Rijksmuseum, Amsterdam (RP-P-2009–3704). Image: Rijksmuseum.

LA MODE ILLUSTRÉE

BUREAUX DU JOURNAL, 56, RUE JACOB, PARIS.

Toilettes de Mme BREANT-CASTEL, rue Gluck, 6.

Mode Illustrée 1883. N° 52

in society. The pressure on women who came from or married into families in the textile or garment sales businesses presumably would have been even stronger. For instance, Nannie Douglas Scott Field was married to Marshall Field and would have had easy access to imported French fashion at the department store in Chicago that bore their name. Yet she also placed orders for French couture when her friend Abbie Louise Spencer Eddy traveled abroad.[75] We may infer that she bought French fashion at both couturiers and department stores, an accepted societal custom, in the same way that women like Mary Swift Thoms and Mary Leiter Curzon bought French couture but also employed local dressmakers. As social leaders, the clothing of the women in department store families was watched and reported on closely, as were the traveling gowns of Mary Leiter on her way to marry British aristocrat George Nathaniel Curzon and Mary Brown Wanamaker, set to marry Philadelphia publisher Barclay Warburton, the subjects of a newspaper feature in April 1895.[76]

Now that we have a sense of how women in the United States came to know and seek out French fashion, we turn to a close study of the couture providers and their interactions so that we may better understand the complexities of the transnational industry in which the women were active participants.

PARIS AS THE CENTER OF HAUTE COUTURE AND COIFFURE

CONNECTIONS AMONG COIFFEURS, COUTURIERS, MILLINERS, AND PERFUMERS

The cover of the March 17, 1894, issue of *Harper's Bazar* shows a woman wearing a *ciel*-blue satin evening gown bordered in black fur, with floral beading on the bodice and skirt and fur straps. The figure gazes to her left, over an open, black lace fan and past a piano in an affluently appointed drawing room, displaying her coiffure to best advantage (fig. 3.1). The hairstyle, with a prominent looped tress at the top, was by Lenthéric, and the gown was by Worth. The fashion plate was signed by artist Adolphe Sandoz. The pairing of Lenthéric and Worth was a favorite in *Harper's*, appearing in at least three other issues that year. The U.S. periodical followed the precedent of the French press, where the two were also coupled in fashion spreads or spaced within a page of one another, as in *Revue illustrée* and *La Grande Dame: Revue de l'élégance et des arts*.[1]

The question of how designs by the houses of Lenthéric and Worth came to be associated in print opens a broad inquiry into the interrelationship of the coiffeur and couture professions in Paris at the end of the century. The coupling is one of many between certain coiffeurs, couturiers, milliners, and perfumers. The mutual reliance and shared business concerns between these practitioners resulted in partnerships but also frictions. "If the milliners had had their way they would have done away with hair," said a statement by the House of Worth later reflecting on the period (fig. 3.2).[2] Here again, the picture diverges from a configuration of the reliance of specific French couturiers on self-representation as venerated artists in order to ensure their success. This point of view is explored by Nancy J. Troy with

HARPER'S BAZAR

Copyright, 1894, by Harper & Brothers. *All Rights Reserved.*

PUBLISHED WEEKLY.
VOL. XXVII.—NUMBER 11.

NEW YORK, SATURDAY, MARCH 17, 1894.

TEN CENTS A COPY.
WITH A SUPPLEMENT.

EVENING GOWN FROM WORTH, COIFFURE FROM LENTHÉRIC OF PARIS.—[See Page 208.]

3.1

Adolphe Sandoz (b. Ukraine, ca. 1845;
active in Paris). *House of Worth Satin Dress.*
Harper's Bazar, March 17, 1894.

3.2

Bonnet. French, 1883. Silk, beads, feathers,
wire. The Metropolitan Museum of Art,
New York, Gift of Mrs. Francis Howard and
Mrs. Avery Robinson, 1953 (C.I.53.68.4).
Image: © The Metropolitan Museum of Art.

regard to Paul Poiret, for instance, and harkens back to Pierre Bourdieu and Yvette Desault's conception of the dependence of haute-couture designers (in their case, referring to avant-gardists in the late twentieth century) on the exclusivity of their creations.[3]

LENTHÉRIC

As was the case with many of the predominant contributors to the fashion industry in Paris, Guillaume Louis Lenthéric (ca. 1846–1912) kept a diversified business. He was trained as a hairdresser, as was his father, and the family may have started the eponymous firm as early as the 1850s, having claimed to style the hair of Empress Eugénie.[4] In 1875, the name first appears in Paris business directories under *modes*. In the 1880s and 1890s, the firm is variously listed as specializing in coiffure, perfume, soap, and tortoiseshell goods, primarily at 245, rue du Faubourg-Saint-Honoré (fig. 3.3).[5]

The Lenthéric establishment seems to have remained at that location at least until the death of Guillaume Louis in 1912, and possibly at least until 1930, although the brand name has carried on through numerous iterations and owners to the present day. The French, British, and U.S. press continuously featured Lenthéric coiffures, a proprietary hair waver tool, perfumes, hats, and cosmetics and ran profile pieces. Prone to hyperbole, the headlines referred to Guillaume Louis as "the Master Coiffeur of Paris," "the Greatest Living Hairdresser," and "the Leading Paris Hairdresser."[6] Studies of fashion publications by Kate Best, Mary E. Davis, Justine de Young, and Agnès Rocamora rightly remind us that periodicals must be considered mediated sources in which publishers and authors have intervened in the selection of the material discussed and reproduced.[7] As the *New York Times* put it in 1886, after a couturier made a toilette for an elegant client: "Then the fashion newspapers take it up, and by the minute description of its details, push it in the circle of their subscribers."[8]

While remaining cautious of these documents and reading them critically, however, it is possible to glean information from them that cannot be found elsewhere. An interview printed in London's *Hearth and Home* in June 1893 is especially revealing. Not only does Lenthéric comment on his methods of following the shape of the client's head and face when crafting a style, rather than blithely complying with the latest fashion crazes, but he also credits much of his success to his collaboration

3.3

The Sale Room on the Ground Floor of
Lenthéric, 245, rue du Faubourg-Saint-
Honoré, *New York Herald* (Paris ed.),
December 21, 1893. Image: Bibliothèque
nationale de France, Paris.

with the fashion-plate artist Adolphe Sandoz. The article reports that the two met on Sundays, when Sandoz would watch Lenthéric testing out various hairstyles on model heads, presumably made of wax: "we used to try and try effects till I produced something good."[9] Further, it provides a glimpse into the working relationship of a master coiffeur and his staff, explaining how Lenthéric listened to the younger men's ideas, observed the work, and then helped them to achieve the desired look. Finally, the article explains that the perfume business was rapidly growing at the time and that the firm had begun to create scents a few years before in response to clients' demands.[10] The company had originally sold other perfumers' products, but clients found them lacking, and when it was discovered that they were made unsatisfactorily with chemicals, Lenthéric turned to producing its own scents. The perfumes, of which the Orkidée series seems to have been the most popular, constituted one of the product lines. There were also monogrammable sachets that could be tucked within gowns, and a pendant necklace (*atyche*) that held perfume, releasing its scent as the vessel warmed from the wearer's body heat.[11] In 1898, Lenthéric published *Physiologie de la toilette*, a well-received handbook that also served as an advertisement for the firm's expertise.

Press coverage and advertisements indicate that Lenthéric succeeded in permeating the market with its diversified offerings. As a trained coiffeur, Guillaume Louis may have been wary of becoming too reliant on each season's hat styles for the success of its hairstyles, per the traditional power structure between milliners and coiffeurs.[12] A clever way to sidestep the dynamic was to specialize in both areas, which Lenthéric did and then some. The company achieved success across multiple categories, with coiffures, wigs, hats, accessories, cosmetics, and perfumes all receiving continuous accolades by fashion writers in France, England, and the United States. As the author with the pseudonym Comtesse Sylvia remarked in *Revue illustrée* in 1895: "Lenthéric saw that he was being led to take care of not just hairstyling and coloring but also everything linked to feminine adornment."[13] At least one interview, however revealed a strain of comparison and competition between hairstyling and dress designing, the latter being an area that Lenthéric did not practice. The article cites Lenthéric's declaration that hairdressing was more challenging because, as opposed to dresses that could have a general appeal, one set hairstyle would not flatter every face, and ingenuity was required.[14] He also admonished the tendency of writers to claim that hairstyles did not change as frequently as dress designs. The reason for this mistaken perception, he said, was the outsized emphasis that writers placed on the rather superficial change of colors in dress.[15]

Although Lenthéric did not design dresses, the firm and other perfumers cleverly infiltrated the specialty and made themselves essential to its success by producing and creating a market for perfume products to be sewn inside dresses. The small silk sachets were filled with flower leaves and powders, sewn onto interior panels or into the sleeves, and meant to provide fragrance to the entire dress.[16] Etiquette books advised that perfumes should be subdued and used in moderation.[17] Many upper-class women chose a signature scent with which they became associated: "It is her freak to be individual," wrote the *St. Paul Daily Globe*.[18] Caroline Astor adopted a "sweet odor somewhat like wild lavender and garden roses mixed."[19] Alice Claypoole Gwynne Vanderbilt preferred verbena, and First Lady Frances Cleveland wore Parma violet.[20] Awareness of their fragrances was an extension of the public's interest in wealthy families' favorite flowers, grown on their estates. Alva Vanderbilt Belmont was known for cultivating pink lotuses in tubs of water.[21]

Perfumers tested different types of sachets and other delivery systems, the goal of which was to sustain the scent in the gown. Some experimented with novel fabrics that could hold the scent longer, from an unnamed fabric that came only in red, to strips of flannel and chamois skin soaked in perfume.[22] Alternatively, perfumed tablets could be placed inside gloves and pockets, and pieces of actual flowers embedded within velvet or silk muffs.[23] In 1897, Lenthéric developed *batons aromatiques*, similar to incense, to burn and scent clothing through proximity.[24] In 1891, one New York theater mounted an atomizer to diffuse a scent throughout the space and permeate the seat cushions and curtains.[25] Atomizers could also be purchased for the home and placed in wooden closets or trunks; an additional benefit was the use of perfume to ward off moths.[26]

The importance of perfumers within the fashion industry is evidenced by their equal inclusion in fashion spreads, in which they are credited by name alongside couturiers, coiffeurs, corseters, and milliners. For example, in *La Coiffure française illustrée* in April, May, June, and July 1897, perfumerie Houbigant (at 19, rue du Faubourg Saint-Honoré) was featured with hairstyles by Cotreau, Camille Croisat, Paul of maison Georges, and Madon, respectively.[27] In *La Mode artistique: Revue de toutes les elégances* of November 1901, the "Céladon" perfume by the L. Legrand firm was paired with a winter outfit by Redfern and the next month its violet-based "Prince Albert" was captioned alongside Redfern's costumes for the production of *La Pompadour* at the Théâtre de la Porte St. Martin, featuring the actresses Jane Hading and Marie Magnier.[28]

The prevalence of the name of the perfume and maker is remarkable given the ephemeral nature of scent. The reader would have had to come with a predisposed olfactory association. If they did not know a particular scent, they might conjure an idea of it through the clothes in colored fashion plates, as certain perfumes were meant to match specific colors of gowns—cherry blossom with a white dress, orchids with mauve.[29] However, periodicals with black-and-white drawings also listed perfumers.[30] Historical interest in perfume and its bottles was also high, with magazine columnists appealing to readers' curiosity in the practices of figures like Cleopatra and Persian kings, for example.[31]

Finally, perfume was part of the overall presentation of fashion. Some gowns arrived in the United States from Paris already scented, further evidence of the partnerships and collaborations that were required in the industry.[32] Perfumery was linked with hairdressing as well. Given the sporadic practice of cleansing the hair, the application of perfumed ointments, tonics, and powder was prevalent. One method recommended by a young woman in Chicago entailed sprinkling sachet powder in the lining of a silk cap and wearing it at home for an hour at a time.[33]

Like other coiffeurs, Lenthéric's daily business took place at the firm's salon, where women came to have their hair styled. Visiting a salon for an upper-class woman was a discreet affair, not a social outing as it was for men going to the barber or as it would become in the twentieth century for women as well.[34] The need for discretion was furthered by the fact that the majority of first-rank hairdressers were male. All of the officers of the hair academies, trade groups, and universal exposition organizers were men. The Lenthéric salon, which was enlarged and refurbished in late 1891 to early 1892, was well appointed with mahogany tables fitted in nickel and could accommodate several customers at a time.[35] On the main floors were the salesroom (see fig. 3.3), a Louis XV salon for demonstrations and lessons, a dyeing room, and a shampoo room with both "American" (with water) and French (*frictions*, dry shampoo) techniques (fig. 3.4).[36] The fact that the salon could offer the former indicates that it had invested in the necessary plumbing and heating apparatus to which U.S. clients had become accustomed in newer architecture at home.[37] One French journal described the "American comfort" of the establishment.[38] The workrooms for wig-making, floral hair ornaments (fig. 3.5), and tortoiseshell craftsmanship were in the basement, as was the perfume laboratory.[39] The building was equipped with electricity, an amenity that had become *de rigueur* in this period but that was also possibly the cause of a large fire in the basement in 1897.[40]

3.4

Shampooing in the "American" and French
Styles at Léntheric. *New York Herald*
(Paris ed.), December 21, 1893. Image:
Bibliothèque nationale de France, Paris.

3.5

The Florists' Workroom at Léntheric.
New York Herald (Paris ed.), December 21,
1893. Image: Bibliothèque nationale de
France, Paris.

By 1895, business had expanded to the degree that clients wanted Lenthéric's services when they were on holiday, and a branch was opened in Nice in a rented space conveniently located above the office of the *International Herald Tribune*.[41] Both branches received French, Russian, English, and U.S. clients, including actresses Sarah Bernhardt and Marthe Brandés; Lady Grey, Countess of Warwick; the princesses Bariatinsky, Obolinski, and Troubetzkoy; and women from the Astor, Vanderbilt, Morgan, Wanamaker, and Mackay families.[42] In summer 1896, for those traveling to lakeside resorts in Aix-les-Bains, Lenthéric set up a temporary shop to sell the latest *Neréide* hairpieces.[43] The firm periodically also provided services at the Hôtel de Paris in Monte Carlo.[44] To keep its foreign clients apprised of the latest styles, some of the wax models retained in the salon may have been modeled after certain women and, after styles were worked out, photographed and sent to the clients for their review. This practice derived from that of circulating models in the eighteenth century.[45]

Wax models were also used in couture and were especially helpful to clients from the United States and South America. As Paul H. Nystrom pointed out in *Economics of Fashion* in 1928, Parisian firms knew how to cater to customers from different climates, citing Buenos Aires, where Paquin operated a branch, as it also did in London, New York, and Madrid.[46] Other businesses set up branches, too. The House of Worth opened salons in London (in 1902, after having an office there since 1897) and in Cannes and Biarritz (by the 1920s) during the years when the late Charles Frederick's sons and grandsons were running the firm. Princess Maud of Denmark, later Queen of Norway, patronized the London shop, which by 1903 was located at 4 New Burlington Street.[47] She also frequented the longstanding British firm Redfern, of Cowes, England, known for its tailoring. It opened shops in London (1878), Paris (1881), New York (1884), Newport (1885), Saratoga Springs (1885), and Chicago (1892), and regularly included lists of royal patrons in its advertisements.[48] Redfern was the epitome of British smart, restrained dress and often was set up as a foil to Parisian styles when they veered toward overly flamboyant. A. E. Lelong, owned by the husband-and-wife team Arthur and Eléonore Lelong, ran its main shop in Paris (first on rue Vignon beginning at least in 1889, and from 1898 at 18, place de la Madeleine). They also opened a branch in London at 1 Brook Street, Hanover Square, and claimed Queen Victoria as a client.[49] Another Parisian firm that established a shop in London was that of Augustine Cohn (at 244, rue de Rivoli in Paris and 39 Conduit Street in London), which presented a large display of dresses at the Philadelphia Centennial Exhibition in 1876.[50]

To promote its Paris and seaside locations to foreigners, Lenthéric placed advertisements targeted to British and U.S. customers in English-language international newspapers.[51] The purchase of ads in the *International Herald Tribune* seems directly relational to the amount of editorial coverage the firm received, with several full-length features, including one on December 21, 1893, that garnished rich illustrations and hefty praise.[52] The article credits Lenthéric with inventing and marketing the "flou-flou" hair waver made out of a shell stick in 1891 (although the *New York Times* reported on it in 1890), which made possible an alternative option to using heated metal tongs to wave the hair, a technique invented by Marcel Grateau in 1872.[53] Lenthéric later credited one of his staff for originating this nonmetal option.[54] Marcel tongs were notoriously dangerous, as the hot iron could burn the scalp and damage the hair to the extent that entirely new styles using false pieces to cover burned-off tresses evolved.[55] Furthermore, the article commends the house for keeping its prices reasonable by eliminating middlemen and producing many of its materials in-house, a curiously specific comment that seems more "advertorial" than editorial but nonetheless signals the competitive nature of the market at the time and a need to distinguish one's business. By 1900, advertisements listed branches of Lenthéric in Nice, London, and Monte Carlo for winter and in Trouville, Deauville, Ostend, and Baden-Baden for summer.[56] Its cosmetic products and hats were carried in stores throughout the United States, from Alcott and Weekes in New York to Platky's in Grand Forks, North Dakota.[57]

LENTHÉRIC AND INTERNATIONAL EXPOSITIONS

For both coiffeurs and couturiers, the most high-profile engagements were fancy dress balls and universal expositions. In 1889, a particularly busy year given the Exposition universelle in Paris, for which visitors came finely dressed and coiffed, *La Grande Revue* described the Lenthéric salon at 245, rue du Faubourg-Saint-Honoré as doubling its efforts to meet the needs of its clients.[58] The same year, Oscar Wilde's magazine *Woman's World* featured Lenthéric's coiffures created specifically for a sea-nymph costume for a ball.[59] Even more fantastical were the coiffures that Lenthéric devised for a fancy dress ball in 1892, including a tripartite, vertical concoction for a woman in a commedia dell'arte–type clown costume (fig. 3.6).[60] Although Lenthéric does not appear to have participated in the 1889 Exposition universelle, the firm may have been involved in the 1893 World's Columbian Exposition in Chicago and played

Costumes travestis de LANDOLFF, coiffures de LENTHÉRIC.

3.6

Costumes by Landoulf, Coiffures by
Lenthéric, *Le Figaro-Graphic*, January 25,
1892. Image: Bibliothèque nationale de
France, Paris.

an integral role at the 1900 Exposition universelle in Paris. Both engagements offer a window into the necessity for collaboration between the coiffeur and couture industries and the extent of their internationalism.

As is discussed at length in chapter 4, Couturiers and International Expositions, international expositions were an opportunity for nations to promote the finest aspects of their culture and enterprise. There is some evidence that Lenthéric may have had a part in styling the historic hair and headdresses of the figures in the French exhibit at the World's Columbian Exposition in Chicago in 1893.[61] The firm's work seven years later, however, received more attention. For France, especially at the 1900 Exposition universelle, hairstyling and fashion design were put forth both in historical and contemporary contexts. At the fair, open from April to November, one of the main attractions was the Palais du costume, in which Émile Martin Poussineau of maison Félix mounted tableaux of historical dress on wax mannequins. Lenthéric styled the coiffures.[62] A claim in the *International Herald Tribune* that Guillaume Louis Lenthéric was an employee of maison Félix must be erroneous, but it is clear that the two houses were associated with one another.[63] Poussineau had begun his career as a hairdresser, and the two may have been acquainted through the Union des coiffeurs, in existence since about 1865, or through the Chambre syndicale patronale des coiffeurs de Paris, founded in 1873.[64] The *International Herald Tribune* reported that in 1890, maison Félix handed over some clients to Lenthéric, providing a glimpse into how the business worked: clients patronized multiple hairdressers, and there was a working relationship between different houses. As they did with Worth, fashion editors considered maison Félix on a par with Lenthéric, and the two firms are paired or appear in close proximity to one another in fashion spreads, as in *Revue illustrée* of June 1893 (Félix with an afternoon gown and Lenthéric for its Orkilia fragrance and Orkidée face powder) and in *Harper's Bazar* in February 1897 (Félix with an opera gown and Lenthéric with a headdress).[65] The two carried the cover of *Harper's Bazar* on March 5, 1898 (fig. 3.7).[66]

In addition to the Projet Félix tableaux of historic dress, the Palais du costume at the Exposition universelle also contained an exhibit of historic French coiffures.

3.7

Cover of *Harper's Bazar*, March 5, 1898, showing designs by maison Félix and by Lenthéric.

HARPER'S BAZAR

PUBLISHED WEEKLY.
VOL. XXXI.—NUMBER 10.

NEW YORK, SATURDAY, MARCH 5, 1898.

TEN CENTS A COPY.
WITH SUPPLEMENTS.

WHITE SATIN EVENING GOWN—PARIS MODEL FROM FÉLIX—COIFFURE FROM LENTHÉRIC.—[See Page 192.]

The proximity and shared space of the two displays substantiates our conception of the mutual reliance of the two professions. The official brochure for the Palais du costume explains that when the plan for the Projet Félix was coming to fruition, the Académie de coiffure expressed interest in collaborating in the artistic venture.[67] A commission was formed to oversee the display of sixty busts showing hairstyles from the time of Henry II through 1900. Camille Croisat, founder of the Académie de coiffure in 1836 and editor of *Le Moniteur de la coiffure* (published since 1858), was president; Henri Dondel (an instructor and editor of *La Coiffure française illustrée*, which began in December 1889) and Auguste Petit were the artistic directors; and Edmond Delot was the secretary.[68] Some thirty-eight hairdressers styled the busts, their names and addresses prominently listed in the brochure. Of the addresses, one in particular stands out: Auguste Petit was located at 7, rue de la Paix, in the same building where Worth had been ensconced since fall 1857 when it opened as Worth et Bobergh (Worth took over after Otto Gustave Bobergh retired in 1870).

PROXIMITIES: PETIT AND WORTH

Following the trail of Auguste Petit (1839–1922) leads to an understanding of how the sharing of space between coiffeurs and couturiers at the Palais du costume at the Exposition universelle in 1900 was just one manifestation of the close affiliations between the two professions. It is known that various design houses employed hairdressers on site, as did maison Félix at 15, rue du Faubourg Saint-Honoré, where the firm was in business from 1846 to 1901.[69] However, their names are unrecorded. French hairdressers were known as the finest in the world, but there were different ranks among them, from the low-paid men's barbers to the middling barbers who worked on men and women, to the elite women's coiffeurs, to which Croisat, Delot, Dondel, Lenthéric, and Petit belonged. As the popular travel guide Baedeker's *Paris and Environs* put it, hairdressers could be found in almost every street, and a haircut could be had for 30 to 50 centimes, but a specialist coiffeur for ladies was best found by recommendation and could charge up to 20 francs for a house call.[70]

Petit was reportedly trained by the hairdresser Sarrazin of 198, rue du Temple, where he gained the attention of and collaborated with Empress Eugénie's hairdresser, Leroy.[71] Petit's salon was located on the mezzanine level (*l'entrecol*) of the five-floor building at 7, rue de la Paix (fig. 3.8). It had existed there as the firm of Hippolyte et Auguste since at least 1865 and continued under that name until 1869

3.8

House of Worth, 7, rue de la Paix. M. Griffith,
"Paris Dressmakers," *Strand Magazine*,
July–December 1894.

or 1870, after which point the now-unidentified Hippolyte was no longer listed, and the name Auguste Petit took over exclusively.[72] Petit won a medal at the Exposition universelle in Paris in 1889, and by 1892, he was director of the Congrès des coiffeurs.[73] By 1886, he offered perfume and cosmetics in addition to hairdressing and millinery. The firm appears to have shifted to 28, place Vendôme after 1910.[74]

The exact relationship between Worth and Petit is unknown, but given Petit's name recognition, the business arrangement was of two established professionals with their own brands, as opposed to maison Félix's anonymous service providers. Petit was well known in Europe and the United States for hairdressing and millinery. He styled hair for the Comédie-Française and for the actresses of maison de Molière, as well as the marquise de Bailleul and the marquise d'Hervey de Saint-Denis.[75] He was in demand for society weddings and gala balls. In 1891, the U.S. magazine *Current Literature* reprinted a piece from the *London Truth* about Petit styling a French woman before a ball, emphasizing how closely he studied the gown before creating the hairstyle:

He takes up the skirt of the gown at the belt, holding it from the ground as high as the waist of his fair *cliente*, studies the "movement" of the train folds, lays the garment deftly where he found it, and then, placing the fingers in the armholes of the corsage, holds that part up, paying particular attention to the outline of the bust. . . . This done, he goes and stands behind the head on which he is to operate, looking intently into the glass wherein it is reflected.[76]

The exaggerated, almost caricatured, tone of the article sounds remarkably similar to literary descriptions of *artiste* male fashion designers, especially the character of Worms (likely based on Charles Frederick Worth) in Émile Zola's *La Curée* (1872), further underscoring the stature of high-ranking hairdressers in Parisian society.[77] From his respected position, Petit judged coiffure contests and signed opinion letters to newspaper editors on behalf of his professional colleagues.[78] He also created hats that were carried in shops in Florence, Italy, with those of the well-known milliner Virot and others, and were featured in such varied periodicals as the *International Herald Tribune* (in which he consistently advertised in the 1890s), New York's society paper *Town Topics*, and the *Millinery Trade Review*.[79] In *Harper's New Monthly Magazine*, Theodore Child compared him to Worth and described how he traveled elegantly in a coupé from "dressing-room to dressing-room" and made his way to London, Madrid, and Vienna when needed for fancy dress balls and theater performances.[80]

Petit and Worth shared several of the same clients, including Princess Pauline von Metternich, who wrote in her memoir about advancing the latter's career through an early order for a ball gown.[81] Mary Crowninshield Endicott, from Salem, Massachusetts, who married British politician Joseph Chamberlain in November 1888, frequented Worth and Petit as well as Raudnitz and Jeanne Hallée for dresses and Perchellet, Monquignon, and Maxen-Gantiez for shoes.[82] In a reversal of the usual dynamics in international marriages, Endicott hailed from a longstanding, wealthy New England family, whereas Chamberlain's modest earnings had derived from manufacturing concerns in Manchester, England.[83] By all accounts the wedding was fairly restrained, owing to the bride's parents' disapproval of the union, even with President and First Lady Cleveland in attendance. The bride wore a gray traveling dress, possibly made by Worth and sold to her by Catharine Donovan in New York; several of her trousseau dresses were by Worth.[84] Phillada Ballard, who has traced Mary Chamberlain's shopping practices in Paris, found that Chamberlain visited Paris at least every eighteen months to order clothes. Her first in-person visit to Worth was on December 5, 1888, during her honeymoon.[85] She returned to Paris in February 1890 en route from a visit to Egypt and once again in late May that year.[86] During that time, she ordered the gray dress of silk with velvet sleeves from Worth that is preserved in the Fashion Museum, Bath, and that she wore for her portrait by John Everett Millais in 1890 (figs. 3.9 and 3.10).[87] She proudly wrote to her mother, Ellen Endicott, that during her visit to Worth she admonished Mademoiselle Berré about the bill, "which I hope impressed her."[88] She further wrote about the selection: "The sleeves are of velvet, with silk cuffs and a regular ruffle of lace—very long—in Paris some of these sleeves covered half the hand like those of Queen Eleanor. . . . This is [what] I had in mind for the portrait. It might be any period and as I told you it was adapted from a picture of Madame Roland. The colour is light and delicate the sleeves a little darker than the silk. What think you?"[89]

For Chamberlain's portrait by Sargent in 1902, the decision for the color and fabric of a dress by the House of Worth was jointly made between sitter, painter, and couturier (fig. 3.11). Chamberlain wrote to her mother, who was paying for the outfit and portrait, on March 18, detailing the collaborative process of choosing the outfit:

Of course the portrait dress was the first thing to be thought about and at 10.30 yesterday we presented ourselves at Worth and found M. Jean and Mme Denise awaiting us. He was most amiable and soon entered into the spirit of it. Mr Sargent is haunted by the scarlet

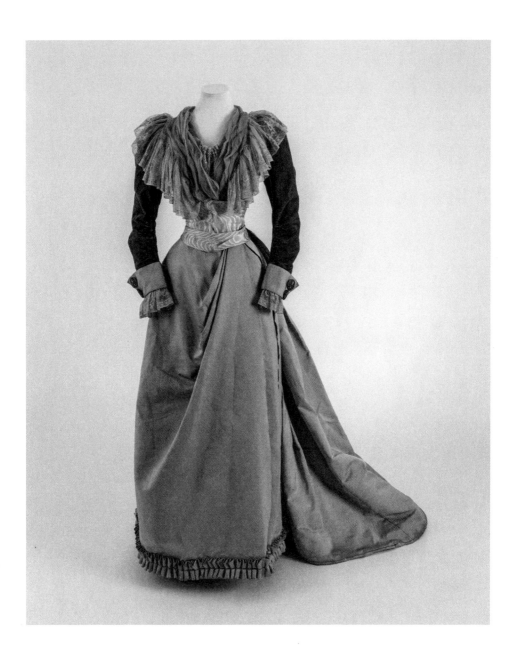

3.9

John Everett Millais (British, 1829–1896). *Mary Endicott Chamberlain*, ca. 1890. Oil on canvas, 134.1×102.4 cm. Birmingham Museums and Art Gallery (1989P60). Image: Birmingham Museums and Art Gallery.

3.10

House of Worth. Gray silk satin and velvet day dress, 1890. Worn by Mary Endicott Chamberlain in portrait by John Everett Millais (fig. 3.9). Fashion Museum, Bath, England (I.09.1342+A). Image: Fashion Museum, Bath / Bridgeman Images.

poppy idea but M. Jean quite agreed with me that it will not do. I said "parrot" rather than "coquettish" was the colour which might do. Mr Sargent also returns to white silk with a "drapery volante" of colour.[90]

The House of Worth produced the dress fairly quickly. Four days later, Chamberlain reported that the final fitting had taken place.[91] Sargent may have held onto the dress in his studio after the in-person sittings were finished, as on November 4, Mary wrote her mother, "My portrait dress has returned from its visit to Paris."[92] As Ballard points out, Chamberlain acquired her wardrobe both on-site in Paris, through ordering by mail, and in custom visits with Parisian couturiers visiting London or at their branches in that city.[93]

It is possible that Petit was responsible for styling Chamberlain's light bouffant hairstyle and dark brown headpiece for the portrait by Sargent. She wrote of Petit as "an *indispensible* part of a visit to Paris" and made a trip to his salon in preparation for the portrait: "we have been there all afternoon and have added two more hats and some 'coiffures.'"[94] Due to the lack of records for the ephemeral business of hairstyling, it is only possible to speculate as to the scope of Petit's enterprise, but clearly the success and longevity of the House of Worth were reliant on close collaborations with other practitioners.

By 1909, Petit was president of the Académie de coiffure. At some point afterward, he appears to have moved his business to 28, place Vendôme, well located near fellow coiffeur Émile Landry and couturier Michniewicz-Cuvée on the same street. Soon after he died in 1922, he was bestowed the Legion of Honor.[95] Baedeker's *Paris and Environs* listed him and only two other high-end coiffeurs throughout the 1890s and early 1900s in its French and English-language editions, and he was one of only two recommended in the widely circulated *Tout-Paris* guidebook of 1899.[96]

3.11

John Singer Sargent (U.S., 1856–1925).
*Mary Crowninshield Endicott Chamberlain
(Mrs. Joseph Chamberlain)*, 1902. Oil on
canvas, 150.5×83.8 cm. National Gallery of
Art, Washington, DC, Gift of the sitter, Mary
Endicott Chamberlain Carnegie (1958.2.1).
Image: National Gallery of Art, Washington, DC.

In 1912, Cassie Mason Myers James of Washington, DC, donated a pair of framed photographs (now unlocated) of Charles Frederick Worth and Auguste Petit to the United States National Museum (now the Smithsonian Institution).[97] The catalog of the year's acquisitions provided little information beyond the name of the donor, the sitters in the photographic portraits, and the identification of Petit as a hairdresser to Empress Eugénie. This seemingly curious donation to the national collection is actually emblematic of the deep-seated reputation of French couture and coiffure in the U.S. consciousness. By 1902, more than 50 percent of buyers of French couture were from overseas, and by 1912, the top three categories of buyers were "middlemen"; English, U.S., and German dressmakers; and overseas individual clients.[98] By the 1920s, the United States was second only to Britain for leading the market for French fashion.[99] At a distance of 3,635 miles (from New York to Paris) to 4,130 miles (from Chicago to Paris), accessible by nine-to-ten-day steamship trips, as opposed to 286 miles between London and Paris, reached by rail and ferry in less than a day, the widespread desire and potent market in the United States deserves critical attention.

FRENCH REPUTATION FOR STYLE

Historians trace the emergence of France as the dominant purveyor of stylish clothing to the late seventeenth century, when finance minister to Louis XIV, Jean-Baptiste Colbert, successfully facilitated the transition of Lyon from a city of importers to manufacturers and exporters of silk cloth.[100] The city had previously brought in Italian, eastern Mediterranean, Chinese, and Japanese silk cloth, but Colbert changed the dynamic, providing silkworms and skilled workers so that Lyon could become self-reliant.[101] Lyon successfully developed into the largest market for silk cloth and maintained the stature until the mid-1890s, when manufacturers in the United States, as a result of industrial improvements, became equipped to produce the fabric.[102] Parisian couturiers benefited from their proximity to the Lyonnaise suppliers of this delicate, "aristocratic fiber" that required hand working, and the House of Worth was one of the most influential customers.[103] The quality of materials and the expertise of creating and presenting fashion emerged among the cultural touchstones of Paris, which have lasted to the present: good taste and good style.

The origin of the reputation of Paris coiffure as unmatched in the Western world is associated with figures who worked for elite clients and the royal court in the seventeenth and eighteenth centuries, beginning with Champagne (d. 1658) and Legros de Rumigny (d. 1770), who published a book on the art of coiffure in 1765 and opened a hairdressing school in 1769.[104] In the late eighteenth century, Marie Antoinette's primary hairdresser was Léonard (Léonard Alexis Autier).[105] In his posthumously published memoirs of 1838, he attributed the intimate relationship of the hairdresser (then always male) to the royal patron as prompting the custom of referring to the hairdresser only by first name.[106] The single-name convention continued in the late nineteenth century, when firms with multiple employees who served long rosters of customers were referred to by the name of the founder (Dondel, Delot).

The link to aristocracy solidified French coiffure in the U.S. mindset as worthy of aspiration (fig. 3.12). The fashion press conveyed French practitioners as superior, a result of their professionalization, which developed from the establishment of organizations and schools. As the *Sun* wrote in 1890, "hair dressers in New York are not artists, as they of the profession are in Paris, and they cannot always be depended upon for their suggestions."[107] People in the United States were aware of the different ranks—from barber to elite coiffeur—that might be claimed. In advertisements, French practitioners in the United States boldly stated their qualifications, like Joannes (John) Rochon, hairdresser to First Lady Frances Cleveland in Washington, DC, who referred to himself as a professor and "first-class hair-dresser from Paris," citing multiple patents and medals from expositions in Paris, Lyon, and Vienna.[108]

The U.S. papers reported on Parisian competitions like the one in October 1891 at the Académie de coiffure at which three prizes would be given to "those who produce styles absolutely new."[109] The styles would then belong to the Académie and officially set the trend for the following season. In the United States, professionalization advanced when the *American Hairdresser* began publication out of Brooklyn in 1878, eventually holding its own contests, and when the Hair Dealer's Association of the United States was founded in 1888.[110] Further, a hairdressing academy was founded by the Frenchmen Brisbois and Federmeyer in Chicago in 1890.[111] In the interim, there were loosely formed societies of hairdressers who gathered to determine styles, as did a certain one in New York that met monthly.[112]

The influence of French styles on these organizations made its way into the mainstream U.S. fashion press, which would painstakingly enumerate each step a woman at home could take to achieve a certain French style.[113] The transmission, however, could lead to exaggerated versions, such as the "French pompadour" that

was popular with U.S. women in 1899 but that towered several inches higher on the head than the original.[114] The French encouraged U.S. women to improve their look by taking up techniques such as ondulating, producing a semipermanent wave: "With care, the waves last fifteen days, and an American hairdresser, having learned the process, could make a fortune by introducing it to New-York," wrote the *New York Times*.[115] Accordingly an extant invoice from the coiffeur Émile Landry at 23, place Vendôme to Mary Rita Wilson Goelet of Newport in 1892 indicates that Landry specialized in ondulations that lasted fifteen days and that English was spoken on the premises.[116]

Women in the United States did not always take to the latest French styles, however, as reported by the *Sun* in 1890, when many women rejected a particular French style that sat low on the neck: "the fashion gains ground slowly among American ladies, who insist that it is untidy and inconvenient, and takes away something from their dignity and smartness."[117] But a good U.S. hairdresser, trained in French techniques, of which there was no shortage of practitioners claiming such, could ably adapt.[118]

INTERNATIONALISM OF THE COUTURE AND COIFFURE INDUSTRIES

As evidenced here, the transnationalism of the couture and coiffure industries was due in large part to the expansion of certain firms into branches outside of Paris and the avid coverage of French fashion in the European and U.S. press. However, an equally important aspect was the internationalism of the practitioners themselves and their movement between countries. There were no requirements for work visas, and France needed laborers, especially in the clothing industries, during periods of depopulation in the nineteenth century.[119] By 1906, the immigrant population of France was 2.5 percent; in Paris alone, it was 6.3 percent.[120] Paging through volumes

3.12

The Marquise and Her Coiffeur, in Theodore Child, *The Praise of Paris* (New York: Harper and Brothers, 1893). New York Public Library, The Miriam and Ira D. Wallach Division of Art, Prints and Photographs: Picture Collection (b17239250). Image: New York Public Library.

of French fashion periodicals of the 1880s and 1890s, especially the advertisements, one notices that most surnames are French but that there is a fair amount of representation from other countries in Europe. By taking a closer look, it is possible to expand on the existing research on migration and garment labor history led so effectively by historian Nancy L. Green. The approach necessitates a focus on the lesser-known manufactures of fashion and accessories, thereby casting light on some of the forgotten women's contributions to the fashion industry.

Morin-Blossier was founded by Viennese seamstresses Marie Blossier and Victoire Morin in about 1879 in Paris.[121] The firm designed and produced court dresses for Queen Alexandra and her daughter, Princess Maud, using fitted linings modeled from the women's bodies.[122] The house was a favorite in the pages of *Woman's World* as well as the *New York Times*, which emphasized patronage by Sarah Bernhardt, opera singer Adelina Patti, and other high-profile clients throughout the United States (reportedly including Alva Vanderbilt), England, Germany, and Russia.[123]

The nationalities of couturiers extended well beyond French and Viennese. In one representative issue of *La Mode illustrée* from April 1883, alongside the French couturiers Delaunay and Coussinet are the children's designer Mademoiselles Hunsinger (Swiss) and the milliner Signorino (Italian).[124] Madame N. Rodrigues of Rodrigues et Cie (active from at least 1875 to 1879), known to have worked with theater performers, was featured by the fashion writer Violette in her book *L'Art de la toilette chez la femme* (1885) and in her columns for *Woman's World*, but surviving garments are exceedingly rare (fig. 3.13).[125] Furthermore, in *Moniteur des dames et des demoiselles* in 1882 and 1883 are dresses by Adolphine Koenig (German) and Madame Brylinski et Cie (Polish), who may have been married to the Monsieur Brylinski, who was president of the Chambre syndicale de la confection et de la couture pour dames et fillettes from 1890 to 1892.[126] The latter is identified as the grandson of Jean Dollfus, who owned a textile company in Mulhouse, France.[127]

The intergenerational change from French to Polish surnames indicates intermarriages that continued to diversify the industry. The Michniewicz-Tuvée millinery house at 28, place Vendôme from 1868 to 1905, is another example of a Polish-French firm. Moreover, the Raudnitz family (French, of German descent) held a significant presence, with two establishments in Paris. The first, Raudnitz et Cie, was founded about 1875 and conducted business at 13, rue de la Grange-Batalière and 21, place Vendôme until 1901, at which time it merged with Huet et Chéruit.[128] In 1883, one of the siblings, Ernest, opened his own firm at 23, rue Louis-le-Grand, later relocating to 8, rue Royale. Marie Callot Gerber worked at

3.13

N. Rodrigues (French, active from at least 1875 to 1879). Dinner dress, blue-green silk satin brocade with woven pattern of red roses, late 1870s. Collection of The Kyoto Costume Institute, photo by Takashi Hatakeyama.

Ernest Raudnitz's firm from 1886 to 1888 and in 1895 founded Callot Soeurs with her sisters, Marthe Callot Bertrand, Regina Callot Tennyson-Chantrell, and Joséphine Callot Crimont; the women were born in Paris to parents of Russian descent. Located at 24, rue Taitbout (it moved to 9–11, avenue Matignon in 1914), it eventually employed some six hundred workers and, by the 1920s, ran branches in Nice, Biarritz, Buenos Aires, and London.[129]

Raudnitz featured prominently in the French fashion press, such as *Le Moniteur de la mode*, and in the U.S. papers, like the *New York Times*, where the name was frequently misspelled, an indication of the foreignness of the name. Prejudices against foreign workers in the garment trades was persistent. Reporting on a tailor and seamstresses' strike in Paris in 1901, the British magazine *Sketch* exaggerated the situation: "ninety-eight per cent of the cutters of Paris tailor-gowns are not French, but foreigners," and several languages were spoken at the meetings of the strikers.[130] It further cites "Tchecks (Bohemians) from Vienna" as the most numerous, having "opened native restaurants on the rue de la Paix and Opéra neighborhood to serve them."[131]

The concern over the presence of so many foreigners in the industry is a reminder of the hundreds of workers who made the houses function as viable businesses and also of the competition within the labor ranks. The top designers and salespeople earned a fine salary plus gratuities from loyal clients.[132] Many of the names are lost, but it is possible to cite here Doucet's chief fitter and designer, José de la Peña de Guzman,[133] and a certain M. Carlsson, who was "first hand" to Charles Frederick Worth. He appears to be Carl Isidore Carlsson of Sweden, who was godfather to Renée Marie Jeanne Worth, daughter of Gaston Worth.[134] Despite the standing of foreigners at all ranks of the businesses, however, at the beginning of the First World War, in 1914, the Chambre syndicale de la couture parisienne disbanded in an effort to dissociate from foreign couturiers within its ranks. After excising certain members, it restarted in 1915.[135]

European Jews claimed a long history in the tailoring trades, having been barred from other professions and from selling goods to Christians. The various bouts of political unrest and anti-Semitism throughout eastern Europe in the nineteenth century, not least of which were the pogroms of Russia and Ukraine in the final two decades, resulted in vast emigrations. From 1800 to 1880, about 250,000 Jews fled eastern Europe; the number grew to one million between 1881 and 1900.[136] Between 1800 and 1925, 100,000 Jews emigrated to France, which generally had been recognized as friendly to Jews since it became the first country to emancipate them in 1791.[137]

In Germany, after unification in 1871, Jews regained political and civil rights that they had been previously denied. Many of the principal ready-to-wear (*konfektion*) manufacturers and department store owners in the country were Jewish.[138] The Nathan Israel store and the Hermann Gerson store in Berlin are prominent examples.[139] They featured French designs, due to clients' demands, and representatives of the businesses traveled to Paris to view the latest styles.[140] German-derived Jewish names appear in Parisian couture, which could be the names of practitioners late in the century who were branching out their businesses or family names that resulted from intermarriages and open borders over generations. As historian Claire Zalc has persuasively argued with regard to the interwar period, in the names that they chose for their shop names, foreigners marked the spaces of Paris.[141]

High-end dressmakers and coiffeurs of various nationalities made their way to the United States as well, although immigration historians cite evidence that larger numbers of European emigrants who may be described as professionals in their trades went to France rather than the United States, probably due to proximity.[142] Nonetheless, as mentioned earlier, many journeyed to the States to attend to clients for special events like fancy dress balls and then returned home. Others opened branches of their businesses, traveling between both, and still others set up shop permanently. Before the infamous Bradley-Martin ball in New York in February 1897 (see chapter 8, Rising Prices: The Impact of U.S. Tariffs), French hairdressers, presumably ones based in Paris, charged $15 (the equivalent of about $453 in 2018) per head, whereas cheaper ones could be hired downtown on Houston Street.[143]

Immigration to the United States was relatively open. From 1866 to 1900, 13.2 million people emigrated to the United States, the majority from western and southeastern Europe.[144] Lower-ranking dressmakers, tailors, and hairdressers were among them, and since the specializations were just beginning to professionalize, people could hang a shingle more easily, rightfully or deceptively claiming French heritage and cultivation. Their work resides next to that of French couturiers' in museums throughout the United States. In the late 1880s, Madame Delphine Michaux of 166 West 23rd Street produced a moss-green silk and velvet dress that is now in the Kent State University Museum.[145] The Museum at FIT holds a mauve silk faille and white wool two-piece dress from about 1889 with the label of Madame Victorine at 60 West 37th Street, who was either an immigrant from France or had advantageously assumed a French name.[146] Similarly, advertisements by self-claimed French hairdressers like Mademoiselle Benoit on East 53rd Street in New York appear frequently; she made house calls, offered the "latest Paris styles," and was looking for "a few more engagements."[147]

Others fled difficult circumstances in their home countries and sought to apply their skills in the burgeoning ready-to-wear market. In a story for the *Independent* titled "The Dressmaker's Life Story," Amelia des Moulins, who learned the trade as a child from her aunt in Paris, wrote about overhearing a conversation between wealthy U.S. clients who were "mostly daughters of working people, common laborers, butchers and shopkeepers who had grown rich some way."[148] In 1899, partially motivated by people from the United States who had complimented her taste, she moved to New York to seek opportunities.[149] Landing on 6th Avenue, she faced demanding shop owners and landlords, two of the many challenges for immigrant workers in the garment district, an entire topic of study in its own right.[150]

When probing the proximities between couturiers, coiffeurs, perfumiers, and related professionals, as this chapter has done, the broad scope of the fashion system in France, with all its personalities, relationships, and conflicts, emerges. It becomes impossible to consider only one or two figures as directing an entire industry, and the tenuousness of individual businesses at any given time, comes into focus. Against this backdrop of multifaceted collaborations and rivalries, the next chapter considers the competitiveness of the market and the speed with which a frontrunner could meet its decline.

COUTURIERS AND INTERNATIONAL EXPOSITIONS

In late spring through summer 1901, the closing of maison Félix, a couturier that had been in business in Paris more than fifty years, became international news. Several papers, especially in the United States, attributed the closure to overspending on a large display of historical costume that the maison organized at the Exposition universelle the year before.[1] A handful of papers, however, cited owner Émile Martin Poussineau's repudiation of the claim.[2] In the absence of business archives, the true explanation for the closing cannot be determined, but the episode raises productive questions about the extraordinary costs that were required for fashion houses to participate in international expositions.

This chapter uncovers the elaborate planning, spending, and execution of the historic costume exhibit for which maison Félix was responsible in 1900 and analyzes the commercial benefits and risks of such involvement. By contrast to the successes of Lanvin, Paquin, and Worth at the 1900 exposition, the chapter argues that participation was a risky endeavor that could either bolster the businesses of couturiers or lead to their demise, even for one that had previously thrived for decades.

COUTURIERS AND INTERNATIONAL EXPOSITIONS

In her steadfast book *The History of Haute Couture, 1850–1950*, Diana de Marly prudently noted that in the nineteenth century the French government encouraged the participation of couturiers in international expositions as a way to promote interest in one of the country's key industries.[3] London had held the first major one, the Great Exhibition, in 1851, launching the worldwide, competitive phenomenon that continued through the end of the twentieth century. The extensive literature on international expositions explains that the opportunity to parade industrial and colonial conquests in a show of national power motivated countries to organize the exhibitions.[4] With scores of buildings across its grounds, the fairs remained open for months and drew immense numbers of visitors. Paris proudly hosted expositions in 1855, 1867, 1878, 1889, and 1900, the last one attracting some fifty million attendees.

Maison Gagelin-Opigez, where Charles Frederick Worth worked early in his career, won accolades at the Great Exhibition of 1851.[5] The house was celebrated again at the 1855 exposition, by which time Worth had been a partner for two years.[6] In 1858, Worth partnered with Otto Gustav Bobergh to open a shop that eventually built the Worth brand, which lasted for generations. Gaston Worth, one of Charles Frederick's sons, appears to have had Worth partake in the Paris exposition of 1889 and at the World's Columbian Exposition in Chicago in 1893.[7] Taking over the business after their father's death in 1895, Gaston and his brother Jean-Philippe put forth the maison for the international exposition in Brussels in 1897 and for the Musée rétrospectif in the Palais des fils, tissus, et vêtements exhibition at the 1900 exposition.[8] At the 1925 Exposition internationale des arts décoratifs et industriels modernes in Paris, it was featured in the Pavilion of Elegance.

The palais, a collective venture, was organized by couturier Jeanne Paquin, whose gown adorned the fifteen-foot plaster statue of *La Parisienne* by Paul Moreau-Vauthier that stood by the main gate to the exposition (fig. 4.1).[9] Business historian Véronique Pouillard has begun to sort out the beginnings of the Paquin firm, determining that Isidore René Jacob opened it under the name Paquin, in 1891 at 3, rue de la Paix after buying out his partner, Madame Lalanne.[10] Jeanne Marie Charlotte Beckers, a former mannequin at maison Rouff, joined the firm in 1888, married Isidore René Jacob (called Paquin) in 1891, and became codirector and lead designer (fig. 4.2).[11] By 1907, the year Isidore Paquin died and Jeanne Paquin took over the business, the Paris location employed 1,350 people.[12]

4.1

Cover of piano sheet music by Domenico Ferroni, *La Parisienne de Paris. Valse de l'exposition 1900. Marche du nouveau siecle* (Paris: Valisi & Giorgi, 1900). Image: Paul van Kuik.

At the 1900 Exposition universelle, the House of Worth's designs were shown on wax mannequins in two of the four displays; one showed "the fitting of the wedding gown" (fig. 4.3). Jean-Philippe Worth later disdainfully recalled that there were too many exhibitors and that Worth was given a dark corner.[13] However unfavorable the placement may have been, it hardly affected future business, as the House of Worth went on to acclaim for decades. In the Musée rétrospectif in the Palais des fils, tissus, et vêtements exhibition at the 1900 exposition, one of Worth's main competitors, maison Félix, was well represented. It showed a "Nile green" evening gown with lace and a low-cut neck embellished with diamonds and emeralds. Other firms—Barroise, Bonnaire, Callot Soeurs, Doeuillet, Doucet, Margaine Lacroix, Sara Mayer, Morhange, the Ney sisters, and Rouff—were also included, many of which showed in later expositions.[14]

Maison Félix, founded in 1846, was located at 15, rue du Faubourg Saint-Honoré from at least 1849 (see chapter 6, Maison Félix and Its U.S. Clients). In 1850, the firm advertised that it had won a bronze medal at the Exposition nationale des produits de l'industrie agricole et manufacturière in Paris in 1849.[15] It was owned and run by Émile Martin Poussineau (called Félix), and its sales and international reputation peaked from about 1870 through the 1890s. It does not appear to have participated in Paris's international expositions of 1855, 1867, or 1878, as the name is not listed in any of the official, and thorough, publications. Félix is also not listed in the records of the exposition of 1889, but it reportedly displayed at least one gown of tan silk with black and white embroidery, which was later purchased, somewhat like a trophy, by May Saunders Harrison of New York through a firm called White and Howard.[16] The maison also designed a gown for the First Lady of France, Cécile Carnot, for the opening of the exposition.[17]

Maison Félix's involvement in earlier, significant exhibitions may be seen as a precursor to that in 1900. First, the firm participated in the Exposition des arts de la femme in Paris in 1892. Organized by the Union centrale des arts décoratifs

4.2

Jeanne Paquin (French, 1869–1936) for the House of Paquin (French, 1891–1956). Evening suit, late 1890s. Silk. The Metropolitan Museum of Art, New York, Gift of Miss Marie Reimer, 1948 (C.I.48.70.1a,b). Image: © The Metropolitan Museum of Art.

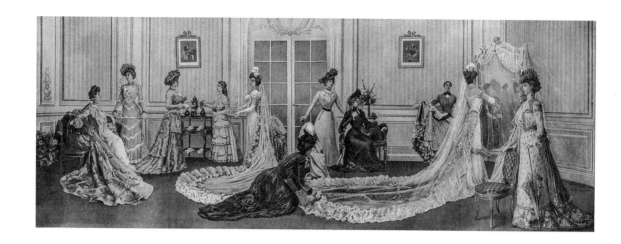

(UCAD), the show was held at the Palais de l'industrie and included historic women's costume and hairdressing on wax models.[18] Félix appears to have been one of the organizers of this section, together with Gaston Worth and others, of the "9th class," which had specialists in clothing, lingerie, hats, and other accessories.[19] The following year, gowns by Félix were included in the French section of the Department of Manufactures at the World's Columbian Exposition in Chicago in 1893, with those by Worth, Pasgner, and Panget.[20] The exposition was visited by some twenty-six million people. Four years later, Félix entered into the Exposition universelle in Brussels, which welcomed six million visitors.[21]

The Exposition universelle opened in Paris on April 15, 1900, and continued until November 12, 1900. The exhibition halls—including Civil Engineering and Transportation, the French Colonies, the Palais de la femme (Women's Building), and the Palace of Electricity, to name a few—spanned more than 250 acres and contained thousands of displays.[22] Fifty-eight countries participated. The goal was to spotlight and promote France's international stature as an owner of colonies

4.3

House of Worth display, Palais des fils, tissus, et vêtements, Exposition universelle, Paris, 1900. In René Baschet, *Le Panorama: Exposition universelle 1900*. Image: Bibliothèque nationale de France, Paris.

and its dominance in various industries, of which textiles and couture were part, but also to celebrate its history. Maude Bass-Kreuger has skillfully elucidated how a collective historical imagination in this period led to the popularity of presenting both authentic artifacts and re-creations of garments, which were recently deemed worthy of collecting.[23] Clothing was featured in several different contexts throughout the exposition: as industry, as history, and as contemporary fashion. The aforementioned Musée rétrospectif in the Palais des fils, tissus, et vêtements showed garments and accessories lent by museums and private owners.[24] The organizing committee comprised an art critic, museum officials, illustrators, and painters, and the project was likely funded by the state, as were many aspects of the exposition.[25]

The privately run Projet Félix, as it was called, was held in the two-story, 3,000-meter-long Palais du costume (fig. 4.4) located on the Champ de Mars near the Eiffel Tower.[26] Also in the Palais du costume was the Académie de coiffure de Paris, headed by prominent hairdressers Camille Croisat, Edmond Delot, Henri Dondel, and Auguste Petit, who erected a display of the history of coiffure executed by contemporary stylists.[27] Brochures explained that the aim of the palais was to show the "glorification of fashion and the apotheosis of woman" through historical tableaux.[28] Wax mannequins were dressed in recreations of historic dress and hairstyles by Lenthéric.[29] They were posed in thirty-one vignettes, including an ancient Roman atrium, a chevalier tournament of the fourteenth century, a portrait statue of Marie de Médici, and an 1830 baptism in France.[30]

The most frequently described tableau in the press was the coronation of Empress Joséphine in 1804 (fig. 4.5).[31] *Harper's* guide for U.S. visitors speculated that Joséphine's original ensemble had cost nearly one million francs and here was "reproduced with scrupulous exactitude, the only difference in the historical garment being that the jewelry with which it is studded is not real, as it was in the original."[32] *Harper's Bazar* reported that it was "supposed to be the only accurate reproduction of the dress of Joséphine on that occasion which has ever been made."[33] Vignette number 32 featured a retrospective of fashion from the Expositions universelles of 1855, 1867, 1878, and 1889, and two Félix costume designs for contemporary theater: Sarah Bernhardt in *La Dame aux camélias* and Réjane (Gabrielle Charlotte Reju), in *La Glu*.[34] Number 33 showed ball gowns from 1867. In a savvy promotion for the business, number 34 presented of-the-moment ball gowns by Félix, and number 35 recreated the Félix salons as "La Mode en 1900 (Créations de Félix)" (fig. 4.6).

The scenes were apparently arranged on the first floor of the Palais du costume, whereas the second floor re-created shopping galleries from the eighteenth-century

4.4

"Le Palais du costume, Exposition
universelle, Paris, 1900," in René Baschet,
*Le Panorama: Exposition universelle
1900.* Image: Bibliothèque nationale de
France, Paris.

4.5

"La Veille du sacres, 1804," *Palais du costume. Le Costume de la femme à travers les âges: Projet Félix* (1900).

Palais-Royal.[35] According to one report, twenty models wore the gowns each afternoon as a novelty entertainment.[36] The event was an extension of the practice of live modeling inside elite couture houses. As Caroline Evans has shown, the evolution from inert dolls or automatons to active modeling occurred in the 1880s, when women walked *en plein air* in the bois de Boulogne and at the Champs-Elysées.[37] Live modeling at the Palais du costume underscores the multiple dimensions utilized by organizers like Poussineau to erect and enact their displays to successful effect. The movement of fashionable models and visitors throughout the grounds of the Exposition counterbalanced the stillness of wax models and display cases. In the formulation of theorists Joanne Entwistle, Elizabeth Wilson, and John Potvin,

4.6

"La Mode en 1900 (Créations de Félix)," in René Baschet, *Le Panorama: Exposition universelle 1900*. Image: Bibliothèque nationale de France, Paris.

here we see the "fleshiness" of fashion worn by human bodies that interact with and act on the spaces through which they move.[38]

COSTS AND BENEFITS FOR MAISON FÉLIX

The Projet Félix was nothing short of "colossal."[39] Poussineau explained that he spent five years working on the palais and that "each of the forty tableaux has been the subject of absorbing thought and care."[40] The papers reported on his large expenditures—as much as $16,000 to make the court mantle of Joséphine alone.[41] A team of colleagues fabricated the exhibition, including architect and theater costume designer Albert-Félix-Théophile Thomas, architect Charles Risler, archaeologist Albert Gayet, scholar and artist Marcel Hallé, and "a host of intelligent women collaborators."[42] Gayet traveled to Egypt and Tunisia to study artifacts for the exhibit and set up a display of excavated objects on the lower level of the palais, accompanied by a companion book he wrote on Egyptian costume from the third through thirteenth centuries.[43] Hallé visited museums throughout Europe, and Poussineau apparently spent weeks in Venice conducting research, perhaps for the scene "Patriciennes de Venise."[44] As the *Irish Times* put it, "The agents of M. Félix have been ransacking Europe for years."[45] The reporter for the *Evening Times-Republican* of Marshalltown, Iowa, described Poussineau as "the fashionable man dressmaker, M. Félix," who has spent a small fortune and years of research in carrying out his idea."[46] Poussineau told the reporter:

I have always been pleased from the first with the interest this plan has excited everywhere. If I had not been thus encouraged I would not have carried this idea thru [sic]. It has cost 400,000 francs ($77,000). Most of this I will never be repaid, tho [sic] we mean to charge a small admission fee. But I think the pleasure I have in the historical interest and significance of my exhibit is sufficient reward.[47]

In light of the enormous personal cost, the question arises as to Poussineau's motivations for taking on such an enormous project. The impulse must have been twofold. First, the exhibition would raise money for his business. The Palais du costume was considered a privately owned side show or novelty rather than a state-sponsored display of industrial prowess. Vendors, entertainment, and amenities abounded at the exposition, from restaurants and cafés to a beauty salon and barber. However, by tapping into the public interest in historical costume, Poussineau cleverly situated maison Félix within the distinguished chronology of French fashion.[48] During private tours for the likes of First Lady of France Marie-Louise Loubet, he would have had exclusive opportunities to promote his work.[49]

Second, this exhibition devoted to the apotheosis, or divine status, of women aligned with Poussineau's civic work. He co-organized the palais with colleagues from the Mutualité maternelle, which he helped found in 1892.[50] The program collected dues from female workers as well as governmental subsidies and private donations, which were distributed when women in the sewing trades and eventually from other groups needed postnatal breaks from work.[51] The overarching goal of the aid society was to support infant health and to combat depopulation, a concern in France at the time, and it constituted a major effort by Solidarists, who believed in the government's social responsibility, which would in turn strengthen the state.[52] The Solidarist movement, lasting from 1889 to 1910, represented the state's republican, conservative turn toward paternalism, which was implemented in many workplaces.[53] Poussineau devoted the rest of his life to the Mutualité maternelle and appears to also have helped open a school in Talant, France, where there is a street named after him.[54]

Poussineau must have known how valuable the exposure at the exposition could be for his firm and for the mutual aid cause. As early as 1897, the U.S. press was predicting the impact the exposition would have on fashion, and during the run of the exposition, magazines ran features on the types of gowns seen on visitors and for sale at French and U.S. stores.[55] Not only did Poussineau display Félix gowns in tableaux 34 and 35, but he also found space for two gowns the firm had made for Elena of Montenegro when she became unable to wear them due to a period of mourning for the assassinated King Umberto I of Italy.[56] The firm's name was advertised on brochures and postcards for the palais. Furthermore, Félix designs were in constant motion throughout the grounds and worn by clients visiting the exposition.[57] The brand recognition extended to another side show: the Guillaume Marionettes performed in a small theater ten to twelve times per day. The first scene showed a Parisian hostess receiving guests at a five o'clock tea, all of whom were dressed in "Worth or Félix gowns and move about with consummate ease."[58] Finally, the association with the history of French fashion held the power to increase sales of its newly designed gowns.

From the perspective of his political leanings as a Solidarist, Poussineau must have seen opportunities to raise support for the Mutualité maternelle at the exposition. The same year, he spoke at a republican feminist congress and championed benefits for mothers.[59] Notably, although Poussineau's name is not attached to them, the exposition provided a number of services for women in the Palais de la femme, including childcare. "You can check your babies at the exposition," wrote a reporter for the *Evening Star*, in an article providing guidance for working women visiting the exposition."[60] In the context of Solidarism, childcare was a mutual responsibility to benefit society rather than a feminist rights concern.[61] The service was one of the efforts to counterbalance the fair's controversial emphasis on consumer interests or, as German literary critic and philosopher Walter Benjamin would later critique world's fairs, as ground zero of commodity culture and fetish.[62] The perception of the morally shallow leanings of visitors to the Palais du costume is accentuated by the disappointing results of a lottery that was set up to benefit the Mutualité maternelle in summer 1900. The drawing of a winner needed to be postponed for more than three months due to a lack of ticket sales, although they cost only one franc.[63]

CLOSING OF MAISON FÉLIX AND THE AFTERLIFE OF THE PALAIS DU COSTUME

Maison Félix's participation in the Exposition universelle constituted a substantial opportunity but also a risk. In the end, the Palais du costume was a critical success—*L'Art et la mode* and *Le Ménestrel* were two of the papers that ran glowing reviews—but did not fare as well financially.[64] In general, the privately run concessions did not turn profits, due to costly leases and fervent competition, and they were dismantled or abandoned. Three weeks after the close of the exposition, one reporter called the dark palais "funereal" and other areas "the city of the dead."[65] After the exhibition, plaster models for the wax figures in the tableaux were sold for 5 to 20 francs at the Hôtel Drouot, and the contents of the palais were purchased by the organizers of the 1902 universal exposition in London.[66] It is unclear to what extent Poussineau benefited from the sale, though he was credited in the official guide for the London exhibition as an ex officio member of the committee for French patronage.[67] Maison Félix's historic tableaux were displayed in the Empress Theatre on the London fair's grounds.[68] Contemporary fashion—including gowns by Doeuillet, Laferrière, Lebouvier, Sara Mayer, Morhange, the Ney sisters, Raudnitz, Redfern, and Worth—were also displayed, possibly in the same building. Maison Félix is not listed in the guide, as the business had closed the previous year.

Based on reports in U.S. newspapers, the assumption has been that Poussineau overextended his spending for the Palais du costume at the Exposition universelle in Paris in 1900 and as a result was forced to shut his doors. On June 29, 1901, the

St. Louis Republic ran the stark headline "Felix, Noted French Dressmaker, Fails," attributing the cause to "investing all his money in the palace."[69] It erroneously reported that the remnants were bought by the Aux trois quartiers department store. In sensationalized terms, it continues: "Worth, Doucet, Paquin and Redfern have all sent condolences, but admit that the bankrupt was their superior. Numerous offers of financial assistance from grandes dames whom he has dressed were made, but Félix, disspirited [*sic*], declined all."[70] The next day, the *Washington Times* colorfully wrote, "For those women who have been in the habit of paying Félix, the world's greatest dressmaker, as much money for a ball gown as would buy a house and farm it must be sad news to learn that he has failed."[71]

In May 1901, at least two of the premier French newspapers reported the closing in stark terms, stating only that good prices could be had during the final days.[72] It is difficult to determine, then, why the U.S. newspapers in June and July 1901 reported the closure as bankruptcy. Poussineau became aware of the reports and apparently told the Associated Press in late June: "This is an idiotic calumny. I have decided to retire from business, after working hard for forty years and amassing a fortune of 6,000,000 francs, with which I intend to retire to the country for life."[73] Only a handful of U.S. papers and magazines, including the *New York Tribune* and *Art Amateur*, ran this counterstory.[74] Concluding the press cycle, *Table Talk* of Melbourne cited Poussineau's retirement and his defense of adequate dollars to his name: "The figures are to be credited when it is understood that M. Félix never charged less than $3,000 for one of his famous gowns, and in an excess of gratitude when his efforts were thought to surpass themselves, his wealthy patrons frequently made far larger payments with apparent satisfaction."[75]

Poussineau's continued work with the Mutualité maternelle until his death in 1930 lends credence to his claim of having money in the bank. Poussineau's leanings toward Solidarism may have come to supersede his private business concerns. Within this social philosophy, the concerns of the group were more important than that of the individual, and women's participation in capitalist shopping, especially in department stores and at universal expositions, became anxiety-producing.[76] In Émile Zola's 1883 novel *Au bonheur des dames*, the department store is a seductive zone in which women circulate, socialize, and spend freely.[77]

In addition to moral concerns, however, labor unrest was also on the rise. The uptick of workers' strikes in this period may have galvanized or necessitated Poussineau's activity in the direction of the mutual aid society and away from the couturier business. For instance, in February 1901, a few months before maison Félix closed, there was a large and influential strike by tailors and seamstresses who worked at high-end clothing establishments on the rue de la Paix and nearby.[78] The feminist-supported strike, lasting thirty-five days, called for shorter work days, higher wages, and a reduction in the employment of subcontractors.[79] The strike involved 700 out of 800 workers from 55 womenswear workshops and likely would have affected maison Félix's business at a time when Poussineau had recently expended immense funds on the exposition. And the very nature of the strikes, motivated by the desires of individual workers for higher wages, was at odds with Poussineau's mutualist leanings.

The afterlife of the Palais du costume continued beyond its tenure at the London exposition of 1902 and further affirms the extent to which investment in exposition displays was a risky proposition. After London, the contents of the palais were bought for the Louisiana Purchase Exposition in St. Louis, on view from April 30 to December 1, 1904. Local investors set up the Palais du Costume Company and bought the tableaux in spring 1903.[80] The coiffure exhibition organized by Camille Croisat, Edmond Delot, Henri Dondel, and Auguste Petit also appeared in St. Louis.[81] Promoters stated the cost as $625,000, with the replica of Joséphine's coronation robe alone valued at $40,000.[82] The historic scenes were housed in a building with the "charm of the Italian renaissance with the strength of detail of the French renaissance," designed by architect Louis Spiering with Ernest Helfensteller and William Hirsch.[83] In addition, there were two displays of fashion in the Palace of Manufactures: the "Salon du costume" and the "Exposition collective de la couture," with dresses by Beer, Callot Soeurs, Paquin, Redfern, and more. A plan to sell the dresses to midwestern stores after the fair closed, however, was foiled by leakage from a massive rain storm in late August that ruined them.[84]

The life of the Palais du costume extended even longer. In 1910, the exhibit was still intact, and a committee in Chicago sought to use it as the basis for a national museum of costumes and material, intended to educate and inspire textile workers in the Midwest.[85] By the time of the Exposition internationale des arts décoratifs et industriels modernes in Paris in 1925 (which spawned Art Deco style), maison Félix had been long since closed, but its line of influence persisted in the fate of two different couturiers. Jeanne Lanvin, who began her career as a teenager in 1883 rimming hats at maison Félix, set up her own workshop in the late 1880s, by 1909 was recognized as a couturier, and joined the Chambre syndicale de la confection et de la couture pour dames et fillettes.[86] At the 1925 exposition, she was vice president of the Pavillon de l'élegance, in which she included her firm's designs (the house employed some eight hundred people) and those of Jenny, maison Myrbor, Poiret, and Worth. Lanvin collaborated with designer Armand-Albert Rateau on the interior decoration.[87] The pavilion was a success, and the Lanvin brand continued well after the founder's death in 1946, until it changed from couture to ready-to-wear clothing in 1993.[88] The Lanvin family may have retained a relationship with the Poussineau family because a men's department for Lanvin was set up at 15, rue du Faubourg Saint-Honoré in 1926 at the building where maison Félix had been in residence until 1901.[89] Lanvin eventually took over all the floors.

Paquin's success was also augmented by the international expositions. Its first branch opened in London (1896), followed by New York (1912; specializing in furs, it was also the first U.S. branch by a French house), Buenos Aires (1912), and Madrid (1914).[90] Jeanne Paquin was awarded the Legion of Honor in 1913 and was president of the Chambre syndicale de la couture parisienne from 1917 to 1919.[91] In addition to the Exposition universelle in Paris in 1900, Paquin was well represented at the Salon du costume at the Louisiana Purchase Exposition in St. Louis in 1904 and at the international expositions in Milan (1906), Brussels (1910), Turin (1911), Ghent (1913), Lyon (1914), and San Francisco (1915).[92] In Turin, she oversaw Le Pavillon Paquin, a Greek temple–inspired building featuring Paquin fashions that stood separately from the work of other couturiers, shown in "La Mode" pavilion.[93] The Paquin brand survived until 1956, long after Jeanne Paquin retired in 1920 and died in 1936. As for the House of Worth, its success and endurance well into the twentieth century hardly needs reiteration here, the name having become synonymous with couture and lasting well after the third generation of Worth descendants had shepherded it. The last turnover of the brand was in 1999 to a company in London.[94]

The misfortunes of Félix after the 1900 Exposition universelle in Paris set against the successes of two of Félix's greatest competitors, Worth and Paquin, and the longevity of a former apprentice's brand, Lanvin, underscores the uncertainty of participating in such massive showcases. The fallibility of couturiers at the fairs is exposed when considered within the context of the diversity and internationalism of the fashion industry as a whole. The circulation of couturiers, coiffeurs, patrons, artists, and celebrities at the Exposition universelle reflected the various classes and communities that comprised fashion culture. The next chapter reconstructs the transnational network of royalty, social leaders, actresses, and singers that mixed with and obscured one another to the great benefit of the industry.

5

INTERNATIONAL CLIENTELE

The great dressmaking shops of the quarter are superb affairs full of pomp and circumstance. They are furnished in splendid fashion and every detail of their management suggests luxury and extravagance. On their books are the names of all the royal personages of Europe, of favorites in Turkish harems, of Japanese beauties, of Americans whose wealth makes them coveted patrons.[1]

Jean Béraud's painting *In Front of Maison Paquin* depicts a bustling shopping day on the rue de la Paix (fig. 5.1). Outside of Paquin at number 3, a pair of women turned out in summer afternoon dresses and hats, parasols in hand, converse, perhaps discussing the next stop on their excursion. Another customer emerges from the store, glancing at the women as a doorman looks on. Meanwhile, a carriage has arrived to let off a woman who has come to shop. We cannot know who the women are—European, U.S., or Russian; socialites or actresses—only that they had the means to patronize Paquin, one of the paramount couture houses (fig. 5.2). Viewers of the painting in its time, about 1900, would not have been able to definitively categorize them either.

The obscuring of social identity in Paris began a generation earlier as a result of open seas and borders that engendered a more international population and a broader distribution of wealth and access to fine clothing. The shift caused great consternation for the likes of author and playwright Alexandre Dumas *fils*, who saw France heading in the direction of general prostitution.[2] Art critic Charles Blanc

5.1

Jean Béraud (French, 1849–1935). *In Front
of Maison Paquin*, ca. 1900. Oil on panel,
36.8×55 cm. Private collection. Image:
Courtesy of Doyle Auctioneers & Appraisers.

5.2

Jeanne Paquin for the House of Paquin.
Ball gown, 1895. Silk. The Metropolitan
Museum of Art, New York, Brooklyn Museum
Costume Collection at The Metropolitan
Museum of Art, Gift of the Brooklyn Museum,
2009; Gift of Mrs. Frederick H. Prince, Jr.,
1967 (2009.300.2115a,b). Image: © The
Metropolitan Museum of Art.

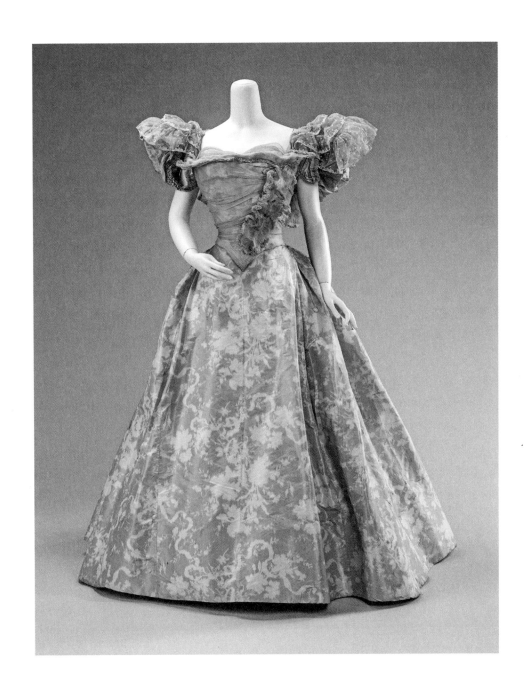

wrote with dismay in 1877: "All was reversed under the Second Empire: family ties were relaxed, and a growing luxury so corrupted manners that an honest woman could no longer be recognised by her style of dress."[3] By the end of the century, actresses and socialites shared the theater, opera, spectators' seats at the Longchamps Grand Prix, and pages of fashion periodicals.[4] Members of the demimonde also wore couture. The openness of the couture market, the prerequisite for entry being only the ability to afford the price tags, allowed different nationalities and classes of people to participate.

The porousness fostered a fluidity that admitted U.S. women, who formerly did not have access owing to lack of royal or noble lineage. In the new configuration, international and interclass marriages led to the exchange of wealth, titles, land and home ownership, and social capital. In turn, a number of European performers married wealthy U.S. men, some elite U.S. women became singers and actresses, and all appeared on the client lists of the principal couture houses. As *Good Housekeeping* remarked in 1888: "In the splendid 'trying on rooms' of the most celebrated man milliners meet the elite of the ancient nobility, the ladies of the financial world, the wives of wealthy merchants and manufacturers, even the world of favorite actresses, and these, forgetting all prejudices of caste and class, discuss proposed modifications and give to them their sanction or their veto."[5] Women from the United States used fashion as one means of becoming significant agents in international society, and couture may be viewed here as a powerful instrument in European-U.S. diplomacy. Remarkably, the women were not discouraged by European denunciations of U.S. taste, mentions of which appear infrequently in U.S. women's writings. Pierre Bourdieu's conceptions of taste as a social construction and the quest for "distinction" as a guiding principal to set the higher classes from the lower classes are useful here.[6] Hailing from the United States, where an entire family's status could catapult in rank from one generation to another after making a fortune in a certain industry, U.S. women were not deterred by European antiquated class barriers.

EUROPEAN ROYALTY AND ARISTOCRATS

Since the late seventeenth-century court of Louis XIV at Versailles, royalty had been the accepted leaders of fashion, given their authority to select the finest couturiers and fabrics and the power to have court clothing made on demand. In the second half of the nineteenth century, several visible figures continued the tradition. Elisabeth ("Sisi"), empress of Austria and queen of Hungary, relished her slim physique and is known to have patronized Worth and Félix. She took pride in her long, thick brown hair, reputedly supervising the techniques of her hairdresser, Fanny Feifalik, to the extent that she was rumored to have her present on a silver dish any hairs that separated from her head during brushing.[7]

Alexandra, Princess of Wales, married Edward VII in 1863, and became queen consort when he was coronated in August 1902. She patronized British firms, including Redfern for tailored walking suits, as did Queen Victoria, but looked to Paris as well.[8] Alexandra commissioned Mrs. James of Hanover Square to design her wedding dress, and she ordered her evening gowns from Morin-Blossier in 15, rue Daunou, Paris, and also patronized Laferrière, Félix, and Rouff.[9] She employed a mistress of the robes to oversee her wardrobe and a dresser, Marianne Skerrett, to whom she later gave some of her used clothing.[10] For her long-awaited coronation gown, she hired the British firm Ede and Ravenscroft but engaged Morin-Blossier to make the underdress.[11] Alexandra's daughter, Princess Maud of Denmark, later Queen of Norway, followed her mother's preference for Morin-Blossier and Laferrière but also patronized Félix.[12] Alexandra's sister, Maria Feodorovna (Dagmar of Denmark), who became the empress of Russia, also ordered gowns from Morin-Blossier and Worth (she was a client for three decades) but contracted local dressmakers in Saint Petersburg for court dresses.[13]

How did royalty throughout Europe and international social leaders learn about the French couture houses' offerings? Information spread in a number of ways. First, advances in railway and ferry transportation facilitated in-person shopping trips, either for the client or her staff. Railway tracks across France had greatly expanded by 1870, easing travel to the capital for those in the countryside.[14] Intra-European travel improved as well, with trips between London and Paris taking only nine to ten hours (fig. 5.3). Passengers would ride a train from London to a British port city, then a ferry to a French port city, followed by a train to Paris. Popular routes were London to Dover to Calais to Paris and London to Folkstone to Bolulogne to Paris.[15] Furthermore, in 1883, the Orient Express began service between Western Europe and Central Europe and the Balkans. Designers and sales staff of local firms in eastern Europe traveled to France to observe the latest styles and convey them to their clients in Vienna, Sofia, Budapest, and other cities.[16] The March train was dubbed the "train des couturières," a reflection of the constant presence of fashion industry staff.

1749

LE JOURNAL DES DAMES ET DES DEMOISELLES
Bruxelles, Rue Blaes, 33.

Couture and hairstyles were also transmitted through magazines and newspapers that carried French fashion plates or, in some cases, were syndicated versions of French magazines. *The Queen, Lady's Realm, Myra's Journal of Dress and Fashion*, and *Woman's World* were some of the most widespread in England. Their significant print runs were part of the larger improvements and efficiencies in printing presses as well as the reduction and eventual repeal of stamp duties in the middle of the century.[17] The expansion in literacy as a result of funded, mandatory education after 1870 increased readership even further throughout Europe.[18] Many English periodicals circulated in Ireland, and the *Irish Times* also reported on French fashion.[19]

In Italy, the high-end *Margherita* and *Corriere delle dame* were published in Milan.[20] In Madrid, *La moda elegante* ran from 1842 to 1937 (favorites in its fashion plates of the 1880s and 1890s were Worth, couturière Madame de Vertus, and Guerlain perfume). *Wiener chic*, related to the Parisian monthly *Paris chic* (1892–1913), was sold in Vienna, Paris, Berlin, London, and New York. In Russia, readers accessed the translated version of *Der bazar, New Russian Bazaar* (*Novyi russkii bazar*), as well as *Fashionable Society* (*Modnyi svet*) and *Fashion Herald* (*Vestnik mody*).[21]

In Japan, after trade opened with Western countries in the mid-1850s, women and men began to adopt Western fashions, which they could observe through the circulation of fashion prints brought in by foreigners.[22] Newspapers and other periodicals in Japan reported on the interest in French fashion at least as early as the 1880s.[23] In Turkey, the *Oriental Advertiser* ran a weekly column titled "Courrier de la mode," and French fashion magazines carried by tourists also communicated styles.[24] In Germany, *Der bazar* ran from 1855 to about 1936 or 1937, despite political strains that lingered between Germany and France since the Franco-Prussian War (1870–1871) ended France's Second Empire and ushered in the Third Republic. Belgium, too, put out editions of French magazines, including the longstanding *Journal des dames et des modes*.

In the United States, *Harper's Bazar* and *Vogue* reported to the upper classes, while *Graham's American Monthly Magazine of Literature, Art, and Fashion, Godey's*

5.3

Jules David (French, 1808–1892).
Toilettes de la Mon. Degon-Pointud, Le Journal des dames et des demoiselles, 1880. Rijksmuseum, Amsterdam (RP-P-2009–3681). Image: Rijksmuseum.

Lady's Book, and *Frank Leslie's Ladies Gazette* catered to the middle classes. A remarkable number of newspapers, from the *Brooklyn Daily Eagle* to the *Los Angeles Herald*, ran Paris fashion features, and especially in the late 1890s, several included detailed drawings and eventually photogravures. With so many of the same fashion plates being reproduced throughout Western countries—with permission from their originators either granted or ignored—French fashion became an international visual language.

PERFORMERS

In addition to fashion plates showing generic female figures wearing the latest styles, international magazines and newspapers covered the fashion choices of actresses and opera singers, who along with royals and aristocrats carried the torch of what would be deemed *au courant*. As foreign correspondent Katharine de Forest wrote in *Harper's Bazar*: "in writing of fashions in Paris one must always remember that the styles are principally launched by the theatre."[25] In her diaries of 1893, Lilla Belle Viles-Wyman of Waltham, Massachusetts, who would become a dance teacher, often recorded new styles that caught her eye at theater performances in New York.[26] Titled by her as "'The Log': An Account of Travel, Adventure and Fashion," the five small notebooks include sketches and fabric swatches. "I have lots of fashion notes. I know someone will be glad to hear them," she wrote in one.[27] In her June "Fashion Supplement," she sketched a shirtwaist (white muslin with black dots) and skirt with a wide hem as "an odd combination that I saw at the theatre yet effective in the extreme."[28] Phrases resonate with those of fashion reporters: "fashion notes," "editorial notice," "a very choice shop of Fifth Avenue," "swell gowns." She addresses "readers of the feminine sex" and signed off one day: "Goodbye. I now go to trip the light fantastic." She frequented department stores B. Altman, Arnold, Constable & Co., Lord and Taylor, and Macy's, where she browsed and obtained pricing for various fabrics.[29] She admired Japanese calico and crepes at a store that stocked Japanese goods.[30]

With audience members like Viles-Wyman tracking their appearances, performers also lent their names and images to (or unknowingly had them co-opted by) product advertisements that proliferated when printing methods became more efficient and less expensive. Sketches of actresses Ellen Terry, Jane Hading, and Madge Robertson Kendal and opera singer Adelina Patti were enlisted for Wakelee's Camelline facial foundation.[31] There was also a large production of trade cards with actresses touting soap, cosmetics, and tobacco. One of the most eccentric series of cigarette cards was put out by W. Duke, Sons, and Co. in 1889, with actresses in fancy dress. Shown at bust-length, headgear is a focal point—Josie Hall as "Light and Shade" wears a lampshade on her head, and Madge Bannister as "The Fisher Maiden" balances a goldfish bowl.[32]

Except for those with top billing, most actresses were responsible for the costs of their costumes, which could run in the thousands of francs or dollars.[33] The *San Francisco Call* remarked, "The prima donna has two duties. The one is to sing, the other is to dress. The cost of the latter is a sum that the public wots (*sic*) not of."[34] Stage costumes could be especially expensive due to the extra fabric and sewing required to make the gowns durable enough to last the theater season, after which they would become unsalvageable.[35] But actresses' income might change from year to year, depending on the success of their performances, a fluctuation that affected their value as customers to the couturiers. As the New York *Sun* explained, "Their fortunes and their credit vary often and violently, and a woman who is a most valuable patron one year may not be the next season."[36] When they were in the limelight, however, they wielded a fair amount of power and were involved in the design of their dresses, exerting opinions and suggesting alterations to the season's offerings.[37]

The English actress Marie Tempest was particularly vocal about the input she believed actresses should have with their costumes: "I always think that a woman ought to have a large share in the designing and arranging of stage-dresses."[38] Other prominent figures were Lillie Langtry, Sarah Bernhardt, and Jane Hading. In the late 1870s, Langtry, hailing from England, became known as a "professional beauty."[39] She wore dresses by Doucet, Félix, Laferriére, Morin-Blossier, and Worth, and her style was copied widely. There was a "Langtry corset," "Langtry bustle," and a "Langtry hat."[40] There was a "Langtry knot" hairstyle, and it was possible to buy "Langtry bangs" ("a little fluffy bunch of waves") so that one did not have to cut one's own hair.[41] As Katherine Armstrong in *Godey's* put it, Langtry was "public property."[42]

Most of the esteemed French houses appear to have dressed Sarah Bernhardt at one point or another, although she was a notoriously difficult client. Jean-Philippe Worth recalled her ordering three dresses from a competitor after causing trouble at Worth during a fitting.[43] She is known to have worn designs by Félix and Laferrière, with the costs covered by her manager, a benefit afforded to her, given her popularity and ticket sales.[44] Her celebrity permeated international popular culture, and her name and image were ubiquitous in papers, magazines, advertisements and testimonials, including Pear's soap, La Diaphane rice powder, and a hair curler. Her "Titian-red" hair was widely emulated, especially after Théobald Chartran depicted her in the role of Gismonda for a Salon painting of 1896.[45] As a sculptor and painter who trained with portraitist Alfred Stevens, Bernhardt was covered in the arts press as well.

DEMIMONDE

The often unauthorized use of performers' names and images to promote cosmetics and other face, hair, and body enhancers draws attention to an adjacent set of customers of couture—courtesans (high-end mistresses) and prostitutes. Art historian Marni Kessler has effectively connected contemporary French writers' concerns about class mixing with that of the superfluity of prostitution in Paris, citing cultural critic Octave Uzanne and others.[46] She argues that the wearing of a fashionable and hygienic veil helped differentiate respectable women from the demimonde, especially in the period directly after the Haussmannization of Paris, with the newly broadened boulevards that made all women more visible.[47] Elsewhere, Kessler notes that the proud patronage of courtesans like Cora Pearl to the upstanding House of Worth was counterbalanced by the heavy application of cosmetics, a telltale visual marker of the demimonde.[48]

In a similar analysis of a fashion accessory, literary historian Susan Hiner elucidates the shift in meaning that the symbol of the cashmere shawl underwent in novels by Balzac, Flaubert, and others.[49] Beginning as a garment of distinction, the shawl lost its prestige when it was adopted by the demimondaine and when reproductions of lesser quality became widely available. The anxieties surrounding the ability of fashion to obscure the wearer's class seeped into the perception of certain workplaces, including that of the lowpaying millinery shops.[50] Workers might be mistaken for prostitutes and indeed were portrayed as liminal figures in paintings by Edgar Degas, for instance. Notably, there is no overt indication in period sources that courtesans or prostitutes played a large role in the France-U.S. trade in fashion, although it is possible that some actresses were also mistresses of high-profile men. The relevant point here is that the wearing of couture by multiple classes of women in Europe does not appear to have lessened wealthy U.S. women's desire for it or the couture houses' eagerness to provide it.

SOCIAL LEADERS FROM THE UNITED STATES

In his 1895 book *Some Memories of Paris*, F. Adolphus recalled interviewing Charles Frederick Worth at the latter's country home in Suresnes.[51] When asked whether there was an average expenditure by clients on his gowns, Worth replied that there was no average and that spending relied on individual circumstances. He continued with some generalizations, however, saying that English and German women often did not overspend but that "some of the Americans are great spenders . . . 'they have faith, figures, and francs'—faith to believe in me, figures that I can put into shape, francs to pay my bills. Yes, I like to dress Americans" (figs. 5.4 and 5.5).[52] The stream of wealthy people traveling between the United States and Europe was steady. Steamships like the Cunard Line's *Campania* (built in 1892), which carried Caroline Astor home from Liverpool in July 1896, transported first-class passengers in style. It could hold fourteen hundred passengers in first-, second-, and steerage classes, and four hundred crewmembers (fig. 5.6).[53] After debarking in Liverpool, passengers might spend time in London and then make their way to Paris.[54]

Several U.S. families owned or rented homes in Europe, as in the case of the Bradley-Martins, who leased homes in London and near Inverness.[55] In Paris, Caroline Astor leased an apartment at 146, avenue des Champs-Élysées, a newly constructed building that opened in 1889.[56] The company Urbaine-Vie commissioned architect Jules Février to design it in 1887, and it was conceived as an investment property, capitalizing on wealthy foreigners.[57] An advertisement in *Le Figaro* described it as "lavishly decorated," with "American installation," electricity, telephones, and "hot and cold water day and night for every floor."[58] The Neoclassical exterior betrayed a Rococo-decorated interior (the building was destroyed in the 1930s).[59]

This rental building is another example of the outgrowth of businesses that benefited from foreign interest in Parisian fashion. Equally fascinating is the apparent lack of a stigma attached to leasing, rather than owning, a second, third, or fourth home. As economist Thorstein Veblen wrote in *The Theory of the Leisure Class* in 1899, owning property was essential to acquiring and maintaining status.[60] For these families that spent hundreds of thousands of dollars on designing, erecting, and decorating their stateside mansions, their standards were more tempered when it came to the homes where they stayed while traveling. The same was true for their yachts, often leased from agencies or from other owners in their social circle. (Lillie Langtry famously received the yacht *White Ladye* as a gift from an Englishman and then swiftly leased it to Ogden Goelet, who used it until his death.)[61]

But renting or hoteling did not signify temporariness, as evidenced by an unusually robust set of extant invoices from the Goelet family, stored and forgotten in a piece of furniture, later to be found and acquired by Salve Regina University in Newport. The invoices record purchases and services rendered in France and England mostly in the early 1890s. In Paris, Ogden and Mary Rita Wilson Goelet

5.4

Charles Frederick Worth for the House
of Worth. Court presentation ensemble,
ca. 1888. Silk, metal, feathers, glass. The
Metropolitan Museum of Art, New York,
Purchase, Friends of The Costume Institute
Gifts, 2007 (2007.385a–l). Image: © The
Metropolitan Museum of Art.

5.5

Ensemble in figure 5.4 configured as dinner
dress. Image: © The Metropolitan Museum
of Art.

5.6

George H. Fergus (U.S., 1840–1911). Poster
for the Cunard Line, 1874. Color woodcut.
Library of Congress Prints and Photographs
Division, Washington, DC.

shopped at Félix for women's and men's couture and accessories, Franck for lingerie and night clothes, Léoty for corsets (figs. 5.7 and 5.8), Morin-Blossier for couture (totaling 3,433 francs), Virot for hats, and others.[62] The length of their stays necessitated trips to the cleaners—at "Jolly Fils" and a generically named "Blanchisserie." They also patronized a tailor who worked on adult and children's clothes and brought their traveling trunks to Bigot for repairs. They must have entertained guests at the Hôtel Bristol where they stayed in fall 1892, as they placed large orders for flowers from Dezilles on the rue de Castiglione. Finally, they bought a French bull dog named "Rabot" for 1,700 francs.[63]

Caroline Astor entertained at various homes throughout the year, including at her rented Paris apartment where she hosted salons. Her annual schedule was public knowledge. In the winter, she was in New York, where she attended the opera and gave teas, dinners, and receptions (fig. 5.9). Debutante coming-out parties were in December, and her annual ball was given on a Monday night in early January. In March, she set off from New York to England and then traveled to Paris.[64] In the last week of June, she returned to London and headed back to the United States, where she spent the summer in Newport. Her husband's wanderings were also notorious: William Backhouse Astor spent much of his time on his boats, first the *Ambassadress* and then *Nourmahal*. As a result, Caroline Astor's travels and parties were associated with her as the primary host, especially after William died in 1892 (the funeral, held at the interdenominational American Church in Paris, was attended by more than twenty U.S. couples).[65] At events, she was surrounded by her children (four daughters and one son) and extended family and friends, of which Ward McAllister (the two devised the infamous list of the Four Hundred worthy members of New York society) was one of the most famous. After McAllister died in 1895, Harry Lehr assumed the position of social leader alongside Astor.

The weddings in New York of the four Astor daughters brought significant attention, of which the gowns and gifts (and in several cases, the eventual demise of the union) were of paramount concern. The eldest daughter, Emily Astor, became engaged to James Van Alen in 1876, against her father's wishes, and split time between Newport and England before her death from heart disease in 1881. The details of their marriage ceremony, often referred to as an elopement, were not heavily publicized, counter to the usual Astor affairs.[66] Her sister Helen Schermerhorn Astor, however, is known to have worn a white satin dress with orange blossoms and old Belgian lace by Worth for her marriage to James R. Roosevelt in 1878 at Grace Church.[67] The bridesmaids' gowns of white satin moiré were also imported, possibly also by Worth.[68]

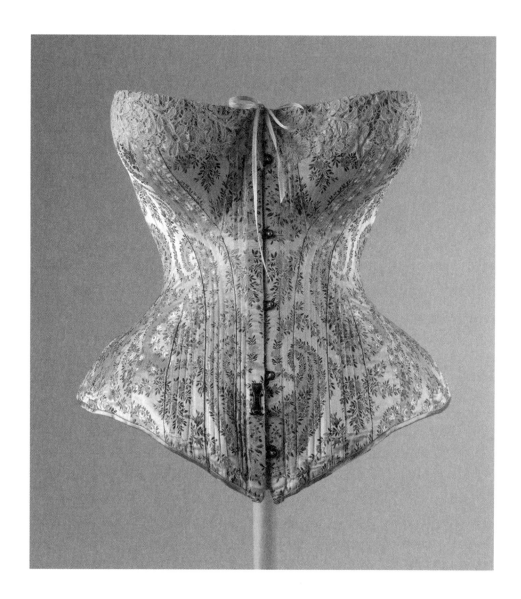

5.7

Maison Léoty (French, active 1868–at least
1917). Corset, 1891. Silk. The Metropolitan
Museum of Art, New York, Gift of Miss Marion
Hague, 1945 (C.I.45.27a,b). Image: © The
Metropolitan Museum of Art.

5.8

Léoty, Tout-Paris: Annuaire de la société parisienne (1899).

The next sister, Charlotte Augusta Astor, and her husband, James Coleman Drayton, garnered a reported half-million dollars' worth of gifts at their wedding in 1879; they divorced in 1894.[69] For her second wedding, to the Englishman George Ogilvy Haig in London in 1896, she wore a plum-colored morning gown, an acceptable choice for divorcées and new brides alike, as white or ivory were not requisite in this period.[70] The youngest daughter, Caroline Schermerhorn "Carrie" Astor, who would live the longest and become the best known, married Marshall Orme Wilson in November 1884 in the art gallery at the Astor house at 350 5th Avenue at 34th Street. She wore a Worth satin and lace dress embroidered with silver, the front and sides trimmed with orange blossoms, and a veil of old lace given by her mother.[71]

5.9

Mrs. Caroline Astor and Mr. Elisha Dyer, Jr. at the 1902 Assembly Ball in New York City, Harper's Weekly, December 20, 1902.

The gown was "said to be one of the handsomest that ever left his establishment."[72] The heavy white satin and lace bridesmaids' gowns were also from Paris.[73] Caroline Astor, the mother of the bride, wore a pale green velvet gown with heavy white satin and point lace by Worth and her diamond tiara.[74] William Backhouse Astor, father of the bride, gave them a house, and the groom's father presented them with "all those one thousand and one things necessary to make it habitable," wrote one newspaper.[75] As for the only son of Caroline and William, John Jacob Astor IV, he married Ava Lowle Willing in Philadelphia in 1891 to much fanfare. She wore a "rich, heavy, creamy duchesse satin with an immense train" by Worth, the bridesmaids donned "Marie Antoinette gowns of pink chiffon," and Caroline Astor wore an embroidered, deep violet satin gown and matching capote with violet-tinted ostrich feathers.[76] Here again the legacy of the wedding outlasted the marriage, as the Jacob Astors divorced in 1910.

In addition to all the Astors' comings and goings, there were many other prominent U.S. families frequenting the Paris couturiers during residential stays in Paris. The King family of Newport and Washington, DC, also kept an apartment in Paris for their annual trips to Europe. In the 1880s and 1890s, Ella Louisa Rives King patronized Doucet, Rouff, and Worth, details that are known from her accounts and the diary of her husband, David King Jr.[77] Their daughter, Gwendolen, favored Raudnitz and Co.–Huet et Chéruit.[78] If families did not own or lease a home in Paris, they stayed at hotels like the steadfast Bristol at 3–5, place Vendôme (the Goelets' preference), the Continental (opened in 1878), or the Ritz (opened in 1898), all a short distance to the maisons on the rue de la Paix.[79]

Hotels served multiple purposes as a home base, as did the centrally located business office of the *International Herald Tribune* (begun in 1887) at 49, avenue de l'Opéra. Travelers held meetings, received mail, and read the latest newpapers there. On registration, the paper printed news of their arrival as well and sent a cable to their respective local newspapers.[80] Other devoted service providers were the locations of the U.S. consulate and from 1895, American Express at 6, rue Halévy.[81] U.S. travelers happened upon one another in the city. As Huybertie Pruyn Hamlin of Albany, New York, wrote in her diary, she and her mother "returned to Paris and found it full of friends."[82] While there, her shopping practices ring familiar. For her 1898 wedding to Charles Sumner Hamlin of Boston, she ordered a gown from Madame Lodaux, who, she noted, packed her boxes beautifully.[83] In a "buying local" selection that we now recognize as *de rigueur* for women at various levels of society, though, she hired a New York dressmaker for her going-away dress.

Travel, socializing, and shopping were facilitated by the ability to speak French, as did Caroline Astor, Frances Cleveland, Anna Gould, and Alva Vanderbilt.[84] The most privileged women studied in France, an advantage that in Bourdieuian terms increased their cultural capital. But foreign languages were also taught in the newly established public high schools in the United States beginning early in the century, albeit often as an elective class.[85] Visitors from the United States joined in the Paris social season, hosting and attending salons, frequenting the theater and opera, and attending fancy dress balls and weddings that would inspire ones back at home (see chapter 7, Gowns and Mansions: French Fashion in U.S. Homes). The extent to which the events were commingled between U.S. citizens and the French is not completely clear and seems to have varied by social circle. The term "American Colony" was used to describe the U.S. citizens residing in Paris at this time, although it was not a cohesive group. As Richard Harding Davis put it in his 1895 book, *About Paris*, there were "Americans who go to Paris for the spring and summer only, who live in hotels, and see little of the city beyond the Rue de la Paix and the Avenue of the Champs Elysées and their bankers.'" And there were those that lived there permanently, essentially relinquishing their citizenship of the United States, according to Davis's view.[86] Immigration historian Nancy L. Green explains that within the contingent, there were the "idle rich" as well as artists and enterprising businessmen. As a whole, she refers to their "elite migration," more commonly termed "expatriation." The classification includes people who owned residences abroad but returned to the States on a regular basis.[87] They established community associations, churches, and newspapers and were a significant precursor to the larger and better studied company of U.S. citizens in Paris, famous artists and writers like Ernest Hemingway among them, between World Wars I and II.[88]

By the mid-1850s, North and South Americans residing in Paris numbered between one thousand and three thousand (the census data combines the United States, Mexico, and South America).[89] In 1876, the amount rose to about six thousand. In 1891 and 1896, the census separated out citizens of the United States, citing about four thousand for each of those years, which was about one third of the British citizens, who held the largest representation.[90] By 1901, the figure decreased to 2,628, about a tenth of the British citizens living in Paris.[91] But the count of U.S. tourists in Paris was significantly higher than the residents, possibly as many as one hundred thousand by 1906, although official records were not kept at the time.[92] Together, residents and visitors from the United States made up the wealthiest foreigners in the city, a credit that must have eased their entry into elite social events.[93]

Accounts such as Albert Sutliffe's *The Americans in Paris* (1887) document citizens from the United States at French-hosted balls at the Tuilieries.[94] In her memoir, Princess Pauline von Metternich recalled the grandness of the balls at that palace and at various embassies and ministries. She once dressed as a black demon in a costume by Worth, embroidered in silver and dotted with diamonds, and with two diamond horns.[95] Likewise, Dr. William Edward Johnston, the Paris correspondent for the *New York Times* in the 1850s and 1860s, described an imperial fancy dress ball in 1863 and the U.S. guests in attendance. The women hailed from Philadelphia, New Orleans, Georgia, New York, Cambridge (Massachusetts), and Washington, DC, and came as Red Riding Hood, Ophelia, Undine, and *en marquise*.[96] He wrote, "Worth and Bobergh, although they are the fashionable house of the season, did not furnish all the dresses."[97] He remarked that the empress invited people from the United States "not only on account of their standing in French society, but also for their beauty and well-known taste in dress."[98]

The U.S. visitors who mixed socially with the Parisians also sat for portraits by the same desirable painters, like Alexandre Cabanel. A French critic wrote about the mutual benefit to the artists and sitters, noting Cabanel's eagerness to accommodate U.S. sitters and the status gained by the patrons: "The effect produced among the American colony in Paris may be readily imagined, and at the present time every American of any pretensions rushes to Cabanel's studio" (see fig. 7.16).[99] The price of a Cabanel portrait could reach 20,000 francs (about $4,000 in 1885), an investment that easily multiplied in social value if the painting was displayed at the hallowed Paris Salon, as was Mary Leiter's portrait by Cabanel in 1888.[100] Leiter married British aristocrat George Nathaniel Curzon in 1895 in a gown by Worth and reputedly received her guests at the wedding reception standing beneath her Cabanel. The marriage would later grant her the title of vicereine of India.[101]

In Paris, the salons hosted by the likes of Caroline Astor and Marie Louise Hungerford Mackay were attended by U.S., French, and other European guests. Mackay's husband made a fortune in the Nevada silver mines, but the couple encountered difficulty when attempting to enter New York society and so moved to Paris in 1876 and to London in 1886.[102] Their U.S. guests at their home at 9, rue de Tilsitt would have comprised those living in Paris and those visiting, many of whom would have been passing through while on shopping trips. A known guest of the Mackays was the soprano Emma Wixom "Nevada" of California, who married Raymond Palmer in Paris in 1886 and set up a residence at 121, avenue de Wagram. While there, they may have dined on the famous Mackay silver-gilt and enamel dinner service that the couple commissioned Tiffany and Co. to make out of silver that came directly from the mines and that was displayed at the 1878 Exposition universelle in Paris.[103] Mackay was also a prominent patron of the jeweler Boucheron, spending hundreds of thousands of dollars on ensembles crafted with sapphires, pearls, diamonds, and turquoise.[104] The elegant dresses that Mackay wore to Parisian social events were eagerly reported on.[105]

By the time their daughter Eva Julia Mackay was married in France in 1885 to an Italian prince, the *New York Times* claimed that "the reception was attended by the fine flower of European and American society."[106] But perhaps the pinnacle of the Mackays' notoriety took place the year before when Marie Louise destroyed a portrait that Ernest Meissonier had painted of her, finding the likeness disagreeable.[107] Shown at three-quarter length, she wore a black satin dress embroidered with beads, a black Gainsborough-style hat, and a brown fur-trimmed mantle.[108] She objected to the appearance of her hands (the left one pulling on a yellow glove), neck, and makeup. At a value of $14,000, the painting's demise constituted big news in Paris and the States, a testament to how ensconced the family was in both arenas.

The stream of patrons making their way to Paris for couture came from cities throughout the United States, most notably New York, Chicago, Albany, and Washington, DC. For her marriage to Potter Palmer, a real-estate businessman and hotel owner in 1870, Bertha Honoré commissioned her wedding dress from Paris.[109] Prominent in Chicago society, in 1891 she was elected to the Presidential Board of Lady Managers for the World's Columbian Exposition to be held in 1893 (fig. 5.10). In 1891 and 1892, she traveled to Paris, where she bought Impressionist paintings by Mary Cassatt, Camille Pissarro, and Claude Monet, building an extraordinary collection, and where she shopped at Callot Soeurs, Paquin, Worth, and more.[110] She was accompanied by her niece, Julia Dent Grant (granddaughter of Ulysses S. Grant), who would marry a Russian prince in 1899 in Newport. Palmer oversaw the procurement of all the gowns in Paris for the event.[111] In 1900, President McKinley

5.10

Anders Leonard Zorn (Swedish, 1860–1920).
Mrs. Potter Palmer, 1893. Oil on canvas,
258 × 141.2 cm. Art Institute of Chicago,
Potter Palmer Collection (1922.450).
Image: Art Institute of Chicago.

appointed her to the United States National Commission at the Exposition universelle in Paris. During her time there, she placed orders at Callot Soeurs, Doeuillet, Paquin, and Worth, and several of the garments survive (fig. 5.11).[112]

Palmer's fellow Chicagoan Abbie Louise Spencer Eddy kept a travel log in 1878 of her shopping trips to Paris, where Pingat at 30, rue Louis-le-Grand was a particular favorite.[113] She purchased a Pingat gown and wore it for her portrait by the U.S. painter George Peter Alexander Healy that year.[114] Her fine taste led her sister, her mother, and a friend, Nannie Douglas Scott Field, to have her proxy shop for them while in Paris. Field was married to Marshall Field, owner of the successful department store and previous business partner of Potter Palmer and Levi Leiter, whose eldest daughter was Mary Leiter. Marshall Field's, like most major department stores, would have carried authentic, imported French couture as well as licensed versions, with which Nannie Field would have been familiar.

The importance with which Chicago society women approached French fashion is further borne out by the record keeping of philanthropist Frances Macbeth Glessner, who traveled to Europe only once, with her husband, her daughter, and a governess in 1890. For the excursion, she recorded the addresses of couturiers and purveyors of myriad goods from bonnets to waterproof boots in a leather-bound book and kept a journal while abroad.[115] The recommendations came from her friends, the frequent travelers Bertha Honoré Potter Palmer and Abbie Louise Spencer Eddy, all of whom would have followed the French fashions in Chicago's society magazine, *Elite*. Eddy suggested a visit to Doucet (in business since 1816 and renowned when Jacques Doucet took over in 1875) for tea gowns. At Pingat, she suggested asking for saleswoman Madame Blanche, who she deemed "perfectly reliable" and "very bright."[116] At Worth, Eddy favored Madame Deve (Eddy's aunt, Delia Spencer, preferred the assistance of Madame Bond).[117] Glessner's journal is incomplete, but she documented visits to Worth, Madame Beer for children's clothes,

5.11

House of Worth. Evening gown worn by Bertha Honoré Potter Palmer. Silk satin with cut velvet, ribbon, rhinestone trim. Chicago History Museum, Gift of the Art Institute of Chicago (1969.1116).

and the department store Le Bon Marché. Finally, her friends endorsed Rouff (13, boulevard Haussmann), Labaudt et Robina (22, rue de Quatre-Septembre), and milliner Kate Weber (6, rue de la Paix next to Worth).[118]

In Washington, DC, too, society women, many of whom hailed from different states but moved to the city when their husbands were elected or appointed to federal offices, were heavily invested in procuring the correct French fashions. Their budgets were lower than the bottomless ones of the millionaire families, but they still sought the highest quality. Harriet Blaine of Augusta, Maine, relocated to Washington, DC, in the winters when her husband was elected Speaker of the House in 1869. When attending an event at which she was escorted through the room by President Chester A. Arthur, she was especially conscious of her appearance in a new dress and expected to see coverage in the newspapers.[119] And when her son was in France, she could not resist asking him, "apropos of nothing," to buy her a black lace parasol cover: "Get it rather large and have some lady like Mrs. Washburne to advise you."[120]

At age twenty-one, Frances Folsom of Buffalo, New York, married sitting President Grover Cleveland on June 2, 1886, wearing a Worth gown. The year before, she traveled to Europe with her mother and purchased part of her trousseau in Paris, choices that the French newspapers reported on.[121] During her second term as First Lady (1893–1897), she patronized couturière Madame Lodaux and most likely the House of Doucet.[122] Her taste in clothing and her hairstyles, like the Grecian coils she wore for her wedding and her signature simple but neat chignon at the middle back of the head, with curled bangs in front, that became known as "à la Cleveland" were widely copied (fig. 5.12).[123] Images of the young First Lady abounded, as did their illegal use on products from perfume bottles to cigar boxes. The result, per reporter Frank ("Carp") Carpenter, was "Seven out of every ten women in Washington have copied her and the style has been adopted throughout the country. . . . A small fortune is spent in hairdressing here every season."[124] Her hairdresser, Joannes (John) Rochon, was a Frenchman located in the capital, who advertised in the papers as having won three patents and five medals at expositions in Paris, Lyon, and Vienna.[125] This type of claim was common, as the expositions doled out hundreds of medals, a credential that was quickly emblazoned on ads and company letterhead.

Among the women traveling from Washington, DC, to Paris for couture was Marguerite Cassini, daughter of the first Russian ambassador to the United States, who became a citizen of the United States and young hostess in the capital. She recalled in her autobiography shopping trips with other U.S. women in Paris.

5.12

Fernand Paillet (French, 1850–1918). *Frances Folsom Cleveland*, 1891. Watercolor on ivory; silver gilt; mother-of pearl, 6.5×5.4 cm. New-York Historical Society, Gift of the Estate of Peter Marié (1905.44). Photograph © New-York Historical Society.

She estimated, for instance, that Mrs. Corey spent $100,000 per year on clothes and had a *vendeuse* assigned to her at the House of Worth.[126] Cassini was acutely aware, especially during visits to Newport, of women who wore the latest French fashions, citing Janet Fish "in her Doucet creations with rows and rows of lace" as well as Alva Vanderbilt Belmont and Ava Lowle Willing Astor.[127] She wrote, "Sometimes the lace alone on their gowns cost two thousand dollars or more, and it took many women working night and day for months to make it."[128] She remembered also seeing Anna Gould in the Worth salon being fitted for an evening gown (that would require a tight corset for her stocky figure).[129] Gould represented another category of society women who heavily patronized the couture houses: U.S. heiresses who married European titled men. Between 1874 and 1911, there were about 115 such marriages.[130] The brides hailed from New York, Boston, Washington, DC, Chicago, Nashville, New Orleans, Portland, Oregon, and Santa Barbara and Stockton, California.[131] The unions were motivated by love interest, mutual gain, or both and elicited a remarkable number of responses throughout the U.S. and French newspapers, which in turn provide one of the clearest entry points into how central and often polarizing fashion was to the business of keeping up international appearances.

The sarcastic comment by the gossip columnist for New York's *Town Topics* that "nothing below an Earl is looked at with favor" was typical of the U.S. response to the marriages.[132] "A union of blood and boodle" is how another paper termed it.[133] The *Saint Paul Globe* ran a sensationalized piece, also characteristic of the press's reaction, about twenty young women in Newport worth $200 million who would return from Europe, "their trunks laden with the latest Parisian frocks and hats."[134] The brides' parents acquired stature while the European men, whose family money was often mostly a memory by late in the century, gained financial stability. One report out of Washington, DC, likened the whole business to a sport played by the brides' mothers and called the real value of the married titles as "bogus."[135] In his novels, William Dean Howells wrote several derogatory comments about the unions, as in *A Fearful Responsibility* (1881), a book that would have circulated this well-respected author's opinion widely.[136] Conservative Parisian papers like *Le Gaulois*, however, listed the millions of francs that each marriage brought to the city and drew attention to the extravagance of the weddings.[137] The wedding festivities were opportunities to observe one another: when Mary Stevens Paget, a U.S. hotel heiress, married Englishman Arthur Paget, "They had come there to see and to be seen, to gossip about the Horse Show, to criticise one another's gowns and to compare Miss Whitney and Miss Vanderbilt as a bride."[138]

Anna Gould, daughter of the late railroad financier Jay Gould, married Count Boniface do Castellane ("Boni") of Touraine, France, in 1895 at her uncle's house on 67th Street and 5th Avenue in New York.[139] The marriage comprised big news in Paris, garnering a page-long announcement in the *Journal du dimanche*.[140] In the States, a full-length drawing of Gould in her bridal gown (the maker is unnamed) appeared in the *World*, referring to her as the "count's prize" and citing the value of the new union as $15 million.[141] *Frank Leslie's Weekly* devoted three illustrated pages to the event.[142] Her steamer gown and hat and much of her trousseau lingerie was imported from France.[143] In addition to procuring items from Paris, however, in a now-familiar practice, she had some evening gowns for her trousseau made at Gosta Kraemer's store on West 23rd Street and matching hats by Madame Louise.[144] After the wedding, the couple lived in the Palais Rose in Paris, a mansion that the count had built in the style of Louis XIV. Their life in France was facilitated by Anna Gould's fluent French. In his memoir, Castellane recalled his wife's interest in fashion: "Anna became superelegant, and the hearts of Paquin and Doucet rejoiced greatly," although counter to Cassini's recollection mentioned above, he boasted, "My wife never went to a *couturière*—the *couturières* came to her."[145] In 1897, the count threw an enormous party, reputedly for four thousand guests, in the bois de Boulogne for his wife's twenty-first birthday. The count's extravagant spending and wayward relationships, however, led to the couple's divorce in 1906.

On the whole, the unions were perceived as constituting acts of soft diplomacy, or peacekeeping arrangements. On the marriage of Mary Endicott, a descendant of settlers in Massachusetts, to British politician Joseph Chamberlain in 1888 (see figs. 3.9 and 3.10), the *Boston Weekly Globe* remarked: "This is one of the pleasant features of our international relations, and goes far to offset disagreeable incidents, like the Sackville affair."[146] One of the most publicized international marriages was between Consuelo Vanderbilt, daughter of Alva and William Kissam Vanderbilt, and Charles Richard John Spencer-Churchill, 9th Duke of Marlborough, in November 1895. By all accounts, including the *Town Topics* columnist who referred to the "elaborate machinery" she devised, Alva Vanderbilt had orchestrated the union in order to secure her daughter's place in international society.[147] Doucet was chosen to design the bridal gown, and the New York dressmaker Catharine Donovan executed it.[148] *Vogue* printed a full-page drawing of the gown on a generic fashion-plate model, perhaps a measure of expedience to rush the dress and several gowns from the trousseau into that month's volume.[149] Consuelo Vanderbilt later recalled how eager the press was for details of her new clothing; she found them greatly exaggerated.[150] Reporters

5.13

Studio of Nadar (French, 1820–1910). *Cora Brown-Potter*. Albumen print. Bibliothèque nationale de France, Paris (FT 4-NA-238 [25]). Image: Bibliothèque nationale de France, Paris.

referred to her as an item of acquisition, using terms like "merchandise," "prize," and "important commercial transaction."[151] Vanderbilt and the duke separated in 1906 and divorced in 1921, and that year she married French pilot Jacques Balsan. Alva, too, remarried, after William Kissam Vanderbilt was found to be unfaithful, to Oliver Hazard Perry Belmont, member of a wealthy banking family.[152]

"Why must Mrs. James Brown Potter act?" asked journalist Katherine Armstrong, writing from Surrey, England, in a piece for *Godey's Lady's Book* in October 1887. London was facing this conundrum, she says, wondering why a woman of high social standing, a confidante of the Princess of Wales, would take to the stage. She names two other U.S. women following the trend: Eleanor C. Calhoun and a singer known in London as "Miss Decca" but plainly known as Miss Johnstone in Philadelphia.[153] Cora Urquhart of New Orleans had married financier James Brown-Potter of New York in 1877 and enjoyed performing at charity events.[154] In the next decade, her interests turned to the professional stage (fig. 5.13), and in 1886 she left for London while her husband and daughter (later Nancy Fowler McCormick, a leader of Chicago society and fashion) remained in New York.[155] Four years afterward, author Alan Dale puzzled over her choice: "Mrs. James Brown-Potter emerged from the lovely insipidity of society in the full belief that she was to be a Charlotte Cushman or a Sarah Bernhardt, with drawing-room amendments."[156] Despite the skepticism, she became a household name and like Lillie Langtry and other well-known performers, patronized the couture houses, including Félix and Worth.[157] In 1895, she persuaded producer Augustin Daly to approve a large budget for her to order gowns for *Le Collier de la reine* from Jean-Philippe Worth.[158] She wrote, "I urge you to let me order the other three. You will never get a chance again to get more exquisite things . . . they are to be trimmed with gold and lace and made splendidly."[159] Worth would make costumes for several more of her performances in the late 1890s.[160]

Brown-Potter's path from society woman to employed actress was so disconcerting because it flowed in the opposite direction from the Veblenian upward stream toward leisure status and away from work.[161] But in terms of the never-ending cycle of conspicuous consumption, the couture industry did not distinguish between socialite, actress, singer, lately titled bride, old or new money. Maison Félix, subject of the next chapter, served them all.

THE U.S. MARKET FOR FRENCH FASHION

6

MAISON FÉLIX AND ITS U.S. CLIENTS

It is somewhat difficult for those who have not traveled extensively abroad to form even an idea of the standing and grandeur of such a house as that of Mons. E. Félix, Paris, which stands at the head of the great fashion modelers of Europe.[1]

The clients of maison Félix represented all the contingents that were key to the success of a couture house: European royalty and aristocrats, European and U.S. social leaders and stage performers (fig. 6.1). The popularity of the house with patrons from the United States, the frequency with which it was patronized and discussed, its abrupt demise (see chapter 4, Couturiers and International Expositions), and the absence of consideration in historical studies of fashion discourse offer a unique opportunity. Evaluating the ways in which U.S. women and the press talked about Félix helps elucidate the mutual reliance between the couturiers and the clients that was essential to maintaining the balance of the fashion system. What emerges is a sense that the U.S. shoppers wanted the finest clothing made with the finest fabrics and were willing to pay but not overpay for it. Given their long history of access to high-quality silks from Lyon and the nation's nurturing of the design process over several centuries, the French couture houses were positioned to meet the U.S. demand. Letters, diaries, and the press indicate that Félix was considered one of the most desirable couturiers and that, in turn, Félix adapted its business to serve U.S. clients. The selectivity of U.S. customers affected how French couturiers distinguished their brands amid heavy competition. The transatlantic relationship of

provider and buyer comes into view as an equilibrium as opposed to the traditional top-down model of imperious couturiers deigning to take U.S. business.

MAISON FÉLIX

The coiffeur Joseph-Augustin Escalier (b. ca. 1815) is referred to in professional publications as early as 1843 and in about 1846 founded maison Félix.[2] He achieved notoriety when he became official coiffeur to Empress Eugénie in the early 1850s and when he was contracted by the Théâtre des variétés.[3] Referring to himself as "Félix," a nickname he purportedly chose after his friend, the famous actress Elisabeth Rachel Félix (1821–1858), Escalier moved in artistic social circles with Sarah Bernhardt and her compatriots. His son, Nicolas Félix Escalier (1843–1920), was a painter and architect, whose 1874 design for "Un palais pour l'exposition des beaux-arts" was used as a prototype for the Memorial Hall at the Centennial Exhibition in Philadelphia in 1876.[4]

About 1857, maison Félix was taken over by Auguste Jean Poussineau (1831–1910), who had trained as a hairdresser with his father, Auguste Poussineau (1803–1886), in Tours before coming to Paris.[5] Auguste Jean's brother, Émile Martin Poussineau (also called "Félix"; 1841–1930), learned the trade in England and Saint Petersburg and joined his brother in Paris about 1860.[6] The business expanded its staff so that it could provide millinery and gowns, eventually employing more than three hundred workers.[7]

Established at 15, rue du Faubourg Saint-Honoré since at least 1849, the firm was well situated on one of oldest and most luxurious streets in the city. Within forty years, it was offering lingerie, hosiery, floral accessories, bonnets, muffs, and hairdressing.[8] The range of available goods and services and the company's varying listings in business directories suggest that in its early to middle years, maison Félix may have been considered a *maison de nouveauté*, becoming a couture house

6.1

Maison Félix (French, 1841–1901). Opera gown, ca. 1887. Fashion Institute of Design and Merchandising Museum, Los Angeles, Helen Larson Historic Fashion Collection (2017.5.50). Courtesy of the FIDM Museum at the Fashion Institute of Design & Merchandising, Los Angeles, CA. Photograph by Brian Sanderson.

in its later years.[9] A *première* would have overseen each specialty, which would have had a number of workers and apprentices, mostly female, except for fur cutting and sewing (fig. 6.2).[10] The milliner's workshop was a training ground for the teenage apprentice Jeanne Lanvin, who proceeded to found her own successful firm (see chapter 4, Couturiers and International Expositions).[11] Émile Martin Poussineau remained the principal of the business throughout its duration, as August Jean Poussineau left Paris around 1876 to pursue real estate holdings in Dinard.[12] The firm's label retained the moniker "A. Félix Breveté," however.

The shop at 15, rue du Faubourg Saint-Honoré was spread out over several floors and received an extensive renovation in 1894 (fig. 6.3). Among the finest decorations of the galleries and showroom were Gobelins tapestries, and panel paintings by Louise Abbéma depicting three of the maison's famous actress clients—Sarah Bernhardt, Sophie Croizette, and Ada Rehan.[13] Marie-Rose Berthé Renault Poussineau (1848–1924), married to Émile Martin Poussineau, circulated among the rooms wearing the designs, as did other live models (called "mannequins").[14] Mahogany-framed mirrors reflected incandescent lighting, and opulent furniture and drapery rounded out the experience of visiting a comfortable, elegant salon.[15] The firm does not appear to have established branches outside of France, but its designs were carried in stores throughout the United States and in London.[16]

The firm was a household name in the United States, spoken in the same breath by patrons and reporters as Worth, Paquin, and Doucet. The maison became known for catering to the desirable slim, hourglass silhouette—the "grace and soft, clinging effects of his gowns"[17]—and was often set up as a foil to Worth, whose gowns were perceived as more heavily adorned. The *Brooklyn Daily Eagle* recounted an 1894 showing with live models at Félix, with one visitor remarking to another: "I wonder where Félix gets all of these young women with such fine figures to exhibit his toilets." Her companion answered: "Well, you know Félix has the reputation of dressing thin, slender women to perfection and Worth's dresses set off stout, portly figures. Félix always uses a lot of lace, filmy goods, chiffons, mousselines de soie, gauzes, and Worth cuts into heavy silks, satins and moirés—cuts the long, straight line, so as not to burden the figure with any more accessories of trimming than it

6.2

Seamstresses at a Couture House, 1890s, in Arsène Alexandre, *Les Reines d'aiguille* (1902).

can gracefully carry." Although their styles were frequently contrasted, Félix and Worth were referred to as "happy rivals" and shared many of the same clients.[18] Félix's best known slender client was Bernhardt, who recalled once being called "thinner than a sparrow" (fig. 6.4).[19] Her body was the subject of continuous comment, not least of which were racially motivated depictions of her as a promiscuous Jew.[20] But Félix's other patrons came in all shapes and sizes, and the firm adapted when necessary. For the more zaftig Lillian Russell, a well-placed bow on the waist would do the trick for slenderizing the look of a gown.[21] The slim aesthetic was well conveyed in the firm's short-lived gazette *Félix-Mode* (1897–ca. 1901), as it was by *au courant* painters like Béraud (figs. 6.5 and 6.6).[22] The small periodical was an

6.6

Jean Béraud. *Parisienne in a Red Dress*,
1900. Oil on panel, 33.3 × 26.7 cm. Clark
Art Institute, Williamstown, Massachusetts
(1955.663). Image: Clark Art Institute.

6.5

Félix-Mode, August 1897. Bibliothèque
nationale de France, Paris.

especially important promotional tool. Unlike Laferrière and others, Félix does not appear to have purchased advertising space in fashion magazines in the 1880s and 1890s, possibly an effort to protect its designs from being copied, although editors still reproduced drawings and provided detailed descriptions.[23]

PRICES

Maison Félix was known for its high prices and eye for profit. One reporter wrote of Émile Martin Poussineau: "His prices were supposed to be state secrets between himself and his patrons, but he did condescend to admit that $3,000 would be about the average cost for a ball gown."[24] Cosima Wagner, wife and promoter of the composer Richard Wagner, placed couture orders from Germany. In spring 1877, she wrote to her friend, the scholar and critic Judith Gautier, asking her to place orders with Félix.[25] In addition to buying new items for spring, including a dark green and white outfit, she wanted the firm to restyle an existing gray silk dress by overlaying it with another material and restyle two existing square shawls; she also commissioned a new hat.[26] Conscious of cost, however, she instructed her friend to compare prices with two other firms: "If the prices are equal I'm for Félix; at lower prices, for Haussemberg and Bizé."[27] Later that month, she became exasperated, offering a sense of the complications that could arise from sending orders from outside the country, relying on postal mail and telegrams: "Nothing but drama! The dressmaker who no longer sews, Haussemberg who takes forever, Félix who doesn't deliver [the goods]."[28] For Bernhardt's lead role in *La Dame aux camélias* at the Porte-Saint-Martin in 1884, the producer, M. Derembourg, balked at a bill totaling 14,010 francs for several gowns. The firm's invoice itemized the premium fabrics that had been utilized: gold tulle, silver brocade, pink satin, and gold lace.[29] Cosima Wagner exclaimed in a letter to a friend: "Félix must be approached with closed eyes and an open purse."[30]

But maison Félix allowed for fluidity in pricing when necessary. In January 1896, to help offset a downturn in the economy, Poussineau lowered his prices and produced dolls in fancy dress and sold them as New Year's gifts.[31] He seems to have respected his customers' acumen as well, recognizing that they would independently visit the drapery houses and educate themselves about the cost of fabrics (see fig. 2.8).[32] The firm also accounted for the inevitable debts by patrons that would go unpaid and took them to court when necessary. The U.S. actress Caroline Louise Dudley Carter was ordered to pay $3,000.[33]

As did Worth and Doucet, Félix facilitated long-distance orders by keeping measurements on file for regular clients.[34] In the absence of business records, an observation from the *Lady's Realm* of November 1900 is tantalizing: "Reaching the office on the first floor of the famous house, you can see the huge account-books of some of those who are its oldest customers, with their names stamped on the red labels on the backs and arranged in alphabetical order in cases. If it were only permissible to take down some of those books and turn over the pages, what a story they would tell, to be sure!"[35] Various sources—garments in museum collections, magazine and newspaper articles, theater records, and individual archives, letters, and autobiographies—make up a working list of patrons in Europe and the United States. Members of European royalty and high society who frequented Félix included Empress Eugénie, Queen Margherita of Italy, Queen consort Maria Pia of Portugal, Princess Maud of Denmark, the marquise de Breteuil, and Élisabeth de Caraman-Chimay, comtesse de Greffulhe.[36] Élisabeth, comtesse de Greffulhe, one of the leaders of Paris society, had been a client since her wedding in 1878.[37] Constance de Castelbajac, marquise de Breteuil, was also a bridal client, ordering twenty dresses for her wedding.[38] In May 1896, Félix sent several gowns to Moscow for Alexandra Feodorovna to wear at the coronation of her husband, Nicholas II, including one of yellow satin with a bodice covered in diamonds.[39] Three years later, the firm supplied garments for the duchesse d'Orléans to wear to her daughter's (Isabelle d'Orleans) wedding.[40]

Félix was well known for its actress clients as well, including Sarah Bernhardt, Sophie Croizette, Jane Hading, Anna Maria Judic, Lillie Langtry, Ada Rehan, Gabrielle Réjane, Lillian Russell, and Marie Tempest (née Marie Susan Etherington).[41] Bernhardt was undoubtedly Félix's most famous client, and her tours in the early 1880s were held to be the catalyst for introducing Félix's fashion to the United States.[42] As did other couturiers, Émile Martin Poussineau acknowledged her difficulties: "No one can be compared to Sarah for being disagreeable when trying on a dress; she often doubles the cost of a dress by tearing it into shreds when in a fit of anger."[43] Bernhardt and fellow actress Sophie Croizette, both patrons of Félix, may have been the connection that brought an especially famous U.S. socialite in Paris to Félix. The New Orleans–born Virginie Amélie Avegno Gautreau is known to have been a house client and may possibly wear a Félix dress in John Singer Sargent's painting of 1883 to 1884, *Madame X*.[44] Gautreau may also have come to know the maison through Sargent and his teacher, Carolus-Duran, whose sister-in-law was Sophie Croizette. In about 1880, Carolus-Duran painted Bernhardt wearing a black Félix dress, a portrait that has been lost.[45]

The maison embraced stage performers' influential power.[46] In 1882, the San Francisco *Daily Evening Bulletin* wrote, "The clever man tells the great ladies that the actresses copy from them—and he says to the actresses that they set the fashions for the great ladies. So both classes are pleased, and no one is any the worse."[47] With each order worth thousands of dollars, the choice of couturier was an invested decision. Other U.S. actresses and singers in the Félix register included Emma Abbott, Sadie Martinot, and Emma Wixom "Nevada" Palmer. Abbott, an opera singer, engaged Félix and Worth each season to produce costumes for her entire company and devoted long hours in helping choose fabrics and decoration.[48] Her biographer observed that Abbott regarded the costumes as part of a contract with the audience, who paid hefty ticket prices and in return expected beautiful sets and costumes together with the performance.[49] Her costumes by Félix and Worth for the 1889 to 1890 season, which totaled at least thirty and cost about $40,000, were so grand that they were exhibited in Paris. One was a reproduction of Empress Joséphine's coronation gown, a precursor to that included by Félix in the Palais du costume at the Exposition universelle in 1900 (see fig. 4.5).[50]

LEADERS OF SOCIETY

Social leaders from the United States sought out Félix, becoming familiar with the maison through magazines, newspapers, the stateside tours of European singers and actresses, and their promotional images. Worth told *Strand Magazine* in 1894 that U.S. shoppers were the best clients,[51] but in general, French couturiers reserved their complete approval. Despite critical remarks, however, they always respected U.S. buying power. In 1897, Émile Martin Poussineau said that he had never visited the United States, but he found that "La Belle Americaine has her decided individualities, her particular charms, and a few peculiar faults in her delightful makeup."[52] He called out shortcomings in their attempts to match dress colors to complexions, but he reportedly declared that U.S. women were responsible for his fortune.[53]

Notably, women's personal writings do not indicate that they were affected by couturiers' often critical attitudes, and at times they shared the same views. Marian

"Clover" Hooper Adams wrote to a friend about going to Worth to try on gowns she had ordered and becoming irked by having to wait for another U.S. woman to first try on her ten gowns. Adams amused herself by watching "a prosperous grocer from Iowa, with a fat wife for whom he wanted a smart dress . . . 'hefting the silks to be sure he was getting his money's worth.'"[54] The account is reminiscent of a character in Mark Twain and Charles Dudley Warner's satirical novel *The Gilded Age* (1873), the Honorable O'Riley, who takes his family to Paris. After remaining there for two years, he changed the family name to Oreille and "they returned home and became ultra-fashionables."[55] Again, the more pliable boundaries of class differences in U.S. society and the ability to declare one's own standing with regard to taste prejudices is evident. For his part, Marian Adams's husband, historian and author Henry Adams, characterized their 1867 visit to Paris as "waiting for ladies' dresses and the milliners' bills."[56] Overall, though, U.S. clients were welcomed in the couturiers' salons, and their orders were appreciated. Félix's and Doucet's drive to serve U.S. customers may have led them to prepare their season's offerings earlier than other couturiers.[57]

At least one magazine profile insinuates that maison Félix charged a U.S. heiress and her mother a higher price than French clients.[58] The customer went unnamed in the article, but a number of others may be identified, based on extant garments and written documents. They included Mrs. George Anderson, Caroline Webster Schermerhorn Astor, Mrs. W. T. Baker, Mrs. Timothy B. Blackstone, Cora Urquhart Brown-Potter, Mrs. Morris Eppenstein, Mrs. Gilroy (whose husband was a Tammany leader), Mary Rita Wilson Goelet, Edith Kingdon Gould, Florine Ross Harrington, Mrs. H. N. Higinbotham, Mrs. Sol Hirsch, Mrs. Thomas H. Keefe, Mrs. Lawton, May Lester, Mrs. Walter P. Little, Mrs. Mary O'Keefe, Mrs. M. L. Towns, Clara Ward (princesse de Caraman-Chimay) (fig. 6.7), Virginia Emiline Cooper Wiley, Mrs. P. J. Willis, and Mrs. Belding Young of the silk family Belding Bros. & Co. Cornelia Bradley-Martin, Anna Livingston Reade Street Morton, and Alva Vanderbilt may also have been clients.[59] They hailed mostly from the east coast from Albany, Baltimore, Newport, New York, and Washington, DC, but also Chicago, Cincinnati, Galveston, Indianapolis, Portland, Oregon, and Los Angeles. Given the amount of press coverage in the *Boston Daily Globe*, clients likely came from that city as well.

One and possibly two Félix gowns owned by Caroline Astor are in the Metropolitan Museum of Art and provide a snapshot example of the peregrinations of couture gowns by maison Félix and its cosmopolitan clients. The first is a historically inspired two-piece ball gown of dark purple velvet with white satin, embroidery,

and lace evoking late sixteenth-century Venice.[60] The dress is not labeled but was donated with a labeled Félix cap by Astor's descendants.[61] In its current state, the dress is believed to date to the 1890s but has been extensively reworked. The original form appears to date to the 1870s and may have been worn by Astor to a fancy dress ball in 1875 (see figs. 9.1 and 9.2). Félix may have created the original dress or may have redone the dress in the 1890s or both.[62] The two iterations of the gown are inspired by the Renaissance period, one of Astor's favorite choices for fancy dress. The embroidered velvet cape, the ruched skirt (the synthetic pearls were added later), and sleeves were retained; the feather fan was worn with the original version.

The second gown is a two-piece dark bluish-black evening dress dating about 1900 that was owned by Astor when she was about seventy years old and bears the Félix label. Made of velvet, the bodice and skirt are decorated with floral-patterned cutwork backed with ivory satin, which is covered with black pailletted net and outlined with plastic or glass beads, plastic or metal sequins, and paste rhinestones. The dress dates about a decade later than the portrait by Carolus-Duran of 1890, also in the Metropolitan Museum of Art, in which Astor wears a dress believed to be by Worth and inspired by seventeenth-century fashions (see fig. 7.1).[63]

Both dresses were gifts to the museum by the brothers Orme Wilson Jr. and Richard Thornton Wilson III, sons of William Backhouse Astor and Caroline Webster Schermerhorn Astor's daughter Caroline "Carrie" Schermerhorn Astor, as were several garments by Worth, Doucet, Paquin, and Redfern. The Wilson brothers were nephews of Mary Rita Wilson Goelet, who patronized Félix during her shopping excursions in 1891 (see chapter 5, International Clientele). Goelet was staying at the well-established Hotel Meurice on the rue de Rivoli when she ordered from Félix a robe de chambre with lace detailing for 350 francs, and several chemises, drawers, and nightgowns. That Goelet was able to buy high-end lingerie and sleepwear indicates the necessity on the part of couturiers to diversify their offerings to meet clients' needs and to contend within the heavy competition that defined

6.7

Studio of Nadar. Clara Ward, princesse de Caraman Chimay, 1898. The designer of the dress is unknown. Image: © Ministère de la culture / Médiathèque du patrimoine, Dist. RMN-Grand Palais / Art Resource, NY.

the transatlantic couture trade. Two days later, Goelet bought lingerie, fabric, and nightshirts at Franck, located in the same building as Worth, Félix's chief rival.[64] By providing more quotidien but still luxurious items like underclothes and sleepwear, brands like Félix remained essential to its clients. This way, they would be top of mind when it came to placing orders for showstopping ball gowns that would become their owners' signature possessions and celebrated to an extent befitting custom-designed mansions and all the complexities and theatrics of their commissioning and outfitting.

GOWNS AND MANSIONS

French Fashion in U.S. Homes

When Caroline Webster Schermerhorn Astor greeted her guests in the drawing room of her new mansion on 5th Avenue, she did so standing in front of the nearly seven-foot-tall portrait of her by Carolus-Duran (fig. 7.1). Painted in 1890 when Astor was fifty-nine years old and the established doyenne of New York society, the picture became a key touchstone in the French Renaissance château-style house she commissioned from Richard Morris Hunt in 1893 and moved into on its completion in 1896.[1] Set against a nondescript background, she wears a dark blue velvet gown with white lace detailing with matching feather fan and headdress. A costume for a fancy dress ball, the dress incorporated elements of seventeenth-century style, including the pointed lace collar with matching lace cuffs.[2] Taking up the majority of the monumental canvas, the painting may well be considered a portrait of the gown. The pride of place that the canvas occupied in the house and the close identification that Astor attached to it presents productive lines of inquiry about the role of fashion inside the mansions erected during the building boom along 5th Avenue in the 1880s and 1890s.

This chapter contends that women wearing costly, elaborate gowns and masquerade costumes effectively activated the newly built homes by filling them with the fabrics and cachet of Parisian couture. The actual wearing of clothing, an understudied component of its consumption, and the interrelationship between interior spaces and fashion drive the inquiry.[3] Hostesses and their guests inserted the powerful institution of French fashion into elite architectural structures. The gowns exerted significant work by displaying status and wealth, but in their volume of fabrics

and jewels, they also contended with the vast square footage, tall ceilings, expertly carved furniture, and outfitting of the rooms. With many of the homes' structures and decor modeled after historical French châteaux, the result is often paradoxical choices and juxtapositions. In the case of fancy dress balls, the garments provided a vehicle for the wearer to masquerade or embody a character, operating within the theatricality that pervaded social life. The act of women first viewing the opera and then wearing specially crafted clothing to a ball infused new meaning into the architectural structures, effectively transforming them into staged arenas. Curiously, many of the costumes were inspired by French royal figures who were ultimately ousted or killed, an ironic association with the monarchy for wealthy U.S. citizens whose families became rich off of capitalistic ventures. Following Veblen's theory of conspicuous consumption, their emulation of royal refinement was pursued at all costs, desperation and discomfort be damned.[4] The question of how conscious they were of their extreme consumption remains an open one. For Veblen and Bourdieu, the behavior was unconscious, and Bourdieu assigns it to the *habitus*, a system of cultural forces that influenced consumer actions.[5] In the context of the Astors, Vanderbilts, and their compatriots, we cannot determine how aware they were of their striving for certain material goods and status, but we can access the paradoxes of some of their choices to give us a sense of the complexities surrounding them.

The homes, gowns, and housewarming balls of Alva Vanderbilt in 1883 and Caroline Astor in 1896 provide apt case studies because they represent the two main categories of Veblen's conception of the leisure class—those who inherit wealth and those who exert effort to earn wealth.[6] The Astors were a respected and old Knickerbocker family, whereas the Vanderbilts were considered *arriviste*. Caroline Astor's father was a Schermerhorn, descended from the settlers who came to America from Holland in the late seventeenth century. Although the family built a fortune through mercantile and real estate businesses, by the nineteenth century, the way in which it had been earned was separated by a sufficient amount of time, and the family was more associated with their cultural capital, as Bourdieu terms it, rather than cash.[7] At this point, the family had put out a few generations of educated, privileged members. The Vanderbilts, on the other hand, although also descended from seventeenth-century settlers, had made money through new shipping and railroad enterprises and were continuously trying to counteract the perception that the family, by one account, was "raised to social eminence by vulgarly-gotten wealth."[8]

ARCHITECTURE AND FASHION

The 1870s through 1890s were booming times in the interrelated industries of elite U.S. architecture, interior decoration, and fashion. Old-money and new-money families sought to mark their territory and display their taste on upper 5th Avenue, as they were doing in Newport, Chicago, and elsewhere by erecting showpiece homes.[9] Astor after Astor and Vanderbilt after Vanderbilt commissioned European-inspired mansions from prominent architects and interior designers. One familial architectural lineup comprised the following: William Henry and Maria Louisa Kissam Vanderbilt's (and two daughters, Margaret Louisa and Emily Thorn's) "Triple Palace" at 640 and 642 5th Avenue and 2 West 52nd Street was designed by the architectural firm Trench and Snook with a neo-Grec exterior, and decoration by Herter Brothers and was completed in 1882. The same year, William Kissam and Alva Vanderbilt's French Renaissance mansion at 660 5th Avenue at 52nd Street was finished, with architecture by Hunt and with multiple interior designers (fig. 7.2). Alice Claypoole Gwynne Vanderbilt and Cornelius Vanderbilt II commissioned a French château-style home on 5th Avenue and 57th Street the same year.[10] Some architectural firms included design services, but many homes were decorated by U.S. firms such as Herter Brothers and George A. Schastey & Co. and French firms like that of Jules Allard et fils. The field of interior decoration was in the process of becoming professionalized in the last decades of the century.[11] Developments in the field paralleled those of couture, with designers signing or labeling their work and consolidating production and sales in their shop (fig. 7.3).[12]

In 1875, Boston's *Cottage Hearth* magazine reported on a "Paris mania" in U.S. furnishings, but the styles of the homes are best described as "historiated"—pastiches that evoke historical styles, in this case, royal European, without a firm

7.2

Photograph by H. N. Tiemann & Co., 1898.
Richard Morris Hunt (U.S., 1827–1895). Home
of William Kissam and Alva Smith Vanderbilt,
660 5th Avenue at 52nd Street, New York.
The Miriam and Ira D. Wallach Division of
Art, Prints and Photographs: Photography
Collection, The New York Public Library.

devotion to authenticity.[13] Architectural historian Bruno Pons refers to the "salon spirit" of French society that imbued French domestic architecture and that was adopted by elite U.S. citizens.[14] But the transmission came through with static, and the homes ended up as patchworks of multiple period styles. Alva Vanderbilt went all in on mismatched French styles in both the 5th Avenue home and Marble House in Newport, built by Hunt and decorated by Allard and Sons in 1888 to 1892. There the exterior was inspired by the Petit Trianon at Versailles, but the so-called Gothic style she favored for the interior actually encompassed art and furnishings from the twelfth through sixteenth centuries.[15] The grand ball at the New York home in 1883 was French mania writ large.

VANDERBILT BALL, 1883

The ways in which fashion activated the newly erected and designed homes along 5th Avenue are best examined through housewarming events, often elaborate balls inspired by the theater. William Kissam Vanderbilt and Alva Vanderbilt moved into their new mansion at 660 5th Avenue at 52nd Street in 1883. The house, which cost a reported $3 million to build, was well known to be their effort to establish themselves in high society, having formerly been derided as *nouveau riche*.

Alva Smith's family was from Mobile, Alabama—"plain Miss Smith, mind you," wrote one reporter[16]—but both her parents' families held money and stature in local and national government.[17] At their cotton plantations, they enslaved laborers, and in her memoir, Alva Vanderbilt Belmont recalled that her mother had "inherited" workers.[18] She remembered a servant named Monroe who had previously been enslaved by her mother and with whom Alva would go to the market after the family moved from Mobile to New York.[19] She wrote of her mother's avid preference of French dress for herself and her daughters, especially from Madame Olympe (see

7.3

Marie de Solar (French, active late 19th century). Fashion plate, *L'Art et la mode*, 1883. The Miriam and Ira D. Wallach Division of Art, Prints and Photographs: Picture Collection, The New York Public Library.

fig. 2.1).[20] Alva recalled that as a child she resented having been made "a pioneer in the matter of clothes," as well as the attention she received for her "extraordinary amount of hair."[21] As an adult, however, especially during the years of her two marriages, her interest in a rich appearance was undeniable.

Despite Alva's childhood summers in Newport, France, Austria, Italy, Belgium, and Germany, her family's fortunes changed when she was a teenager and when her father's businesses declined in about 1875. From then onward, both she and William Kissam Vanderbilt sought approval from the old-money Knickerbocker families like the Astors, Schermerhorns, Stuyvesants, and Van Cortlandts and courted newspaper editors to help the cause.[22] The four-story limestone house was conceived as a French Renaissance "petit château" in the style of François I, a deliberate choice that associated it with French royalty and that would be copied by a number of elite homes in New York, including the Henry G. Marquand House on Madison Avenue at 68th Street.[23]

Alva Vanderbilt had lived and studied in Paris with her mother and siblings between 1866 and 1870 and recalled fondly her formal education there, including etiquette lessons on how to conduct oneself at an evening entertainment.[24] After returning to New York, she remembered that her mother shipped their French furniture to their rented home at 14 East 33rd Street and that it was an unusual decision at the time.[25] Vanderbilt retained a taste for all things historically French and presumably followed the progressions of French interior design, which, as design historian Anca I. Lasc has shown, were amply circulating throughout the world in collecting and decorating manuals.[26]

Vanderbilt worked closely with Hunt on the design of the house at 660 5th Avenue and later referred to him as one of her closest friends.[27] She instructed him on her preference for what she called medieval style but that was truly a combination of French Gothic and Renaissance.[28] Herter Brothers designed the banqueting hall, and Jules Allard's well-known French firm was contracted for the eighteenth-century Régence salon.[29] The entrance hall was executed in Caen limestone, and the dining hall had ceilings of oak and windows created with pieces of medieval stained glass. Other rooms were appointed with Aubusson carpets and Gobelin tapestries, the latter evoking the grandness of the court of Louis XIV, as the Gobelins manufactory had become the Royal Manufactory of the Crown's Furnishings in 1664.[30]

Shortly after the house was finished in 1883, William Kissam Vanderbilt published several catalogs of his art collection and engaged Edward Strahan (pseudonym for artist and critic Earl Shinn) to write the text of a four-volume handbook, *Mr. Vanderbilt's House and Collection*, with lavish illustrations of the decorative highlights.[31] The Vanderbilts became known for using this type of self-promotion to amplify their taste as publicly as possible, an effort that for the most part was successful, although the level of societal acceptance remained varied. In her memoir, Alva Vanderbilt Belmont remained proud of the house, which by then had been destroyed but whose plans had been shared by request in France, England, and Germany.[32]

On Monday, March 26, 1883, the Vanderbilts held a fancy dress ball with hundreds of guests (at least one thousand invitations were sent), spending a rumored $250,000 in total. The impetus for the event was a housewarming and also a welcoming to their close friend Consuelo Yznaga, Lady Mandeville, who was visiting. Without a specific theme from the hostess, people arrived in costume from multiple eras (fig. 7.4).[33] Vanderbilt dressed as a Venetian princess (fig. 7.5), based on a painting by Alexandre Cabanel, and her husband was the "Duc de Guise," possibly after a painting in his art collection—not as Cinderella and Mine Host of the Inn, as was rumored beforehand.[34] As did most balls, this one began late at night. Advancing past the police-patrolled spectator crowds, they arrived at about 11:00 p.m., the eight-course dinner was served at 2:00 a.m., and they departed at daybreak (fig. 7.6).[35] The timing indicates that the majority of partakers was not required to report to jobs in the morning.[36]

Attending the opera was an act that had become coded for the leisure classes, warranting entire chapters in etiquette books on the specifics of appropriate dress.[37] The multifarious influences of the opera on the ball that followed are worthy of consideration. On March 26, *Rigoletto* played at the Academy of Music on East 14th Street and Irving Place, the most highly respected venue at the time. (The Metropolitan Opera opened further uptown in October 1883 on Broadway between 39th and 40th Streets.)[38] *Rigoletto*, composed by Giuseppe Verdi with libretto by Francesco Maria Piave, premiered in Venice in 1851. The first scene is a ball held at the palace of the sordid Duke of Mantua. The duke takes a liking to Gilda, the daughter of his jester, Rigoletto. Gilda has only seen the duke in his disguise as a student and wishes to be with him, but her father explains the man's true identity and attempts to dissuade her. He has her dress as a man so that she may escape safely to Verona; however, she manages to return and, still dressed in men's clothes, is killed in a case of mistaken identity.

7.4

The Vanderbilt Ball, Frank Leslie's Illustrated Newspaper, April 7, 1883. Image: New York Public Library Digital Collections.

7.5

Jose Maria Mora (b. Cuba ca. 1849; active in New York until 1893). Alva Vanderbilt at her ball, 1883. New-York Historical Society, PR 223, Costume Ball Photograph Collection, 33756. Photograph © New-York Historical Society.

7.6

Paul René Reinicke (German, 1860–1926),
*Fish out of Water; or, Leaving the Fancy Dress
Ball*, 1893. The Miriam and Ira D. Wallach
Division of Art, Prints and Photographs:
Picture Collection, The New York Public
Library.

Guests at the Vanderbilt ball, including the socialite Cora Urquhart Brown-Potter, who was also an actress, would have watched and listened to these scenes of artifice leading to tragedy before donning costumes themselves and enacting their own show at the party. The themes ranged from allegorical and historical to technological, with Alice Claypoole Gwynne Vanderbilt famously wearing a Worth dress representing electric light (figs. 7.7 and 7.8).[39] Outfitted with a battery-powered torch, it was the height of contemporaneity, as Thomas Edison's lightbulb invention was then available in only a few private homes.[40] During the ball, "the house was in a blaze of light, which shown upon profuse decorations of flowers" by the society florist Charles F. Klunder, who created the ambience of a "garden in a tropical forest."[41] The *New York Times* noted that a certain Miss LaFarge came as Diana in a white satin dress with petticoat embroidered with silver stars and crescents and with drapery of tiger skin. Brown-Potter came as the eponymous opera character Madame Favart (an eighteenth-century actress), holding a mandolin, and she danced a quadrille with her husband.[42] Brown-Potter was also a client of Worth and Félix, and the soprano Adelina Patti who played Gilda in *Rigoletto* that night was a client of Worth. Sarah Hewitt, who patronized Worth and Félix, dressed as a Persian princess in a blue brocade robe trimmed with white fur; accessories included a feather turban and two daggers tucked into her belt. Worth created a phoenix-themed gown for Emily Taylor Lorillard, the long train of which was decorated with a crimson cashmere border embroidered with "leaping flames."[43] Caroline Astor wore a dark, Venetian-inspired dress of velvet and satin, with a diamond aigrette in her loose, long hair.[44] A significant number of guests dressed as opera characters, from Carmen (Fanny Gage Horton Benkard) to Serpolette (Jennie Smith Yznaga) and La Perichole (Caroline Morris Kean Rives).

The costume selections derived from such handbooks as Ardern Holt's *Fancy Dresses Described: Or, What to Wear at Fancy Balls*, first published in 1879 and followed by five more editions through 1896. The guide provides a fascinating glimpse into the zeitgeist of the mid- to late 1880s.[45] Listed alphabetically rather than by categories, the themes of electric light, newspapers, photography, postage, and telegrams were included with those of allegorical, historical, and Shakespearean figures, and among the most intriguing were doll pin cushion, chocolate cream, and hornet. The latter two were taken up, with some interpretation, at the Vanderbilt ball by Jennie (Jenny) Bigelow, who came as La Belle Chocolatier, and Constance Rives Borland, who came as a hornet in yellow satin and a brown velvet skirt (figs. 7.9 and 7.10). Borland was not the only hornet that night: Eliza (Lila) Osgood Vanderbilt Webb

7.7

Jose Maria Mora. Alice Claypoole Gwynne
Vanderbilt in "Electric Light" ensemble seen
in figure 7.8. New-York Historical Society.
Photograph © New-York Historical Society.

7.8

House of Worth. "Electric Light" ensemble.
Silk satin and velvet with silver and gold
metallic tinsel and silver paillettes. Museum
of the City of New York, Gift of Countess
László Széchenyi (51.284.3A–H).

7.9

Hornet costume in Ardern Holt, *Fancy
Dresses Described: Or, What to Wear at Fancy
Balls* (1879).

7.10

Jose Maria Mora. Constance Rives Borland
at the Vanderbilt ball, 1883. New-York
Historical Society, PR 223, Costume Ball
Photograph Collection. 49007. Photograph
© New-York Historical Society.

wore nearly the same costume, a testament to how closely readers adhered to Holt's suggestions.[46]

Holt ranked French and English historical figures as most notable, with Marguerite de Valois, Marie Antoinette, Marie Stuart, and the "Louis XIII, XIV, XV, and XVI periods" especially highlighted. Cornelius Vanderbilt II, Alva's brother-in-law, dressed as Louis XVI, a Bourbon monarch destined for the guillotine, as did seventeen other men, according to the *New York Times*, which was prone to exaggeration in its fancy dress ball coverage, as were many news outlets.[47] In Alva's memoir, though, there is no acknowledgment of the ironic association with a counterrevolutionary deposed king. And this was at a time when the Vanderbilts and other prominent families were continuously criticized for monopolizing entire industries and lampooned for their opulent lifestyles, as were William Henry Vanderbilt, Jay Gould, and Cyrus W. Field in the humor magazine *Puck*.[48] William Henry Vanderbilt was alternately called a "merciless millionaire" and the "modern colossus of (rail) roads" in its pages.[49] Rather, in Alva's memoir, she wrote about fashion: "Many of the costumes, including Lady Mandeville's and mine, came from Paris." She recalled that Yznaga came as Queen Maria Theresa of Austria and that her own dress was of white satin with elaborate gold embroidery, a velvet mantle, diamond diadem, and additional diamond and emerald jewelry completed the outfit.[50]

This loose, vaguely escapist historicism also manifested in dressing as the subjects of old master painters like Titian, Velàzquez, Watteau, Reynolds, and Gainsborough. Servants, however, were required to dress as wait staff of a historical period.[51] When partygoers toyed with dressing below their station, they could choose from peasant options from multiple countrysides, Romanian and Sorrentine among them. And when a hostess wanted everyone to dress down, she might throw a calico ball, for which the costumes were constructed from cotton or other inexpensive fabrics.[52] Holt prescribed that net and tarlatan should be used instead of tulle, for example. At one such party in Los Angeles, dance partners were paired by having each man select an envelope that contained a remnant of patterned fabric. He would then match the pattern to the dress of one of the women in attendance.[53]

Guests at the Vanderbilt ball, however, were dressed in the finest that was to offer, and after attending the opera, they would have first returned home for their own costume change or, attended by servants, used one of the dressing rooms made available by the hostess of the ball. They would not have attended the opera wearing a Russian peasant or Cinderella costume, for example (fig. 7.11). The evening's

7.11

Willard Poinsette Snyder (U.S., 1853–1934),
The Talking Boxes, Harper's Weekly, April 2,
1892. Image: The author.

proceedings, especially this interlude between the two main events, suggest a poignant blending of the experience of watching the opera and then embodying a different character at the ball, realized through a change of clothing, hairstyle, and makeup. In terms of the setting, the scene changed from the established opera house to that of the new mansion of an *arriviste* family.

The theatrics of debuting fancy dress ball costumes were not lost on the press, which was an integral part of the institution of fashion.[54] (Paul Poiret famously took full advantage of this strategy in the early twentieth century.) *Godey's Lady's Book* covered the Vanderbilt ball thoroughly, and photographs of guests in costume taken by Jose Maria Mora were distributed widely via cabinet cards.[55] Mora's black-and-white photographs provide an invaluable record of the costumes worn by prominent attendees.[56]

At least one representation in color exists in a painted miniature of Mary Stevens Paget that was based on a photograph of her at either the Vanderbilt ball or another contemporary ball (figs. 7.12 and 7.13). Painted by Fernand Paillet in watercolor on ivory, the image shows Paget in her Cleopatra costume, gold jewels abounding. The miniature attests to the impulse for recording the outfit, which no doubt was a costly investment and long in the making. As Paillet was a French artist who painted the miniatures of many U.S. socialites, the piece may have been executed in Paris or the United States. Paget's taste for elaborately dressing as the Egyptian queen is further demonstrated by the photograph of her at the Devonshire ball in 1897 (see fig. 8.3), to which she wore an ensemble created for her by Worth that differs from the one she wore in 1883.

Formal portraits and miniatures are also helpful when viewed alongside photographs from balls as testimony that couturiers furnished a range of garments from daily wear to fancy dress ball costumes and that the latter were not considered a lesser endeavor (as they were regarded later in the twentieth century). There was no strict division between costume and fashion as there is today. The equality derives from the previously discussed synergistic relationship between theater and the fashion system. Although we do not know the names of the makers of Frederika Belmont Howland's costume for the Vanderbilt ball or the jeweled ensemble with ermine-lined cape she wore for her portrait miniature in 1898, the fastidious detail of both attests to Howland's exacting eye (figs. 7.14 and 7.15). A photograph by Mora of another guest, Olivia Peyton Murray Cutting, shows that her eighteenth-century costume for the ball was completed by a powdered updo and floral hairpiece. Dressing in character may have emboldened the sitter to adopt a direct gaze

7.12

Fernand Paillet. *Mary Stevens Paget*, 1891. Watercolor on ivory; silver gilt, 7.3×6.4 cm. New-York Historical Society, Gift of the Estate of Peter Marié (1905.182). Photograph © New-York Historical Society.

7.13

Jose Maria Mora. Mary Stevens Paget in Cleopatra costume. New-York Historical Society, PR 223, Costume Ball Photograph Collection, 80437d. Photograph © New-York Historical Society.

7.14

Jose Maria Mora. Frederika Belmont (later Mrs. S. S. Howland) at the Vanderbilt ball, 1883. New-York Historical Society, PR 223, Costume Ball Photograph Collection, 83888d. Photograph © New-York Historical Society.

7.15

Carl A. Weidner (U.S., 1865–1906) and Fredrika Weidner (U.S., 1865–1939). *Mrs. Samuel Shaw Howland (Frederika Belmont)*, 1898. Watercolor on ivory; silver gilt, 9.8 × 7.6 cm. New-York Historical Society, Gift of the Estate of Peter Marié (1905.112). Photograph © New-York Historical Society.

at the camera.[57] Four years later, for her portrait by Alexandre Cabanel, her attitude is more traditional, her pale pink satin and lace ballgown was formally arranged with complementary fan, and her chestnut-colored hair is set in a conservative high chignon (fig. 7.16).

Finally, Emily Thorn Vanderbilt Sloane, a daughter of William Henry Vanderbilt, who would live with her husband in part of the "Triple Palace" on 5th Avenue, opted for a Little Bo Peep costume. It was made for her by Catharine Donovan at the dressmaker's 315 5th Avenue location (figs. 7.17 and 7.18).[58] Donovan may have consulted a guidebook like Holt's, which includes a Bo Peep listing that recommended a short skirt and black velvet bodice for the whimsical ensemble. However, Donovan seems to have used her own design for the red satin quilted skirt with diamond patterns, overskirt with embroidered red poppies, and sewed-on poppy decoration on the skirt trim and bodice.[59] Five years later when Sloane sat for her portrait by Benjamin Curtis Porter, she chose a formal white ball gown with yellow taffeta trim (fig. 7.19).[60]

Once inside the mansion, the guests-turned-characters flooded the elaborate rooms of 660 5th Avenue. A set of young guests performed six quadrilles (dances with four couples) that they had practiced for weeks; two multipiece bands provided the music.[61] In the case of the Dresden Quadrille, the women dressed and powdered their faces in white to resemble Dresden china, becoming living statues within a home that abounded with sculpture, painting, and decorative arts.[62] Other quadrilles, including one with life-size hobby-horses attached to the waists of the dancers, flowed from the third-floor supper room (called the "gymnasium"), down the grand staircase, and into the drawing room on the second floor.[63] The choreographed dances crossed through several sections of the house, inserting bodies, fabric, and props into spaces that had not yet been fully inhabited, the house having been finished only days before. Hundreds of other unchoreographed guests also enlivened the rooms, their costumes often voluminous with formidable headdresses. Kate Fearing Strong famously wore a stuffed white cat to top off her feline outfit,

7.16

Alexandre Cabanel (French, 1823–1889). *Olivia Peyton Murray Cutting*, 1887. Oil on canvas, 132×99 cm. Museum of the City of New York, Gift of the daughters and granddaughter of Mrs. William Bayard Cutting through Mrs. Bayard James, 1950 (50.60.1).

7.17

Jose Maria Mora. Emily Thorn Vanderbilt
Sloane as Little Bo Peep at the Vanderbilt
ball, 1883. New-York Historical Society, PR
223, Costume Ball Photograph Collection.
Photograph © New-York Historical Society.

7.18

Catharine Donovan (b. Ireland, ca. 1826–d.
1906). Little Bo Peep costume seen in
figure 7.17. Silk velvet, lace, velvet ribbon,
brocade, and faux flowers. Courtesy of
the FIDM Museum at the Fashion Institute
of Design & Merchandising, Los Angeles
(2012.5.32A-C). Photograph: FIDM Museum.

the skirt of which was composed of sewn white cat's tails (fig. 7.20).[64] Her nickname, "Puss," is inscribed on a blue ribbon around her neck, from which hangs a bell.

The notion of the guests wearing their outfits and setting them into motion within the freshly built Vanderbilt house is a poignant demonstration of how fashion interacts with interior spaces. As John Potvin, Louise Crewe, and Heidi Brevik-Zender have shown in their pioneering studies, fashion and spaces work upon one another, leaving lasting impacts.[65] It is fitting to invoke here what theorists Joanne Entwistle and Elizabeth Wilson have so astutely termed the "embodied practices" of fashion.[66] Although the skeleton of the Vanderbilt house was filled with a sizeable collection of furniture, paintings, sculpture, textiles, and decorative objects by the most desired artists and designers of the period, the space did not function as a home and showpiece for the owners until it was activated by the bodies, heat, and fabrics of the guests who actually warmed the house.

The satirical "Town Terrier" columnist in *Puck* magazine joked that "the most richly dressed person in the ball-room" had "two certified checks for $250,000 each" enwreathed in her hair.[67] The "Fitznoodle in America" feature in *Puck* jested about the spectacle of a ball being similar to the chaos of a battle.[68] In the article "Wicked Extravagance," a reporter in Maine condemned the elaborate affair for taking place not all that far from impoverished neighborhoods. Tellingly, they used language describing materials but not distinguishing between interior decoration and people to conjure the overall atmosphere: "And so throughout the whole affair—there was the artistic manipulation of velvet, satin, ermine, silk, diamond, pearls, silver and gold."[69]

ASTOR BALL, 1896

Standing under her portrait by Carolus-Duran on the night of Monday, February 3, 1896, Caroline Astor welcomed six hundred guests to the housewarming ball for her new French Renaissance château–style house at 840 5th Avenue at 65th Street, to which she had moved sometime in January.[70] Astor had held annual balls at her brownstone on 5th Avenue at 34th Street (she had added a ballroom there in 1875, and Stanford White enhanced the interior in 1879) and in Newport, always with exclusive guest lists (the famed list of Four Hundred selected by her and Ward McAllister).[71] Her decision to move uptown was in part motivated by scorn for her nephew William Waldorf Astor's decision to build the Waldorf Hotel, in her view an undesirable commercial venture, next to her private home.[72] The enormous ballroom in the new house was sixty feet long and one-and-a-half stories high, and doubled as an art gallery displaying paintings by mostly French artists, including Jules Breton, William Bouguereau, and Carolus-Duran.[73] Hunt designed a tremendous fireplace for the room and a stained-glass skylight above. Caroline, whose husband, William Backhouse, had died in 1892, resided in the house, and her son, John Jacob, and his family owned an adjoining home.[74] The latter hosted their own, slightly smaller, housewarming dance on February 10, 1896, after the performance of *Die Meistersinger* at the Metropolitan Opera House.[75]

The performance before the Astor ball on February 3 was *Carmen* at the Metropolitan Opera House, which the *New York Times* called the "best of the season."[76] The relatively new opera, composed by George Bizet with a libretto by Henri Meilhac and Ludovic Halévy, was first performed in Paris in 1875. Deemed controversial, it showed the life of common gypsies, including that of Carmen, a girl with whom a Spanish corporal, Don José, falls in love and later kills out of jealousy over her ardor for a bullfighter, Escamillo. Emma Calvé played the role of Carmen; the Australian soprano Nellie Melba played Micaela, a peasant girl.

As with the Vanderbilt ball, the evening for many guests proceeded from watching a richly costumed tragedy (often from their family-owned private boxes) at the opera house to enacting their own drama as the first players in the grand ballroom of the Astor house. Other guests evidently attended dinner parties instead of the opera and then proceeded to the ball.[77] The ball was not themed, and costumes were not required, so the guests wore gowns by the French couturiers who were dressing some of the stage performers. Melba was a client of Worth. Astor was an avid patron of Worth and Félix, making regular visits to the Parisian maisons and placing seasonal orders (see chapter 5, International Clientele). At the New Year's Ball at the Metropolitan Opera House in 1890, Astor wore a Worth brocade gown and her renowned stomacher of diamonds together with a diamond tiara.[78] The stomacher was purportedly owned by Marie Antoinette, herself an enthusiastic host of historically themed costume parties. As Caroline Weber and Kimberly Chrisman-Campbell have demonstrated, the queen was a masterful implementer of diamonds and big hair as symbols of power, which generations of elite women would emulate.[79] For the February 1896 ball, Astor wore a purple velvet gown with lace, a coronet of diamonds, and the same stomacher.[80] A seated dinner, prepared by the society caterer Pinard, was served at midnight. A cotillion, a French court dance, began at about one o'clock in the morning, led by Elisha Dyer IV and Ava

Lowell Willing Astor, who wore a "rich gown of heavy white silk" and an "aigrette of diamonds" in her hair. In the middle of winter, the house was replete with "huge tropical plants" and American Beauty roses.[81]

Edith Wharton and Ogden Codman Jr.'s *The Decoration of Houses* (1897) explains that "gala rooms" were sparsely furnished and are "never meant to be seen except when crowded: the crowd takes the place of furniture."[82] People were needed to fill the space, indeed to take up space, for which the architecture and fabrics of their clothing were essential. The gowns and costumes that were enlisted at the Vanderbilt and Astor balls allowed guests to try on the garb of European kings, queens, and knights; boast the cost of commissioning creations from the finest couturiers; and also embody a theatrical production by putting on their own show and christening a new stage. By doing so, the U.S. elite used fancy dress balls at newly built mansions—spaces of spectacle par excellence—to claim their rightful place within the transnational fashion industry that relied as much on them for its success as on the French couturiers. Further underlying the theatrics was a fervent grip on past monarchal practice, mostly French, that might at first appear out of step with the complexities of contemporary society but, on second consideration, may be viewed as part of the overall claiming of rightful power.

In the portrait of her by premier French society portraitist Carolus-Duran, Astor commemorated the centrality of French fashion and its attendant stature within her social life and in her homes. Seven years after the portrait was made, she apparently wore the same dress, or one modeled closely after it, to the extravagant ball

7.19

Benjamin Curtis Porter (U.S., 1845–1908). *Emily Thorn Vanderbilt Sloane*, 1888. Oil on canvas. Collection of Vanderbilt University Fine Arts Gallery, Nashville, Tennessee.

given by Bradley and Cornelia Martin.[83] The newspapers often claimed the dress was made by Carolus-Duran—he may have helped design it, but it would have been produced by a couturier such as Worth. The Bradley-Martin ball, which "eclipsed, even the memorable Vanderbilt ball of 1883," was held at the Waldorf Hotel on 5th Avenue and 33rd Street on February 10, 1897.[84] The hotel was a contested space that had originally fueled Astor's desire to build a new home uptown. By wearing the same gown and re-creating her image from the portrait that stood as a monument to her in her own French château-styled home, Astor made a decisive statement of her presence. When Astor died in 1908, the portrait was shrouded in black fabric and stationed in the salon, materially imbuing its iconic power (fig. 7.21). The extent of the investment that women like Astor made in couture, embodying it and inserting it into their homes, was a reflection of the time, effort, and money they exerted to procure it. This fidelity was so substantial that it affected government efforts to reduce the influence of foreign goods, an action that arguably instilled greater devotion to obtaining French garments, as is discussed within the context of tariffs in the next chapter.

7.20

Jose Maria Mora. Kate Fearing Strong at the Vanderbilt ball, 1883. Museum of the City of New York (F2012.58.1460).

7.21

Portrait of Caroline Webster Schermerhorn
Astor by Carolus-Duran (1890; figure 7.1)
shrouded with black fabric, in photograph of
Astor's home upon her death in 1908. *The
Burr McIntosh Monthly*, January 1909. Image:
The author.

8

RISING PRICES

The Impact of U.S. Tariffs

The towering influence of Paris on production and of the United States on consumption for the couture market is set into further relief when viewed against efforts by the U.S. government to curb the flow of goods. Two tariffs in particular affected the influx of French fashion—the Tariff of 1890 (McKinley Tariff) and the Tariff of 1897 (Dingley Tariff). Looking closely at the reactions of elite customers and shrewd business owners to the protectionist government's institution of lawful measures to limit luxury purchases sharpens our view of what fashion historian Alexandra Palmer terms the "investment in couture."[1] The transnational dynamics of the tariffs and their effect on consumption practices reinforces the extent to which fashion was intertwined with politics and the economy, a point that Ilya Parkins and Elizabeth M. Sheehan have highlighted.[2] Changing outfits as many as five or six times per day—from dressing gowns to afternoon dresses to fancy dress ball outfits (figs. 8.1 and 8.2) to tea gowns to ball gowns, and more—upper-class women invested extraordinary amounts of money and time into couture. Elaborate routines of planning, scheduling, shopping, ordering, dressing, cleaning, packing, transporting, and storage contributed to the substantial value, both monetary and perceived, of couture garments. The U.S. government took notice. Signficantly, the French couture houses grappled with how to adjust to new ordinances, reactions that emphasize the complexities of the enterprises. Although they might bear the name of a founder or family, decisions were hardly made by a single figure.

In late December 1890, two gowns that Caroline Astor had ordered from maison Félix in Paris arrived at the United States Custom House in New York. On the lookout for undervaluation of goods and delinquent luxury duties, federal officers seized the dresses and sent them to a local shop for appraisal. The assessment came in at 3,500 francs ($694.80), which was 1.5 times the price of 2,000 francs ($400) that Astor and the dressmaker agreed to and Astor paid, and 3.5 times the low-ball value (1,000 francs; $200) declared by the dressmaker's agents when they arrived at the Custom House.[3]

The saga of the famous Astor gowns—an embroidered apple- and dark-green silk and velvet dress and a sky-blue silk dress with ostrich-feather trimmings—played out in the international press over the course of ten months.[4] The papers speculated as to whether Astor would pay the remaining duties and penalties of $300 to $400. Even after the case was escalated to the office of the secretary of the treasury, Astor refused to pay, and the gowns were sent to auction. Competitive bidding between a theater owner and two other men ran up the price of the green dress, with Bloomingdale Brothers winning it at $660. John Koster of Koster and Bial's Music Hall bought the blue one for $770.[5]

The Astor gowns episode encapsulates a particular moment in the government's protectionist efforts to discourage the purchase of foreign goods and encourage domestic production. Historian Sven Beckert calls the tariff the "guiding theme of the politics of the 1880s and 1890s."[6] The Tariff of 1890 (McKinley Tariff) became law on October 1, 1890, two months before Astor's gowns were seized. William McKinley—a Republican Representative from Ohio, chair of the House Committee on Ways and Means, and future president of the United States—championed the new tariff, which applied to a broad swath of goods and materials, including oil paints, wood, sugar, and tobacco. Schedule L was concerned with silk and silk goods and encompassed velvets, fringes, tassels, laces, embroideries, and other trimmings.[7] Other sections covered related categories but applied to less expensive

8.1

Maison Félix. Afternoon dress, 1890–1891.
Silk with lace. Albany Institute, Gift of
Mr. and Mrs. J. D. Hatch Jr. (1946.56.2ab).

clothing: Schedule I (cotton manufacturers), Schedule J (flax, hemp, and jute, and manufacturers of those materials), and Schedule K (wool and manufacturers of wool). The average tariff rate on these items was 48 percent, up from about 38 percent. The duties for completed gowns are difficult to generalize because they were based on the weight of the fabric and included a value-added tax on the actual manufacture, but the duty could be as high as 100 percent of the original price.[8] The goal was to extend protectionism in the name of nationalism. The tariffs aimed to safeguard and boost U.S. manufacturing, but the rich and poor both took ire, as the former scorned their reduced access to materials, and the latter saw higher prices for certain staples without an increase in their wages.[9]

As historian Andrew Wender Cohen points out, public opinion in the United States was divided over tariffs, but in political offices, protectionists prevailed over reductionists and free traders.[10] Furthermore, attitudes toward tariffs did not always adhere to party lines: some Republicans (like William Backhouse Astor and New York congressman Ashbel P. Fitch) opposed steep tariffs, whereas some Democrats were pro-tariff. For the most part, the opportunity for personal gain guided individual positions. If tariffs helped keep competition and wages low, industry leaders supported them, lobbying for certain amendments to bills that would work in their favor.[11] For example, the steel magnate Andrew Carnegie, a Republican, was a protectionist, and some smaller-scale merchants supported duty-free imports of raw materials but not free trade.[12] New York's Reform Club, founded in 1888 and lasting until 1928, held meetings and events to aid tariff reform, like formal dinners at the Metropolitan Opera House.[13] The names of the founders comprised a Who's Who of New York society, with philanthropist Anson Phelps Stokes and architect Russell Sturgis among them.[14] The humor magazine *Puck* captured the sentiment of opposing factions amid tariff reform in its centerfold of January 2, 1884, titled *The Slave-Market of To-day* and illustrated by Bernhard Gillam. In the scene, trade

8.2

House of Worth. Fancy dress ensemble, ca. 1870. Silk, metal. The Metropolitan Museum of Art, New York, Brooklyn Museum Costume Collection at The Metropolitan Museum of Art, Gift of the Brooklyn Museum, 2009; Designated Purchase Fund, 1983 (2009.300.1363a,b). Image: © The Metropolitan Museum of Art.

union laborers are auctioned off by a protectionist statesman for bargain prices to industry leaders, including Cyrus W. Field and William H. Vanderbilt, two favorite targets.[15]

Caroline Astor would have ordered her dresses from maison Félix when tariffs were being discussed in national politics but had not yet been ratified. She apparently planned to wear at least one of the gowns to a Patriarch's ball organized by the Society of Patriarchs in New York that she and Ward McAllister led.[16] Although Astor could afford to pay an additional few hundred dollars to release the gowns from the Custom House, she was likely upholding her family's and social circle's objections to the McKinley Tariff. Her husband, William Backhouse Astor, was a Republican who reputedly favored free trade, which would benefit his real estate and railroad investments.[17] The Vanderbilt family came into a large and public arbitration with the tariff the same year, an ordeal that was often discussed in tandem with the case of the Astor gowns. Frederick W. Vanderbilt (Alva Vanderbilt's brother-in-law) bought a yacht, *The Conqueror*, in England for $75,000, and it was seized in United States waters with the claim that duties were due. The case stated that Vanderbilt attempted to avoid duties by having the boat fully crafted abroad rather than properly first importing the furnishings to the United States. Vanderbilt filed a libel for wrongful seizure against the Collector of Customs of the Port of New York, Jacob Sloat Fassett, with the District Court of the United States for the Southern District of New York. The suit proceeded through the court system, eventually reaching the U.S. Supreme Court, which ruled in favor of Vanderbilt.[18]

As for the Astor gowns, the actress Jennie Joyce ended up wearing the one purchased by her employer, Koster and Bial's Music Hall.[19] The press opined on Astor's decision to give up the dresses. The *Watertown Times* favored the tariff and opposed Astor: "And it serves her right. American dressmakers could have made as good and she would have had no trouble about them."[20] The *Morning Oregonian* shamed her for allowing elite gowns to land in the hands of a music hall proprietor.[21] The *Evening World*, for its part, had no trouble taking the money of Bloomingdale Brothers, which ran a prominent advertisement in January 1892 for the Astor gown it had won at auction, noting that the green silk and velvet dress was shown in its establishment to some half a million people. It also boasted four outfits of another society woman, whose name it did not reveal—a walking ensemble and a dinner gown by Félix, with outfits by Laferrière and Raudnitz.[22] Astor and the anonymous woman were not alone in contending with the U.S. Customs Service. In September 1892, the *Evening World* ran a story on the quantities of French garments that passed through the appraisers' offices, which had expanded to ten divisions, each with forty appraisers who quickly became experts on the styles of the foremost couture houses and handled up to one thousand dresses per day.[23]

Cohen writes about the immense size and power of the Port of New York operations—by 1884 it employed more than 1,500 people and received two-thirds of the nation's imports.[24] Given how high the stakes were, with customs proceeds going directly (except in the cases of dishonest officials) to the U.S. Treasury, detectives were also sent abroad to investigate the purchase prices of luxury items.[25] Major seizures of goods from unnamed Paris couturiers were also reported in October 1891 and in December 1893 of gowns by Félix, Worth, Pingat, Raudnitz, Laferrière, and Lebouvier.[26] The humor magazine *Puck* captured the mood in its caricature "McKinley and the Fashions"—in one vignette a popular theater bills a "grand spectacular display of Mrs. Van Astorbilt's seized gowns," conflating the names of the two families with the most at risk in the face of the tariff.[27]

In April 1893, five days before her wedding to William George Robert Craven, 4th Earl of Craven, sixteen-year-old Cornelia Martin—the only daughter of Bradley and Cornelia Sherman Martin—had her wedding gown stopped at the Custom House. She and her parents were returning from a trip to Europe where they acquired her trousseau for the wedding that was to be held at Grace Church and that *Town Topics* would say resembled a "national event."[28] When queried—such society betrothals were well-publicized and would have been known by officials at the ports—her father claimed the gown was old and soiled, previously worn.[29] The family and gown were reluctantly allowed to pass. The papers later reported that the white satin dress was by Worth, the "perfection of simplicity."[30] The efforts by the Bradley-Martins—buying and transporting couture from Europe to New York, only to presumably ship it back again to England after the wedding when the newlyweds would settle there—underscores the immense commitment by U.S. patrons to obtaining French couture. The Bradley-Martin family would continue to test the limits of how much extreme wealth could be devoted to fashion and its display.

BRADLEY-MARTIN BALL, 1897

Rates were reduced slightly, by about 15 percent, when the Revenue Act of 1894 (Wilson-Gorman Tariff) replaced the McKinley Tariff.[31] However, they rose again with the Tariff of 1897 (Dingley Tariff), named for Republican Representative Nelson

Dingley Jr. of Maine, chair of the House Ways and Means Committee, who had been involved in preparing the 1890 McKinley Tariff.[32] The Dingley Tariff, which passed on June 7 and took effect on July 24, 1897, was intended to counteract the treasury deficits that had resulted from the depression following the Panic of 1893. Several circumstances in the United States and abroad—including the collapse of the Philadelphia and Reading Railroad and European investors' exchange of U.S. stocks for gold—caused the panic. The Treasury's gold reserves were drained, the stock market fell, and unemployment rose.

Two aspects of the heavily protectionist Dingley Tariff, which raised duties to an average of 49 percent, were the implementation of weight duties for dress and piece silks and the limitation of luxury purchases to $100.[33] Dingley believed so strongly that luxury "articles of voluntary consumption" would bring in such high revenue that he included a clause in the bill that made the rates retroactive to April 1, 1897.[34] *Godey's Magazine* noted that $100 covered only one high-end gown and strained the purchase of other desirable French products like perfumes and soaps.[35] The magazine, however, also acknowledged the potential benefit to U.S. dressmakers whose business would presumably increase.[36] They would need to use local fabrics, as did the creator of the ball gown that First Lady Ida Saxton McKinley wore to her husband's inauguration on March 4, 1897.[37] Some retailers cleverly advertised garments that had been made with French fabrics imported before the Dingley Tariff and promoted them at pretariff prices.[38] The tariff would stay in effect until the passage of the Tariff of 1909 (Payne-Aldrich Tariff) in July 1909.

The political machinations that led to the passage of the Dingley Tariff in June 1897 had been in the works during McKinley's presidential campaign of 1896. The infamous Bradley-Martin ball was held at the Waldorf Hotel on February 10, 1897, three months after the election, and was railed for its shameless lavishness. The hosts were Bradley and Cornelia Sherman Martin (referred to as the Bradley-Martins), parents of the newly titled Countess of Craven. The Bradley-Martins were considered *arrivistes* in New York because although Bradley was a banker, a considerable amount of their wealth came from Cornelia's inheritance of several million dollars from her merchant father, Isaac Watts Sherman.[39]

The Bradley-Martins' goal was to outdo the Astor and Vanderbilt balls of years past—Veblen's conspicuous consumption par excellence—and the hubris here was even more telescoped than at those former balls. They engaged some of the same society purveyors, including the elite caterer Pinard, who provided a French menu from *consommé de volaille* to *glaces de fantaisie*.[40] Some six to seven hundred guests (out of a reported one thousand or so invitees) came in dress inspired by the six-teenth through eighteenth centuries, with Cornelia Bradley-Martin as Mary Queen of Scots. The queen was a favorite choice of women who wished to claim a heritage with royal families or at least a proximity. As with the Vanderbilt ball of 1883 (see chapter 7, Gowns and Mansions: French Fashion in U.S. Homes), the efforts to align with monarchal figures known for dubious actions and violent demises, was in full, nonsensical, often desperate effect. At least one source erroneously cited Bradley-Martin's costume as Marguerite de Valois, a typical melding of historic figures in the press coverage of the balls.

Later in 1897, however, Alexandra, Princess of Wales, dressed as Marguerite de Valois at the Devonshire House Ball in London on July 2. The celebration was coor-dinated with Queen Victoria's diamond jubilee, the sixtieth year of her reign. Seven hundred people dressed in allegorical and historical costumes dating to before 1815, with many made by Paquin and Worth.[41] Guests included many of the newly titled U.S. wives of European men. Mary Stevens Paget paid $6,000 for an emerald-studded Cleopatra costume by Worth (fig. 8.3). Mary Endicott Chamberlain came as an eighteenth-century shepherdess in a pink satin and silk ensemble, also by Worth (and despite her Massachusetts-bred mother's suggestion that she dress as one of their Puritan ancestors).[42]

At her own ball, Cornelia Bradley-Martin's Mary Queen of Scots costume was black velvet with cerise satin over a petticoat of white silk with silver embroidery; she wore a jeweled stomacher and multiple diamonds (fig. 8.4).[43] Kate Brice wore a white satin and organza "Infanta Margarita" ensemble inspired by a Velázquez painting, and created for her by Jean-Phillipe Worth, reportedly on a rush order.[44] Marie Churchill dressed as a French marquise, Harriet Cocker Alexander came in a Venetian-inspired costume by Callot Soeurs, and Matilda Davis Cabot Lodge was made up as an eighteenth-century lady (fig. 8.5).[45] Caroline Astor apparently wore the same dark blue velvet gown with white lace detailing from her 1890 portrait by Carolus-Duran or one modeled closely after it (see chapter 7, Gowns and Mansions: French Fashion in U.S. Homes).[46] As they had at the Astor and Vanderbilt balls, guests at the Bradley-Martin ball were inspired by historical figures as well as popu-lar culture, adhering to recommendations in sourcebooks like Ardern Holt's *Fancy Dresses Described: Or, What to Wear at Fancy Balls*. Interior designer Elsie de Wolfe took up Holt's option of dressing after celebrity actress Sarah Bernhardt, coming as Gismonda, a role Bernhardt played in 1894; it was rumored that her feet were bare.[47] Others enlisted theater costumer Maurice Herrmann to create their looks, from a

Louis XIII–era cranberry red and gold gown to a Marie Antoinette gown of white satin with silver-embroidered flounce.[48]

The Bradley-Martins claimed that the affair, purportedly costing between $300,000 and $500,000, provided an impetus to local tradespeople because the party employed hundreds of workers.[49] By several accounts, the Bradley-Martins spent close to $1,400 on silk stockings for the servants, who were required to wear period uniforms.[50] Social economist George Gunton supported this motivation, preferring that the hundreds of thousands of dollars spent to mount such social events be given to local laborers rather than have wealthy U.S. citizens hold their events in Europe.[51]

Clergymen took various stances on the matter, with the most vocal being Reverend William S. Rainsford of St. George's Episcopal Church in New York, whose words against the frivolity were reproduced in papers throughout the country.[52] The *Rocky Mountain Christian Advocate* praised his position and condemned the ball as barbaric and selfish, as "unAmerican, unphilanthropic, and unChristian."[53] New York's society paper *Town Topics*, however, accused Rainsford of grandstanding, and the *Washington Post* called his protest silly and impertinent.[54] *Harper's Bazar* wrote favorably about the affair, explaining that fifteen dressing rooms at the Waldorf were filled that evening with hairdressers, costumers, and maids.[55] *Munsey's Magazine* also praised the spectacle.[56]

But the overall consensus of the press was that the event was a gross indulgence of wealth, a view that sealed the ball's legacy. The *World* seemed to take pleasure in printing cameo drawings of society women who chose not to or were unable to attend.[57] *Harper's Weekly* covered the details of the party in depth and then condemned the press for stoking public interest in such an extravaganza.[58] The ultimate ridicule came in the form of a three-act burlesque at Hammerstein's Olympia Theatre at Broadway and 44th Street the following month.[59]

Even when the increase in work for laborers was acknowledged, the criticism held that the toll was too heavy and assigned without ample notice. One paper

8.3

Photogravure by Walker & Boutall, 1897; published 1899. Mary Stevens Paget in a Cleopatra costume by the House of Worth at the Devonshire House Ball, London, July 1897. National Portrait Gallery, London (Ax41154). Image: National Portrait Gallery, London.

claimed that local dressmakers were strained: "sitting up at night at work that is most injurious to the eyes and health."[60] Some of them seem to have used local materials when available, rather than relying on imported materials that were the subject of political dispute and that would have required long lead times to order and ship. *Vogue* and the trade magazine *The Standard Designer* related that featherbone, a U.S. invention, was used in place of whalebone to support the waists of certain gowns worn at the ball.[61] The historical theme also brought the opportunity to wear heirloom laces rather than buy entirely new outfits, but those efforts were counterbalanced by others who placed orders abroad and at home to acquire additional pieces of antique lace.[62]

Other service providers—like hairdressers, florists, caterers, and photographers—were not as reliant on international materials and did swift business for the ball. Some premier French-trained hairdressers reputedly raised their prices for the event, based on the skill and time required for historical styles.[63] In addition to large amounts of powder, hairdressers also inserted formed pieces and extensions to achieve the volume dictated by certain eighteenth-century styles. The enormous international trade in human hair, however, was affected during the McKinley Tariff and Dingley Tariff periods. France, Spain, Italy, and Germany were several of the major exporters to the United States, and yearly totals could reach 100,000 pounds.[64] Under McKinley, raw hair was on the free list, but manufactured hair pieces were taxed at 35 percent.[65] Under Dingley, hair that was clean or drawn but not manufactured was taxed at 20 percent; manufactured hair was listed at 35 percent.[66] Raw hair required more labor to shape it into extensions, padding, braids, or buns.

Town Topics excitedly described the furor of activity for the top hairdressers and perruquiers (wigmakers) who began work early in the morning on the day of the ball: "I heard of one woman to whom the hairdresser could only give the hour between 7 and 8 A.M. yesterday morning. She received the capillary composer in her bedroom in a wrapper, and after the operation was finished went again to bed, where, placing herself in sitting posture with pillows around her, she remained all day until the time to dress after dinner."[67] Hairdressers of lower rank, who worked downtown, were able to take up some of the overflow business for the ball.[68]

Many hairdressers would have been employed again on February 26, when a number of guests rewore their costumes and staged tableaux-vivants at a benefit for St. Mary's Free Hospital for Children at the Madison Square Assembly Rooms.[69] The charity function must have been held in part as a counterreaction to the negative press the ball continued to receive. It was common practice for flowers from society events to be donated to hospitals. Per Veblen, however, the very creation of so much conspicuous waste signaled the excess that was engaged to begin with.[70] Representatives of the working classes and their champions reacted vehemently toward the Bradley-Martin ball. The progressive Boston newspaper *Woman's Voice and Public School Champion*, run by a group of Protestant independent women voters, assailed the insensible association of costumes with the French Revolution:

As though to flaunt defiance into the faces of the poor, the ball was a representation of the court of ball [*sic*] Louis XV of France, of the period just before the French Revolution, fifty ladies being dressed up to represent Marie Antoinette, and the shameful intrigues and licentiousness of the French king were characterized by certain ladies (?) at the ball.[71]

The most haunting response was a caricature in the Christian magazine *Our Day* showing gaunt-faced, disenfranchised people weakly dancing a quadrille.[72] The extreme and divisive notoriety of the Bradley-Martin ball resulted in increased property taxes for the family, a punitive act by government authorities and the reason they decamped for London and Scotland permanently the following year.[73]

The Bradley-Martin ball was the flashpoint for exorbitant spending, but outside of that spectacle at the Waldorf, the long run of the Dingley Tariff had a significant impact on other upper-class women's shopping practices, with myriad points of friction along the way. The posturing of stakeholders on all sides of the tariff as they settled into the new scenario were especially heightened. As a national industry that was central to the economy of the state, the French government raised concerns about the luxury tariff, calling it excessive and potentially harmful to the future of French products.[74] In August and September 1897, Emma Bullet of the *Brooklyn Daily Eagle* reported on the challenges that the new tariff brought to Parisian suppliers, couturiers, U.S. buyers, and fashion writers. She predicted that U.S. women would be more selective in what they would be willing to purchase in Paris but yet would expect the same high quality in the silk-lined, tailor-made dresses that they had always received.[75] She found that Parisian couturiers were apprehensive about losing business from U.S. clients, whom they had come to rely on for profits.[76]

The French business newspapers followed the effect of the U.S. tariffs on fashion and materials for the industry and ran letters from regional presidents of the chambers of commerce, the trade unions, and ministers of commerce or foreign affairs on behalf of their constituents. For instance, in 1898 the Chambre de Commerce in Saint-Étienne expressed concern over the Dingley Tariff on ribbons, which it found to be draconian.[77] By late in the century, the elevated rates had severely impacted exports of goods from France.[78] In September 1897, London's *Sketch* ran a hearsay piece about couture houses on the rue de la Paix that were considering opening branches in New York. They feared that the tariffs would "[spell] ruin for them," a statement that encapsulates the houses' reliance on U.S. clients and the lack of control that any individual had over the vast fashion system.[79]

In 1900, Émile Martin Poussineau of maison Félix offered his perspective to a London reporter: "But the new American tariffs are, from my point of view, a misfortune; not so much because they prevent Americans from getting their clothes in Paris—for American women seem to have, where clothes are concerned, limitless purses—but the new laws concerning the importation of foreign dress lead to the most shameful cheating on the part of certain American dressmaking houses."[80] The account expresses a sense of powerlessness over rampant copying that was taking place. Dressmakers from the United States notoriously sent spies to Paris to retrieve and replicate the latest styles. Toward the end of Dingley, the government took the step of curbing the dissemination of new designs from Paris into U.S. fashion magazines. In 1908, the Board of United States General Appraisers ruled that fashion plates drawn by U.S. artists temporarily located abroad and intended for publication in U.S. weekly magazines were subject to the 20 percent duties on "pen-and-ink drawings." Harper and Brothers filed the case, declaring that the drawings should be considered in the category of "works of art" and should not be dutiable. The judge saw through the publisher's savvy claim and ruled that the purpose of the sketches was to convey the latest fashions and products to U.S. consumers.[81] Harper and Brothers filed an appeal but lost in the United States Circuit Court in May 1909.[82]

Searches of personal baggage may not have always have been as rigid as the *New York Times* predicted a few days after Dingley passed in June 1897—"ruthless exposure of one's belongings have begun"—but unpleasant incidents had been chronicled with some regularity for years (fig. 8.6).[83] In September, several women boycotted the Merchants' and Manufactures' Board of Trade in opposition to their new practice of placing spies to watch over the customs' inspectors at the port of New York. The spies were meant to catch any officers overlooking garments purchased abroad that were worth more than $100. Their methods involved emptying trunks and unwrapping and laying out garments, laces, and embroideries, to the consternation of the owners.[84] Not only would it have been embarrassing, but also it was a frustrating disturbance of the packing for which clients paid professionals

like E. Deraisme and Bigot, two packers and sellers of trunks and other luggage, whom Mary and Ogden Goelet patronized.[85] The tactility of the process underscores the mutually understood value of the investment in couture. Customs officials justified their efforts as a way to counteract illegal smuggling. Avoiding tariffs was one of the motivations behind the widespread practice of smuggling French garments into the United States and, in turn, points to the expansive and multifaceted secondary life of the clothing, the subject of the next chapter.

8.6

G. A. Davis (U.S., d. 1901). Wood engraving on paper. *New York Customs Officers Examining the Baggage of Returning Tourists, Frank Leslie's Illustrated Newspaper,* October 24, 1891. Clark Art Institute, Acquired by Sterling and Francine Clark before 1955 (1955.4383). Image courtesy Clark Art Institute.

THE UNDERWORLD AND AFTERLIFE OF FRENCH COUTURE IN THE UNITED STATES

The secondary life of French fashion in the United States encompasses the various practices and outlets that arose from the desire to own or traffic in the latest styles from Paris. The pervasive tariff laws cast an interrogative light on consumer fervor. In public opinion, a taste for foreign luxuries could be seen as antinationalist.[1] As a result, French couture entered and circulated throughout the country by legal and illegal channels. Rampant smuggling and theft as well as a large trade in counterfeit dresses forced some French houses to adapt quickly or else see their profits thinned significantly. Some of them chose to license their patterns to U.S. retailers in an attempt to recapture a portion of the profits, thereby partaking in the market for copies, rather than holding fast to being the sole, authoritative creator, as Paul Poiret would later do, and which proved unsustainable.[2] Engaging here with what Nancy J. Troy terms the "discourse of the copy," we may agree with her take on couturiers who, like modern painters, sought to "maintain their elite status as creators of unique and original objects while at the same time they capitalized on the potential of copies," but we broaden the pool of couturiers and shift the focus to how consumers forced the hands of the couturiers to adapt to the new market forces.[3] Tracing the ways in which the garments were exchanged between makers, patrons, retailers, and thieves elicits a more tactile understanding of the shared investment of the various parties in the system.

REUSE AND CASTOFFS

Wealthy women who spent thousands of dollars on French gowns maximized their investment by repurposing them—wearing them on multiple occasions over the course of several seasons or years, not unlike what they did with their most valuable pieces of jewelry. They either wore a gown in its original form, reaccessorized it, or hired the original maker or a local dressmaker to rework it. The concept of reuse may seem counter to Veblen's assignment of "conspicuous waste" to elite consumers, but it reinforces his concept of class emulation. The practices reflect the value placed on the textiles and were well ensconced in European royal culture. Alexandra, Princess of Wales, had her British-made wedding gown converted by her dressmaker, Madame Elise and Co. (a firm run by Mr. and Mrs. Wootton Isaacson), into an evening dress only a few days after her wedding with Edward VII in March 1863.[4] For the Marlborough House ball in 1874, the Elise firm appears to have remodeled a costume that Alexandra wore to the 1871 Waverley ball in London. The gown bears the Elise label and is kept today in the Royal Ceremonial Dress Collection at Kensington Palace.[5]

When attending two separate court functions in London in March and July 1893, Mary Endicott Chamberlain wore the same House of Worth pale blue silk dress with lace, beading, and velvet.[6] The first event was a reception in Queen Victoria's drawing room at Buckingham Palace, and the second was the wedding of the Duke and Duchess of York (later King George V and Queen Mary). She also made a practice of sending her Worth gowns back to the maison for remodeling, as she did when she wanted a Van Dyke lace collar attached to a red satin dress.[7]

Upper-class U.S. women adopted the royal precedent for repurposing garments early in the century. When Elizabeth Patterson of Baltimore married Jérôme Bonaparte in 1803, she wore an embroidered white muslin dress that she subsequently wore on multiple occasions.[8] Nancy Fowler McCormick's French dresses, now in the Chicago Historical Society, show signs of alterations for rewearing.[9] With her husband, millionaire Cyrus Hall McCormick, she attended numerous social events, and in 1904, she wore a gown by Worth to her son's wedding.[10] Caroline Astor reworked gowns, too. A dark purple velvet ball gown in the Metropolitan Museum of Art, in its current state believed to date to the 1890s, has been significantly reworked (fig. 9.1). The

9.1

Possibly maison Félix. Fancy dress, 1890s. Velvet, satin, and metal. The Metropolitan Museum of Art, New York, Gift of Orme Wilson and R. Thornton Wilson, in memory of their mother, Mrs. Caroline Schermerhorn Astor Wilson, 1949 (49.3.1a–c).
Image: © The Metropolitan Museum of Art.

original form may date to the 1870s and possibly could be the dress that Astor wore to a fancy ball in 1875 (fig. 9.2). Astor also rewore dresses to the extent that specific ones were understood to be her favorites, like her dinner gown of dark blue satin with gold embroidery, sometimes paired with a blue and gold hat.[11] For her portrait by Charles E. Drake, Frances Katherine Drexel Paul wore a wine-colored velvet dress by Melanie Pascaud, who was located at 157, rue du Faubourg Saint-Honoré in Paris (figs. 9.3 and 9.4). She removed the long-sleeved, lace-trimmed bodice and replaced it with an evening bodice that she had made by Mrs. Jacobs of 20 North 19th Street in Philadelphia.[12]

Many elite gowns became heirlooms, written into wills, with the inheritors then choosing how they would wear them, with or without alterations. Alva Vanderbilt Belmont recalled how strongly she and her siblings valued a camel-hair shawl and the lace flounces from their mother's wedding outfit that were left to them in her will.[13] Both Alva and her daughter, Consuelo, later used the lace on their own wedding dresses. Similarly, a dark blue velvet ensemble with chinchilla fur trim bearing the label of maison Lipman was purchased by philanthropist Caroline Louisa Williams French of Boston, Massachusetts, in 1883 for 1,600 francs (fig. 9.5). The maison, run by Madame Camille Lipman, operated locations in the 1880s, alternately at 7, rue Drouot and 2, rue de la Paix (sharing a building with British dress-case maker Leuchars) and counted among its clients queen consort Maria Pia of Portugal. Some thirty-seven years later, French's descendant, Alice Williams Pearse, wore the gown and chinchilla muff, without the coat, in a photograph taken at an event to celebrate the Nineteenth Amendment, which granted voting rights to women (fig. 9.6).[14] The string of donations by Orme Wilson Jr. and Richard Thornton Wilson III of gowns by Worth, Doucet, and Paquin to the Metropolitan Museum of Art further provides a sense of how couture garments passed through the branches of one family (figs. 9.7 and 9.8). The Wilson brothers were sons of William Backhouse Astor and Caroline Webster Schermerhorn Astor's daughter Caroline "Carrie" Schermerhorn

9.2

Caroline Webster Schermerhorn, 1875. Photograph. Astor Family Papers, 1792–1916, Manuscripts and Archives Division, The New York Public Library. Image: New York Public Library.

Astor, and their aunt was the aforementioned Mary Rita Wilson Goelet, who widely patronized Parisian couturiers.

For events like the centennial balls that took place across the country in 1876, women commissioned dresses to be modeled on those worn by their ancestors in portrait paintings and photographs.[15] Couturiers who were regularly engaged to make historically inspired stage costumes were well equipped to make reproduction gowns. Some women utilized pieces from their personal antique lace holdings for the occasions, as did the Astors, who collected Flemish and French eighteenth-century lace, fragments of which have survived.[16] At the wedding of her daughter Helen to James R. Roosevelt in 1878, Caroline Astor proudly wore a black velvet gown with two-hundred-year-old lace trimmings.[17]

Another outlet for reuse came via castoffs from owners to their maids or to charity recipients. Caroline Astor donated dresses to a women's hospital, and Cornelia Stewart, who was married to retailer A. T. Stewart, reputedly passed some of hers to a singer in need of stage wear.[18] The practice was an outgrowth of the European convention of royalty handing down their finery to their ladies-in-waiting, as did Queen Victoria and Alexandra, Princess of Wales.[19]

Yet another stream was to sell gowns to secondhand dealers, descendants of the long-established history of the European trade in old clothing. In Paris, the trade had been in existence since the thirteenth century, and by the eighteenth century, it was centered in the Les Halles neighborhood. In the nineteenth century, there were dress agents to whom royals would sell.[20] Since the early eighteenth century, England also had a history of selling royal and aristocratic clothes in the Old Clothes Exchange in East London.[21] George IV's wardrobe was made available for public sale in 1831, at which Madame Tussaud's bought his coronation robe.[22]

In New York, large populations of recent European immigrants who had arrived between 1880 and 1920 fueled a robust secondhand trade on the Lower East Side, run mostly by Jews who had experience with peddling and tailoring.[23] Some advertised in local newspapers offering to buy castoff garments.[24] The advertising may have been necessary because the peddlers appear periodically to have been banned

9.3

Melanie Pascaud (French, active late 19th century). Dress, ca. 1890. Drexel University, Philadelphia (889). Image: Drexel University.

from buying garments at charity rummage sales.[25] Anti-Semitism was in action here, as Jews historically were seen as dominating the trade, which had derived out of necessity when they had been outlawed from participating in professions and instead they took to itinerant, pushcart sales.[26]

Actresses became creative in how they obtained and disposed of their costly costumes. When Emma Abbott died in 1891, fellow actress Jennie Kimball bought the gowns by Worth and Félix that Abbott had worn in *Carmen* several years earlier. Kimball purchased them for her daughter Corinne, a rising star on the stage.[27] And when Elena of Montenegro could not make use of several new Félix gowns due to a period of mourning for the assassinated King Umberto I of Italy (killed by an anarchist), the couturier first placed them on view at the Exposition universelle in Paris in 1900 (see chapter 4, Couturiers and International Expositions). While visiting the exhibition, Francesca Redding admired the green silk and chiffon gown with winding leaf pattern, bought it, and promptly wore it on stage.[28] Performer Sadie Martinot sold her own Worth and Félix stage gowns at auction in May 1894, raising $35,000 in income.[29] Actresses also sold their stage gowns to secondhand dealers with storefronts like the one described by the *Sun* in 1892 as "hung three and four deep with dresses and skirts and basques."[30]

The buyers at secondhand stores were middle-class women who were capable of making clothes last for several years. Hannah Ditzler Alspaugh of Illinois recorded in her diary and extant scrapbook of fabric the dresses and suits that she would remake, or "rip," over the years, including one suit that she wore for several visits to the World's Columbian Exhibition in Chicago, an event that notably, was held during a nationwide financial panic in 1893.[31] With careful planning and maintenance, garments could be preserved and worn with frequency. Multiple layers of undergarments served as a barrier between bodily oils and dirt and the main part of the dress, although rain, mud, moths, and mold caused further concerns.[32]

9.4

Charles E. Drake (U.S., 1865–1918).
Frances D. Drexel, ca. 1890. Drexel
University, The Drexel Collection (1901).
Drexel wears the Pascaud dress seen in
figure 9.3. Image: Drexel University.

A new, pristine couture dress held the most value, and theft was rampant. Some thieves sought to resell the ill-gotten dresses in the secondhand market. Others were dressmakers whose aim was to copy the styles and techniques for their own businesses. The aforementioned Edith Kingdon Gould, an actress who married the financier George Jay Gould (eldest son of the railroad baron Jay Gould) in 1886, encountered incidents of theft over the course of her years in high society. She patronized Parisian couturiers and local dressmakers in New York. In an 1898 portrait of her by Théobald Chartran, she wears a red velvet Worth gown with fur stole that survives in the collection of one of her descendants (see figs. 1.1 and 1.2).[33] In January 1893, some of her dresses, worth up to $2,500 each, were stolen from dressmaker Phebe A. Smith's shop.[34] The following winter a white-and-pink satin gown and other garments of hers from Worth and Félix, valued at $1,600, were taken from photographer Mendelssohn's studio at 5th Avenue and 45th Street by a boy put up to the task by an older man posing as a messenger.[35] The dresses were then delivered to a dressmaker or retailer with plans to copy them.

Part of what made society women like Gould so vulnerable to theft was that their couture purchases were reported on thoroughly in the press. Their trips to Paris and their return voyages to the States were public knowledge, and along with the news of ship arrivals came details of their purchases. In August 1895, *Life* magazine wrote that Astor owned a new lace dress valued at $28,000, and socialite Theresa Alice Fair Oelrichs's wedding gown, once worth $10,000, appreciated in value to more than $50,000.[36] Coverage of society events also regularly detailed the guests' gowns and jewelry. A women's reception at the Montauk Club in Brooklyn in 1893 garnered nearly two columns of dress descriptions in the *Brooklyn Daily Eagle*.[37] And in Washington, DC, beginning in 1882, Frank ("Carp") Carpenter reported on society events for the *Cleveland Leader*, the readership of which was keen to hear how midwestern transplants were faring in the capital. In fall 1888, one of their own, Benjamin Harrison,

9.5

Maison Lipman (French, late 19th century). Ensemble, 1883. Velvet, satin, fur. Courtesy of Historic New England. Gift of Nancy Olive Morison Allis (1990.507A–G).

was elected president.[38] Carp recalled that First Lady Caroline Scott Harrison dressed "in quiet taste" and preferred that her clothing was made in Washington, DC, or New York rather than at Worth.[39] Her inauguration dress was U.S.-made, but a number of the guests wore "Paris dresses," delineated down to the last pink ostrich feather and princess pearl ornaments in the *Washington Post*.[40] Carp reveled in it: "We are lavishing fortunes on clothes. There is enough silk worn here every winter to carpet a whole state; there are pearls by the bushel, and diamonds by the peck."[41]

If a thief wanted details of exactly which items of jewelry were available at the home of Jane Lathrop Stanford (founder of Stanford University, with her husband, Leland Stanford) in Washington, DC, they would need only to obtain a copy of *Cosmopolitan* magazine of October 1889 for an itemized list.[42] Her jewels were ranked in the top three U.S. collections, with Caroline Astor and Marie Louise Hungerford Mackay, and their values commented on in papers in France and as far west as San Francisco.[43] The previous year, the lavish gifts presented to Mary Crowninshield Endicott on her marriage to British politician Joseph Chamberlain of England in Washington, DC, were eminently newsworthy (see fig. 3.9). The bride's New England blueblood grandparents gave a "bank check for a large amount," and other family members presented a diamond and sapphire necklace and bracelets, and a diamond crescent.[44] Similarly, the costumes (by Worth, Félix, and New York dressmakers) and jewels worn by the Four Hundred at the Metropolitan Opera's ball on January 2, 1890, were described in extraordinary detail throughout thirty-seven pages in the book *Titled Americans*.[45] Caroline Astor wore a light brocade gown by Worth, with her diamond stomacher and tiara and "famous necklace of brilliants."[46] Finally, itemized lists of property willed to descendants were publicized when wealthy people passed away. Two years after Edith Kingdon Gould died, the *New York Times* printed the appraisal of her property—home furnishings, jewelry, clothing (a monkey fur cape valued at $100, and a sable stole, possibly the one in the Chartran portrait [see fig. 1.2])—at $2,200.[47]

The practice of smuggling by customers to avoid paying duties was fairly consistent throughout the latter part of the century, and it was also prevalent by

9.6

Bachrach Photograph Studio (U.S.).
Photograph of Alice Williams Pearse in 1920
wearing the ensemble seen in figure 9.5.
Courtesy of Historic New England.

dressmakers and retailers.[48] In 1888, before the McKinley Tariff took effect (see chapter 8, Rising Prices: The Impact of U.S. Tariffs), high-end gowns from abroad were subject to taxes, whereas actresses' costumes were not. Rose Ludvigh, a downtown dressmaker who sold original Worth gowns to socialites and performers, set up an international scheme facilitated by her brother, who was located in Paris. When the dresses were ready, she enlisted a friend to travel with her to Paris. The friend posed as an actress while Ludvigh postured as her maid. On the return trip, the two claimed to the U.S. Customs Service that the garments were costumes and did not require payment of a duty. She then sold the gowns to her customers, having saved on her initial costs.[49] Smuggling, or at least the reporting of it, seems to have peaked during the first years of each new tariff. In 1892, after the first full year of the McKinley Tariff, officials at the United States Custom House in New York (mostly male but some female) explained that they caught more women smuggling goods than men. They had honed their skills for detecting women who claimed to have purchased gowns for their own use but in reality were bringing in samples to copy in their shops. They would measure the width of the gown against the woman's waist, often finding that they did not match.[50]

COUNTERFEIT COPIES

Theft and smuggling contributed to the widespread availability of counterfeit copies of original patterns. In 1868, Worth and others founded the Chambre syndicale de la confection et de la couture pour dames et fillettes, one of the purposes of which was to advocate against illegal copying, but piracy of fashion designs in France was difficult to prosecute. The French law of July 19–24, 1793, which ended sumptuary laws, stipulated that property rights in some cases could be applied to

9.7

House of Worth. Ball gown, 1898–1903.
Silk. The Metropolitan Museum of Art, New
York, Gift of Orme Wilson and R. Thornton
Wilson, in memory of their mother, Mrs.
Caroline Schermerhorn Astor Wilson, 1949
(49.3.8a,b). Image: © The Metropolitan
Museum of Art.

9.8

U.S. or Europe. Dress, 1881–1884. Silk.
The Metropolitan Museum of Art, New
York, Gift of Orme Wilson and R. Thornton
Wilson, in memory of their mother, Mrs.
Caroline Schermerhorn Astor Wilson, 1949
(49.3.31a,b). Image: © The Metropolitan
Museum of Art.

couturiers, as could the 1806 law for industrial design, but it was not until the 1902 law on artistic and literary property that couture design was securely protected.[51]

On the whole, however, France made greater attempts to protect its economically critical fashion industry than did the United States, but the international nature of the industry proved challenging.[52] Prosecution of copying in foreign countries was prohibitively difficult. In the United States, copyright laws often interpreted clothing as a utilitarian item, not art, and did not provide protection.[53] Certain couture houses, becoming aware of illegal copying in the United States and unable to stop it, eventually embraced the opportunity to claim a piece of the secondary market. Worth began sewing in labels in the mid-1860s but faced continuous troubles with copyists and brand infringement, including the London corsetmaker who ran her business under the name Madame Worth and whom the Parisian Worths successfully sued.[54] In the late 1880s, fake labels began appearing in garments. To preserve its business, Worth began selling models that could be legally copied by department and dry goods stores, hence allowing the local makers to avoid import duties.[55] Worth also sold designs to middle-class magazines like *Godey's*, which in turn made them available to readers to make at home. A copy of a Worth dress in the Fashion History Museum, Ontario, may be either an illegal copy or a sanctioned one and is a rare survival (fig. 9.9).

The methods of disseminating styles varied. Department stores and other retailers sent official buyers or agents to Paris, as did Catharine Donovan (known to her customers as Mrs. Donovan). Donovan's shop, which had been in business since the early 1860s and had a few employees, carried French couture and also crafted new designs for its clients. Her 1906 obituary in the *New York Times* referred to her as the "400s Dressmaker," citing Goelets, Astors, and Vanderbilts as patrons; her funeral was held at St. Patrick's Cathedral.[56] In an unplanned course of events, Donovan designed Alva Vanderbilt's wedding gown in 1875 when the one she had ordered from Paris did not arrive on time.[57] Vanderbilt was displeased that she needed to have "old Donovan" make the dress, but she was satisfied enough to engage her again years later for her daughter, Consuelo's, wedding gown when she married the Duke of Marlborough.[58]

Vanderbilt's offhand, derogatory reference to "old Donovan" is a reminder of the mutual reliance of patrons and dressmakers and the power differential that came along with the familiarity. Regardless, the money and dresses flowed between them, and Donovan made out particularly well in 1883, when she created several ensembles for the Vanderbilt ball.[59] She was also responsible for providing Mary

Crowninshield Endicott's wedding dress in 1888.[60] Endicott was a devoted customer of the House of Worth and purchased several dresses for her trousseau from the firm. She also procured dresses to wear as a newly married hostess, including a lilac tulle ball gown that she wore in February 1889, and wrote home to tell her mother about its success.[61] In a testament to the strength of Donovan's brand, the business continued after the founder's death, under the name "C. Donovan and Co." Katherine A. Brennan served as president, Edward T. Brennan as vice president, and Kate Hannon as secretary. Their names were publicized in 1913 after a failed smuggling plot with thousands of dollars' worth of French garments.[62]

Some firms sent spies to sketch the latest styles they observed in the couturiers' salons, at the theater, and at the races at Longchamps.[63] Designs were also leaked by employees.[64] Félix began sewing in labels about 1885, and garments with the Félix name appeared at B. Altman's, Bloomingdale Brothers, Mandel Brothers, and James McCreery and Co., among other U.S. retailers, since at least 1889.[65] The goods were presumably made expressly for the U.S. trade or legally licensed.[66] In 1900, for example, Arnold, Constable & Co. in New York bought Doucet and other couture designs directly from Paris and sold them in its store on Broadway and 19th Street.[67] Félix and Laferrière had made patterns available for sale to the British readers of *Le Follet* (a periodical published in London) and likely did the same for the U.S. market.[68]

By 1913, however, U.S. retailers could order packs of "A. Félix Breveté" labels from wholesalers, and there was concern within the industry about false representation of French brand names.[69] Hats with the maison Félix name were featured in French fashion periodicals as late as 1908 and 1915.[70] There were also hybrid garments by which a U.S. dressmaker would buy a French garment but then partially alter it with cheaper materials that did not need to be imported and dutied, as did one dressmaker in Detroit in 1891 with a Félix design.[71] By 1896, Félix, Doucet, Laferrière, and others are confirmed as making models in multiples for the U.S. trade (figs. 9.10 and 9.11).[72] In an interview in the London periodical *The Woman at Home* in September 1900, Émile Martin Poussineau acknowledged that he had business relations with U.S. retailers but conveyed his dismay at hearing about unlicensed designs:

9.9

Copy of House of Worth dress,
ca. 1893–1897. Fashion History Museum,
Ontario. Image: Courtesy Jonathan Walford.

Quite recently one of my American clients told me that she had been shown a number of model dresses bearing my name at a New York establishment with whom I have never had any direct or indirect dealings. When this kind of thing occurs I am doubly injured, for the garments attributed to me are very often of very inferior cut and make. The same thing applies to hats.[73]

Coverage of French fashion in mass-circulated periodicals and newspapers also fueled the legal and illegal dissemination of styles. The proliferation of the fashion press resulted in some one hundred titles by the end of the nineteenth century, with many distributed internationally.[74] In addition to elite publications like *L'Art et la mode*, mainstream magazines like the weekly *La Mode illustrée* contained hand-colored fashion plates. *L'Art et la mode* eventually used photographs, mostly after 1890, the clarity of which facilitated copying.[75] In the United States *Harper's Bazar* and *Godey's Lady's Book*, most prominently, included patterns for women to follow at home, and Demorest, Butterick, and McCall led the market by issuing paper patterns.[76]

Another channel for transmitting the latest styles, supporting local businesses, and also contributing to a worthy cause was charity events. One of the most influential was the International Costume Exhibition held at New York's Madison Square Garden in 1895 to benefit the Young Women's Christian Association and the St. James's Mission. In addition to the historical fashions, which were mostly early court dress, and artifacts on view at the exhibition, Gosta Kraemer, owner of a store on West 23rd Street selling imported couture, sponsored an exhibit of gowns by Worth and Doucet and planned to change the display on a daily basis.[77]

The emphasis here is to acknowledge the traditional focus on couture houses' concerns about authenticity but, in equal measure, to show that U.S. consumer desire put pressure on the French providers, ultimately forcing them to change their business practices and supply licensed goods. Consumer ingenuity in creating multiple

9.10

Possibly made in Paris; retailed by Stern Brothers, New York. Evening dress, 1894. Embroidered silk velvet with glass beads and sequins, Victoria & Albert Museum, London (T.272&A-1972). Image: © Victoria & Albert Museum, London.

channels (both legal and illicit) for obtaining desired goods and then reusing, circulating, and exchanging them helps explain the wide dissemination of French couture in collections around the world. As Kate Strasdin points out, Queen Alexandra's gowns were auctioned by the American Art Association and Anderson Art Galleries in 1937, where Irene Lewisohn purchased a quarter of them and founded the Costume Institute at the Metropolitan Museum of Art.[78] And Mary Rita Wilson Goelet's wardrobe, so carefully tracked in an archive of invoices that has proved invaluable to the present book, was reportedly sold after her death to the New York theatrical costumer Eaves and worn by various actresses.[79]

9.11

Designed by Madeleine Laferrière (French, 1847–1912); made in New York and retailed by E. Wiggins. Evening dress, 1887–1888. Embroidered velvet, silk, and satin. Victoria & Albert Museum, London (T.278 to C-1972). Image: © Victoria & Albert Museum, London.

10

CONCLUSION

Follow the Dresses

Mary ("May") Goelet, whose parents Mary Rita Wilson and Ogden Goelet had shopped for her childhood clothes at Marindaz on the rue de la Paix during their visit in 1893, married the Duke of Roxburghe in 1903. It was one of the most fashionable international marriages of the day, with the bride's worth estimated at $20 million. Her enormous trousseau from Paris, packed in multiple trunks, was eagerly awaited stateside, the image of which encapsulates the volume of Parisian couture landing and circulating in the United States (fig. 10.1). By marrying an Englishman, Goelet followed suit with her aunt Leila "Belle" Wilson, who wedded a British ambassador to the United States in 1888 and resided in Europe. From there, Belle wrote letters to her parents, Richard Thornton Wilson and Melissa Johnston Wilson, detailing the importance of wearing the correct clothing.[1]

The transmission of French fashion between generations and across the extended branches of elite U.S. families is one of the mechanisms by which the present volume has sought to access the widespread, international, and diplomatic reach of the couture system. The pervasiveness of French fashion in the U.S. market and consciousness in the late nineteenth century has been traditionally difficult to harness into a single definition or image. Instead, it is often reduced to a general abstraction—the so-called lure of Paris and its transcendent couturiers. As an alternative, this book demonstrates that a more accurate and productive framework is to first study the complex workings of the fashion industry—from the large, multicultural labor force to the interconnections of the various professionals in each specialization. From there, the adoption of French fashions into the U.S. market through

10.1

May Goelet's trousseau from Paris arriving in the United States. *Tatler*, November 25, 1903. Image: © Illustrated London News Ltd / Mary Evans the various channels of the press and local imports in the early to mid-nineteenth century comes more clearly into focus. Against this backdrop, the later engagement with couture and coiffure by influential patrons like Caroline Astor, Alva Vanderbilt Belmont, Mary Rita Wilson Goelet, and their compatriates is further understood as rooted in practices that were established some generations earlier. The peak of French fashion in the United States, from 1870 to the turn of the century, was the culmination of a partiality that had been maturing in U.S. culture for decades.

The emphasis on U.S. women's shopping practices situates the consumption side of the fashion system on a proper equilibrium with that of design and production. Centralizing extant garments from women's collections as well as firsthand written accounts demonstrates the breadth and depth of the market that the women navigated, expanding the discourse far beyond the legend of one or two famous couturiers. The considerable U.S. spending on French couture that was established in the nineteenth century continued well after the First World War and persisted despite the increasing prevalence of readymade garments and sophisticated retailing. By following the dresses and the women who owned them, we discover an extraordinarily powerful center of a transnational network of cultural exchange.

ACKNOWLEDGMENTS

With gratitude to Niv Allon, Charlotte Balliett, Deborah Cantor-Adams, Susan Clark, Gabriela Bueno Gibbs, Emily Gutheinz, Victoria Hindley, Lauren Knighton, Katie Lewis, Sarah McFadden, Jim Mitchell, Kevin D. Murphy, Mary Reilly, Rosemary Winfield, Kathy Woodrell, Christopher Zichello, The Aileen Ribeiro Grant, established and funded by The Association of Dress Historians (ADH), the Association for Art History, and the Pasold Research Fund.

NOTES

CHAPTER 1

1. Yuniya Kawamura, *Fashion-ology: An Introduction to Fashion Studies* (London: Bloomsbury Academic, 2018), 39–54.

2. Ulrich Lehmann, *Fashion and Materialism* (Edinburgh: University of Edinburgh Press, 2019), 4.

3. Nancy J. Troy, *Couture Culture: A Study in Modern Art and Fashion* (Cambridge, MA: MIT Press, 2003).

4. Heidi Brevik-Zender, *Fashioning Spaces: Mode and Modernity in Late Nineteenth-Century Paris* (Toronto: University of Toronto Press, 2015); Louise Crewe, *The Geographies of Fashion: Consumption, Space, and Value* (London: Bloomsbury Academic, 2017); John Potvin, ed., *The Places and Spaces of Fashion, 1800–2007* (New York: Routledge, 2009).

5. Joanne Entwistle and Elizabeth Wilson, eds., *Body Dressing* (Oxford: Berg, 2001), 1–10.

6. Alexandra Palmer, "New Directions: Fashion History Studies and Research in North America and England," *Fashion Theory* 1, no. 3 (August 1997): 299, 302.

7. Kawamura, *Fashion-ology*, 33.

8. Charles Woolsey Cole, *Colbert and a Century of French Mercantilism* (Hamden, CT: Archon Books, 1964), 2:141 and chap. 10 passim.

9. Cole, *Colbert and a Century of French Mercantilism*, 2:190, 205–206; Valerie Steele, *Paris Fashion: A Cultural History*, rev. ed. (New York: Bloomsbury USA, 2017), 26; Valerie Steele, "Paris, Capital of Fashion," in *Paris: Capital of Fashion*, ed. Valerie Steele (London: Bloomsbury Visual Arts, 2019), 11–15; Pamela A. Parmal, "La Mode: Paris and the Development of the French Fashion Industry," in *Fashion Show: Paris Style*, ed. Pamela A. Parmal and Didier Grumbach (Boston: MFA Publications, 2006), 14.

10. Mary E. Davis, *Classic Chic: Music, Fashion, and Modernism* (Berkeley: University of California Press, 2006), 2–3; Justine de Young, "Not Just a Pretty Picture: Fashion as News," in *Getting the Picture: The Visual Culture of the News*, ed. Jason Hill and Vanessa R. Schwartz (London: Bloomsbury, 2015), 112. See also Hazel H. Hahn, *Scenes of Parisian Modernity: Culture and Consumption in the Nineteenth Century* (New York: Palgrave, 2009), 65–66; and Kimberly Chrisman-Campbell, *Fashion Victims: Dress at the Court of Louis XVI and Marie-Antoinette* (New Haven, CT: Yale University Press, 2015), 14–17.

11. Kate Best, *The History of Fashion Journalism* (London: Bloomsbury Academic, 2017), 30–33; Steele, *Paris Fashion*, 7.

12. Green, *Ready-to-Wear and Ready-to-Work: A Century of Industry and Immigrants in Paris and New York* (Durham, NC: Duke University Press, 1997), 2.

13. Green, *Ready-to-Wear and Ready-to-Work*, 2.

14. Sophie Kurkdjian, "The Cultural Value of Parisian Couture," in Steele, *Paris: Capital of Fashion*, 143.

15. Véronique Pouillard, "Managing Fashion Creativity: The History of the Chambre Syndicale de la Couture Parisienne during the Interwar Period," *Economic History Research* 12 (2016): 77; Kurkdjian, "The Cultural Value of Parisian Couture," 141–143.

16. Kurkdjian, "The Cultural Value of Parisian Couture," 143–145.

17. Linda Baumgarten, *What Clothes Reveal: The Language of Clothing in Colonial and Federal America: The Colonial Williamsburg Collection* (Williamsburg, VA: Colonial Williamsburg Foundation, 2002), 76.

18. Baumgarten, *What Clothes Reveal*, 82–84.

19. Kate Haulman, *The Politics of Fashion in Eighteenth-Century America* (Chapel Hill: University of North Carolina Press, 2011), 96–97.

20. John Singleton Copley (U.S., 1738–1815). *Mary and Elizabeth Royall*, ca. 1758. Oil on canvas, 145.7 x 122.2 cm. Museum of Fine Arts, Boston, Julia Knight Fox Fund, 25.49.

21. Baumgarten, *What Clothes Reveal*, 84, 94.

22. Baumgarten, *What Clothes Reveal*, 95–99, 156; Hilary Davidson, *Dress in the Age of Jane Austen* (New Haven, CT: Yale University Press, 2019), 265.

23. Nicola Shilliam, "The Sartorial Autobiography: Bostonians' Private Writings about Fashionable Dress, 1760s–1860s," *Textile and Text* 13, no. 3 (1991): 10.

24. Giorgio Riello, *A Foot in the Past: Consumers, Producers and Footwear in the Long Eighteenth Century* (New York: Oxford University Press, 2006), 191, 205. Paris fashion began appearing in British periodicals as early as 1797. Davidson, *Dress in the Age of Jane Austen*, 238, 244–245.

25. Greg King, *A Season of Splendor: The Court of Mrs. Astor in Gilded Age New York* (Hoboken, NJ: John Wiley, 2009), 212–215; Amy De la Haye and Valerie D. Mendes, *The House of Worth: Portrait of an Archive* (London: V&A Publishing, 2014), 21; Caroline Evans, *The Mechanical Smile: Modernism and the First Fashion Shows in France and America, 1900–1929* (New Haven, CT: Yale University Press, 2013), 13.

26. Aileen Ribeiro, *Clothing Art: The Visual Culture of Fashion, 1600–1914* (New Haven, CT: Yale University Press, 2016), 326–336.

27. Anna Reynolds, "John Singer Sargent Painting Fashion," *Metropolitan Museum Journal* 54 (2019): 113–114.

28. "These Three Women Are the Most Beautiful Types of Lovely Womanhood in France, England, and America," *San Francisco Call*, April 10, 1898, 21.

29. Joel H. Kaplan and Sheila Stowell, *Theatre and Fashion: Oscar Wilde to the Suffragettes* (Cambridge, UK: Cambridge University Press, 1995), 9.

30. Michele Majer, ed., *Staging Fashion, 1880–1920: Jane Hading, Lily Elsie, Billie Burke* (New York: Bard Graduate Center, 2012), 28, 31, 37; Kawamura, *Fashion-ology*, chap. 5; Maureen E. Montgomery, *Displaying Women: Spectacles of Leisure in Edith Wharton's New York* (New York: Routledge, 1998), 137.

31. Majer, *Staging Fashion*, 6, 26.

32. Pierre Bourdieu. *Distinction: A Social Critique of the Judgement of Taste*, trans. Richard Nice (Cambridge, MA: Harvard University Press, 1984, 6–7).

33. Rebecca Edwards, *New Spirits: Americans in the "Gilded Age," 1865–1905* (New York: Oxford University Press, 2011), 97; Emily Remus, *A Shoppers' Paradise: How the Ladies of Chicago Claimed Power and Pleasure in the New Downtown* (Cambridge, MA: Harvard University Press, 2019).

34. Kevin D. Murphy, "The François Premier Style in New York: The William K. and Alva Vanderbilt House," in *New York: Art and Cultural Capital of the Gilded Age*, ed. Margaret R. Laster and Chelsea Bruner (New York: Routledge, 2019), 41–55.

CHAPTER 2

1. "A Card: Mad'lle J. Houdbert," *New York Herald*, April 17, 1837, 1.

2. Louisa Iarocci, *The Urban Department Store in America, 1850–1930* (Burlington, VT: Ashgate, 2014), 73; William Leach, *Land of Desire: Merchants, Power, and the Rise of a New American Culture* (New York: Pantheon Books, 1993), 123; Jean L. Parsons, "No Longer a 'Frowsy Drudge': Women's Wardrobe Management: 1880–1930," *Clothing and Textiles Research Journal* 20, no. 1 (January 2002): 35–37.

3. Anita A. Stamper, *Clothing through American History: The Civil War through the Gilded Age, 1861–1899* (Santa Barbara, CA: Greenwood, 2011), 145.

4. "Madame Jamme from Paris," *New York Herald*, April 17, 1837, 1.

5. For example, "At Mme. Elvina Guerin's," *New York Herald*, April 3, 1859, 2.

6. For example, *New York Herald*, October 24, 1859, 2.

7. See Bourdieu, *Distinction*, 1–2.

8. *Doggett's New-York City Directory* (New York: J. Doggett, Jr., 1845), 158, 397.

9. "Millinery and Dressmaking," *New York Herald*, March 23, 1854, 5.

10. "Millinery and Dressmaking," 5; "Help Wanted," *New York Herald*, September 26, 1855, 6.

11. *Official Catalogue of the New-York Exhibition of the Industry of All Nations* (New York: G. P. Putnam, 1853), 147–153.

12. *Official Catalogue of the New-York Exhibition of the Industry of All Nations*, 36–41, 57–71.

13. "Fall Fashions," *New York Herald*, September 26, 1859, 2.

14. For example, Culp and Burogyne of Plymouth, Ohio, in *Plymouth Advertiser*, May 19, 1855, 3.

15. Françoise Tétart-Vittu, "Who Creates Fashion?," in *Impressionism, Fashion, and Modernity*, ed. Gloria Groom (New Haven, CT: Yale University Press, 2012), 75.

16. Barbara Brackman, "M. T. Hollander and the Abolitionist Baby Quilt," *Civil War Quilts: Quilts & Women's History Focusing on the American Civil War* (blog), November 8, 2014, http://civilwarquilts.blogspot.com/2014/11/mt-hollander-and-abolitionist-baby-quilt.html. See L. P. Hollander & Co. (U.S.). Cape, 1897–1900. Silk, beads. The Metropolitan Museum of Art, New York, Gift of Mrs. Lee Woodward Zeigler, 1952, C.I.52.52.1; L. P. Hollander & Co. (U.S.). Wedding gown, 1884. Silk velvet and satin. The Mint Museum, Charlotte, Museum

Purchase: Auxiliary Costume Fund, 2003.74A-B; Billhead for L. P. Hollander & Co., 82 & 83 Boylston Street and Park Square, Boston, Mass., dated January 1888. Historic New England, EP001.01.059.02.02.01.018.

17. Samuel E. Brown, "Mrs. Hollander's Case of Children's Clothing, on Exhibition at the Crystal Palace, New York," September 10, 1853, The Miriam and Ira D. Wallach Division of Art, Prints, and Photographs: Picture Collection, New York Public Library, New York Public Library Digital Collections, https://digitalcollections.nypl.org/items/510d47e0-ccb6-a3d9-e040-e00a18064a99; *Report of the Committee on Awards of the World's Columbian Commission* (Washington, DC: Government Printing Office, 1901), 207.

18. Alva E. Belmont, Alva E. Belmont Memoir, 1917, Matilda Young Papers, Rare Book Manuscript and Special Collections Library, Duke University, Durham, NC, 30–31.

19. "At Gaynor's,"*New York Tribune*, October 22, 1867, 3; "At Mrs. Gaynor's," *New York Herald*, November 14, 1869, 1.

20. "Paris in New York," *New York Herald*, October 24, 1869, 1.

21. Invitation, Joaquin et Cie, March 26 and 27, 1879, Historic New England, EP001.01.023.06.01.025.

22. "A Vanderbilt Married," *New York Times*, November 22, 1877, 5. See "New York City—The Wedding of Miss Florence Adele Vanderbilt to Mr. Hamilton McK. Twombley," December 8, 1877, The Miriam and Ira D. Wallach Division of Art, Prints, and Photographs: Picture Collection, New York Public Library, New York Public Library Digital Collections, http://digitalcollections .nypl.org/items/510d47e2-d17d-a3d9-e040-e00a18064a99. An 1890 portrait of Florence Adele Vanderbilt Twombley by John Singer Sargent is owned by Columbia University, New York.

23. "A Vanderbilt Married," *New York Times*, November 22, 1877, 5.

24. *Trow's New York City Directory* (New York: J. F. Trow, 1878–79), 287. For example: M. A. Connelly (U.S.). Dress, 1882–1886. Silk. The Metropolitan Museum of Art, New York, Gift of Mrs. Vanderbilt Webb, 1939, C.I.39.100.4ab.

25. "Another Arrival," *New York Herald*, September 9, 1855, 5.

26. Iarocci, *The Urban Department Store in America, 1850–1930*, 69, 73.

27. For example, "Spring Fashions," *New York Herald*, February 23, 1859, 8.

28. "Fashionable Hats for City Ladies," *New York Herald*, April 3, 1859, 2; "New Paris Dress Goods," *New York Herald*, June 1, 1862, 3.

29. *The Millinery Fashion Magazine*, January 1886, 13.

30. Iarocci, *The Urban Department Store in America, 1850–1930*, 69.

31. Kate Smith, "Sensing Design and Workmanship: The Haptic Skills of Shoppers in Eighteenth-Century London," *Journal of Design History* 25, no. 1 (March 2012): 3–4.

32. Deborah S. Gardner, "'A Paradise of Fashion': A. T. Stewart's Department Store, 1862–1875," in *A Needle, a Bobbin, a Strike: Women Needleworkers in America*, ed. Joan M. Jensen and Sue Davidson (Philadelphia: Temple University Press, 1984), 69; "The Ladies behind the Counter," *New York Herald*, July 29, 1870, 10.

33. Leach, *Land of Desire*, 95. By 1900, women buyers numbered in the hundreds of dollars and earned salaries in the thousands. "Successful Women Buyers," *Woman's Journal*, December 8, 1900, 390.

34. See, for example, Brevik-Zender, *Fashioning Spaces*, 114.

35. See Michael B. Miller, *The Bon Marché: Bourgeois Culture and the Department Store, 1869–1920* (Princeton, NJ: Princeton University Press, 1981); Leach, *Land of Desire*, passim; Lisa Tiersten, *Marianne in the Market: Envisioning Consumer Society in Fin-de-Siècle France* (Berkeley: University of California Press, 2002); Anca I. Lasc, *Interior Decorating in Nineteenth-Century France: The Visual Culture of a New Profession* (Manchester, UK: Manchester University Press, 2018), 152–189.

36. Charles P. Kindleberger, "Origins of United States Direct Investment in France," *Business History Review* 48, no. 3 (Autumn 1974): 394. For example, *New York Herald*, October 24, 1859, 2.

37. "Stewart's Store," *Appleton's Journal*, April 9, 1870, 411–113.

38. Nancy L. Green, *The Other Americans in Paris: Businessmen, Countesses, Wayward Youth, 1880–1941* (Chicago: University of Chicago Press, 2014), 149.

39. Advertisement for Leubrie Brothers, *Memphis Daily Appeal*, December 10, 1874, 2; Advertisement for Bain & Son, *Daily Ohio Statesman*, July 12, 1861, 2.

40. "Paris Fashions," *Boston Weekly Magazine: Devoted to Polite Literature, Useful Science, Biography & Dramatic Criticism*, May 17, 1817, 126.

41. Charles Sumner, *Memoir and Letters of Charles Sumner*, ed. Edward Lillie Pierce (London: Sampson Low, Marston, Searle, and Rivington, 1878), 1:312.

42. Sumner, *Memoir and Letters of Charles Sumner*, 3:530.

43. Margaret Fuller Ossoli, *At Home and Abroad*, ed. Arthur B. Fuller (Boston: Crosby, Nichols, 1856), 192.

44. Emma Willard, *Journal and Letters from France and Great-Britain* (Troy, NY: N. Tuttle, 1833), 164–167.

45. Willard, *Journal and Letters*, 166–167.

46. Willard, *Journal and Letters*, 162.

47. Willard, *Journal and Letters*, 168.

48. Willard, *Journal and Letters*, 169–170.

49. Joy Spanabel Emery, *A History of the Paper Pattern Industry: The Home Dressmaking Fashion Revolution* (London: Bloomsbury Academic, 2014), 24–25.

50. Steele, *Paris Fashion*, 7.

51. Emery, *A History of the Paper Pattern Industry*, 26–27.

52. Commercial and domestic ephemera scrapbook, 19th century. Historic New England, Purchased from John Hardy Wright, HGO-01-001-O-C-102.

53. "The Great Textile Invention at the Centennial Exposition," *Scientific American*, September 16, 1876, 176.

54. *Frank Leslie's Illustrated Historical Register of the Centennial Exposition 1876* (New York: Frank Leslie's Publishing House, 1877), 271.

55. "Notes on Ocean Travel," *Mme Demorest's Semi-Annual What to Wear and How to Make It* (1878), 33–40.

56. Sarah Josepha Buell Hale, *Manners: Happy Homes and Good Society All the Year Round* (Boston: Lee and Shepard, 1889), 130.

57. Claire Jessup Moore, *Sensible Etiquette of the Best Society, Customs, Manners, Morals, and Home Culture* (Philadelphia: Porter and Coates, 1878), 252.

58. Shilliam, "The Sartorial Autobiography," 17.

59. Quoted in Shilliam, "The Sartorial Autobiography," 17.

60. Shilliam, "The Sartorial Autobiography," 20. For Roger (alternately Rodger), see Mme Roger (French, active mid-19th century). Woman's evening dress, ca. 1865. Silk plain weave (faille) and satin, trimmed with silk satin ribbon, net, and silk lace. Museum of Fine Arts, Boston, Gift of Mrs. Robert Homans, 46.209a-c; and Mme Roger (French, active in mid-19th century). Woman's evening dress, ca. 1868, restored ca. 1962. Silk plain weave patterned with weft floats, net, satin and blond lace. Museum of Fine Arts, Boston, Gift of Mrs. Robert Homans, 46.207a-b; Parmal, "La Mode," 60–62.

61. Frances Willard, Frances Willard Journals, February 24, 1869, Frances Willard Historical Association, Evanston, IL.

62. Willard, Frances Willard Journals, May 28, 1870.

63. Willard, Frances Willard Journals, February 24, 1869.

64. Willard, Frances Willard Journals, May 24, 1870.

65. Willard, Frances Willard Journals, December 31, 1868.

66. Justine de Young, "Representing the Modern Woman: The Fashion Plate Reconsidered (1865–75)," in *Women, Femininity, and Public Space in European Visual Culture, 1789–1914*, ed. Temma Balducci and Heather Belnap Jensen (Farnham, UK: Ashgate, 2014), 97–116.

67. U.S. woman's travel diary, May 24, 1878, David M. Rubenstein Rare Book & Manuscript Library, Duke University.

68. "At John Wanamaker's," *Lancaster Daily Intellegencer*, May 30, 1882, 3.

69. *Paris and Its Environs, with Routes from London to Paris, Paris to the Rhine and Switzerland: Handbook for Travellers* (Leipsic: K. Baedeker, 1874), 33–34.

70. Similar fashion plates to that in figure 2.8 were reproduced in U.S. periodicals—for example, *Frank Leslie's Lady's Magazine* in 1879.

71. Cynthia Amnéus, *A Separate Sphere: Dressmakers in Cincinnati's Golden Age* (Lubbock: Texas Tech University Press, 2003), 86.

72. Nicola J. Thomas, "Embodying Imperial Spectacle: Dressing Lady Curzon, Vicereine of India 1899–1905," *Cultural Geographies* 14, no. 3 (July 2007): 385.

73. Belmont, Alva E. Belmont Memoir, 7. The memoir was dictated to poet and social reformer Sara Bard Field in the summer of 1917 in Newport, Rhode Island. Amanda Mackenzie Stuart, *Consuelo and Alva Vanderbilt: The Story of a Daughter and a Mother in the Gilded Age* (New York: Harper Perennial, 2007), 375–380.

74. Belmont, Alva E. Belmont Memoir, 110a.

75. Elizabeth Jachimowicz, *Eight Chicago Women and Their Fashions, 1860–1929* (Chicago: Chicago Historical Society, 1978), 47.

76. "Their Wedding Journey," *Wheeling Sunday Register*, April 28, 1895, 12.

1. For example, Adolphe Sandoz, *Toilettes by Worth, Coiffures by Lenthéric*, in "La Vie Mondaine," *Revue illustrée*, December 1890, 87.

2. House of Worth, *A History of Feminine Fashion* (London: Ed. J. Burrow, 1928), 67.

3. Troy, *Couture Culture*, 16–17; Pierre Bourdieu and Yvette Delsaut, "Le Couturier et sa griffe: Contribution à une théorie de la magie," *Actes de la recherche en sciences sociales* 1, no. 1 (1975): 12.

4. Information about Lenthéric is culled from period sources, primarily "Lenthéric: The Master Coiffeur of Paris," *Hearth and Home* (June 8, 1893): 115; "Lenthéric," *International Herald Tribune*, December 21, 1893, 5; and *Annuaire-almanach du commerce, de l'industrie, de la magistrature et de l'administration* (Paris: Firmin Didot et Bottin, 1870–1907).

5. *Annuaire-almanach du commerce, de l'industrie, de la magistrature et de l'administration* (1880s and 1890s). A claim that Lenthéric was an employee of maison Félix appears in "Lenthéric: The Master Coiffeur of Paris," 5.

6. "Lenthéric: The Master Coiffeur of Paris," 115; "Society," *St. Paul Globe*, July 18, 1897, 14; Ignota, "A Chat with the Leading Paris Hairdresser," *Hearth and Home*, August 6, 1896, 491.

7. Best, *The History of Fashion Journalism*, 30–33; Davis, *Classic Chic*, 3–4; De Young, "Not Just a Pretty Picture," 109–115; Agnès Rocamora, *Fashioning the City: Paris, Fashion and the Media* (London: I. B. Tauris, 2009), 35; Agnès Rocamora, "Pierre Bourdieu: The Field of Fashion," in *Thinking through Fashion: A Guide to Key Theorists*, ed. Agnès Rocamora and Anneke Smelik (London: I. B. Tauris, 2016), 239.

8. "How Fashions Are Made," *New York Times*, April 4, 1886, 5.

9. "Lenthéric: The Master Coiffeur of Paris," 115.

10. For the French and British presence in the perfume industry in the mid- to late nineteenth century, see Jessica P. Clark, *The Business of Beauty: Gender and the Body in Modern London* (London: Bloomsbury Visual Arts, 2020), 126–128. For the history of perfumery in France, see Morag Martin, *Selling Beauty: Cosmetics, Commerce, and French Society, 1750–1830* (Baltimore, MD: Johns Hopkins University Press, 2009), 32–51.

11. "Courrier de la mode," *Revue illustrée*, December 1, 1892, 1; "Les Nouvelles Étrennes," *Revue illustrée*, June 15, 1893, 441.

12. Steven Zdatny, ed., *Hairstyles and Fashion: A Hairdresser's History of Paris, 1910–1920* (Oxford: Oxford International, 1999), 1–34; Steve Zdatny, *Fashion, Work, and Politics in Modern France* (London: Palgrave Macmillan, 2006), 14.

13. "Lenthéric s'est vu amené à s'occuper non seulement de la coiffure et du teint, mais aussi de tout ce qui se rattache à la parure féminine." Comtesse Sylvia, "La Parure de la femme," *Revue illustrée*, December 15, 1895, 376 (trans. Sarah McFadden).

14. Ignota, "A Chat with the Leading Paris Hairdresser," 491.

15. "Paris Fashions," *San Francisco Call*, April 3, 1898, 27.

16. "Mermaid Bead Bodices," *St. Paul Daily Globe*, June 5, 1887, 19; Elliam, "Interview Chez Lenthéric," *La Revue mondaine illustrée*, November 25, 1892, 3; "Perfumed Sleeves," *Sea Coast Echo*, July 27, 1895, 3.

17. John H. Young, *Our Deportment, or, The Manners, Conduct and Dress of the Most Refined Society* (Detroit: F. B. Dickerson, 1882), 352.

18. "French Fashion Fancies," *St. Paul Daily Globe*, October 30, 1887, 19.

19. "Known by One Rich Scent," *St. Paul Daily Globe*, July 1, 1888, 19.

20. "Known by One Rich Scent," 19.

21. "Flowers Their Fad," *Morning Times*, May 3, 1896, 21.

22. "Cloth Carries Perfume," *Herald and News*, November 30, 1899, 4; "Talks about Womankind," *Freeland Tribune*, November 2, 1900, 3.

23. "Talks about Womankind," 3; "Some Stylish Muffs," *Evening Star*, January 18, 1896, 16; Ella Adelia Fletcher, *The Woman Beautiful* (New York: Brentano's, 1901), 473.

24. Marquise de Fontenoy, *Eve's Glossary: The Guidebook of a Mondaine* (Chicago: Herbert S. Stone, 1897), 36.

25. "Woman of Fashion," *Seattle Post-Intelligencer*, August 16, 1891, 11.

26. "Woman of Fashion," 11; Christina Walkley and Vanda Foster, *Crinolines and Crimping Irons: Victorian Clothes: How They Were Cleaned and Cared For* (London: Owen, 1978), 174.

27. *La Coiffure française illustrée* 97 (April 1897); *La Coiffure française illustrée* 98 (May 1897); *La Coiffure française illustrée* 99 (June 1897); *La Coiffure française illustrée* 100 (July 1897).

28. *La Mode artistique: Revue de toutes les elégances*, November 1901, 25; *La Mode artistique: Revue de toutes les elégances*, December 1901, 19. Jane Hading's name is misspelled as "Jeane."

29. "Women of Fashion," *Roanoke Times*, January 17, 1891, 5.

30. For example, Le Masque de Velours, "La Vie mondaine," *Revue illustrée*, May 15, 1895, 388.

31. Anne Hathaway, "Scent and Scent Bottles," *Woman's World* 2, no. 6 (May 1889): 321–325.

32. "Ladies' Perfumes," *St. Paul Daily Globe*, August 14, 1887, 12.

33. "To Perfume the Hair," *Southern Herald*, May 12, 1893, 1.

34. Carol de Dobay Rifelj, *Coiffures: Hair in Nineteenth-Century French Literature and Culture* (Newark: University of Delaware Press, 2010), 173–174; Zdatny, *Fashion, Work, and Politics in Modern France*, 3.

35. "Le Dernier mot de la mode," *Le Figaro-graphic*, November 28, 1891, 192; "Fashions in Head-Dresses," *International Herald Tribune*, December 15, 1895, 2.

36. "Fashions in Head-Dresses," 2; "Carnet Mondaine," *La Nouvelle revue*, March 1889, 630. "French Ideas about Hairdressing," *The Sun*, October 15, 1899, 4.

37. Geoffrey Jones, *Beauty Imagined: A History of the Global Beauty Industry* (Oxford: Oxford University Press, 2010), 48.

38. "Interview chez M. Lenthéric," *La Revue mondaine illustrée*, November 25, 1892, 3.

39. *Figaro-salon* (suppl. to *Le Figaro*, April 25, 1895), 2.

40. "Fire in the rue Saint-Honoré," *International Herald Tribune*, August 24, 1897, 1.

41. "Where Is Lenthéric?," *International Herald Tribune*, December 29, 1895, 3.

42. "Fashions in Head-Dresses," 2; "Lenthéric's Natural Scents," *International Herald Tribune*, September 15, 1901, 4.

43. "Après le Grand Prix," *Gil Blas*, June 16, 1896, 2.

44. "Les Modes et l'élégance," *Le Monde illustrée*, January 14, 1899, 38.

45. "Various Manifestations," *The Sun*, March 13, 1892, 19.

46. Paul H. Nystrom, *Economics of Fashion* (New York: Ronald Press, 1928), 178; Lourdes M. Font, "International Couture: The Opportunities and Challenges of Expansion, 1880–1920," *Business History* 54, no. 1 (February 2012): 34; Véronique Pouillard and Waleria Dorogova, "Couture Ltd: French Fashion's Debut in London's West End," *Business History* (February 2020): 4–5, 8.

47. Anne Kjellberg and Susan North, *Style and Splendour: The Wardrobe of Queen Maud of Norway* (London: Victoria & Albert Museum, 2005), 77, 82.

48. Susan North, "John Redfern and Sons, 1847 to 1892," *Costume* 42, no. 1 (2008): 152–153; *Life*, October 27, 1892, 226 (new branch in Chicago); Otto Charles Thieme, "With Grace & Favour: Victorian and Edwardian Fashion in America," in *With Grace & Favour: Victorian & Edwardian Fashion in America*, ed. Otto Charles Thieme (Cincinnati, OH: Cincinnati Art Museum, 1993), 69.

49. Jacqueline Demornex, *Lucien Lelong* (London: Thames & Hudson, 2008), 9, 135.

50. See Augustine Cohn & Company (French). Dress, ca. 1879. Silk. Peabody Essex Museum, Salem, Mass., Gift of Miss Helen F. Pettes, 1932, 121199. See also Centennial Photographic Company, *Augustine Cohen's exhibit—Main Building*. Silver albumen print, 1876. Print and Picture Collection, Free Library of Philadelphia, call number c020658.

51. "Fashions in Head-Dresses," 2; *International Herald Tribune*, March 11, 1893.

52. "Lenthéric," 5.

53. "Lenthéric," 5; "Telephone 'Communicated,'" *International Herald Tribune*, January 1, 1896, 3; "Paris Gowns and Wraps," *New York Times*, August 3, 1890, 11. On Marcel Grateau (also known as François Marcel), see Jones, *Beauty Imagined,* 46; Zdatny, *Fashion, Work, and Politics in Modern France*, 8–10.

54. "Paris Fashions," 27; "Le Flou-flou," *Revue illustrée*, December 15, 1894, n.p.

55. "French Ideas about Hairdressing," 4.

56. "Fashions at Lenthéric," *International Herald Tribune*, August 5, 1900, n.p.

57. "Fine Assortment," *Grand Forks Daily Herald*, March 25, 1900, 4; *Vogue*, October 24, 1901, iv.

58. Baronne de Spare, "Carnet parisien," *La Grande revue*, 1889, 215.

59. Violette, "Paris Fashions," *Woman's World* 2, no. 6 (May 1889): 304–305.

60. "Soirées et bals," *Le Figaro-graphic*, January 25, 1892, 4.

61. "Women and Home," *San Francisco Call*, September 3, 1893, 13. Further documentation has not yet been found.

62. *Palais du Costume: Le Costume de la femme à travers les âges. Projet Félix. Exposition universelle de Paris 1900* (Paris: Lemercier, 1900), 4.

63. "Lenthéric," 5; Nicy as Lenthéric's teacher: "Cours Chevrel-Dufour," *Le Journal des coiffeurs*, January 1, 1873, 3.

64. Joseph Barberet, *Le Travail en France: Monographies professionnelles* (Paris: Berger-Levrault, 1887), 388.

65. "Le Masque de velours," *Revue illustrée*, June 15, 1893, 76; Illustration, *Harper's Bazar*, February 27, 1897, n.p.

66. *Harper's Bazar*, March 5, 1898, cover.

67. *Palais du Costume: Le Costume de la femme à travers les âges*, 61.

68. *Catalogue illustré des coiffures* (Paris: L'Academie de coiffure, 1900), unpaginated; *Palais du Costume: Le Costume de la femme à travers les âges*, 61–64; "Les Attractions à l'exposition," *The Nineteen Hundred* 9, no. 1 (July 15, 1899): 13.

69. For example, "New French Gowns," *New York Times*, November 11, 1888, 2.

70. For example, *Paris and Environs with Routes from London to Paris: Handbook for Travellers* (Paris: K. Baedeker, 1891), 38 and (Paris: K. Baedeker, 1910), 27.

71. G.P., "M. Auguste Petit," *Le Panthéon de l'industrie*, September 5, 1886, 1.

72. "No. 3.—Coiffure de M. Auguste, Maison Hippolyte et Auguste, 7, rue de la Paix," *Le Moniteur de la coiffure*, November 10, 1865, 4; *Annuaire-almanach du commerce, de l'industrie, de la magistrature et de l'administration* (Paris: Firmin Didot et Bottin, 1870–1907). One source cites Petit opening the firm at 7, rue de la Paix in 1864 but does not mention Hippolyte: G.P., "M. Auguste Petit," 1.

73. The medal is listed in *Annuaire des coiffeurs* (Paris: Bureau central de placement, 1895), 25; "Echos de Paris," *Le Gaulois*, July 22, 1892, 1.

74. The firm was still listed at 7, rue de la Paix in 1910: *Paris and Environs with Routes from London to Paris: Handbook for Travellers* (Paris: K. Baedeker, 1910), 27. By 1907, three further businesses were listed at 7, rue de la Paix: Fontana brothers (jewelers); maison Franck (lingerie, trousseaux, and layettes); and the journal *Le Goût de jour*. *Annuaire-almanach du commerce, de l'industrie, de la magistrature et de l'administration* (Paris: Firmin Didot et Bottin, 1907), 581. Franck had been at the location since at least 1891, when Mary Rita Wilson Goelet made a purchase (see chapter 6, Maison Félix and Its U.S. Clients).

75. G.P., "M. Auguste Petit," 2; "Fashions in Head-Dresses," *International Herald Tribune*, December 15, 1895, 2.

76. "My Lady's Hairdresser: The Artist in Coiffure," *Current Literature* 6, no. 1 (January–April 1891): 59.

77. See Brevik-Zender, *Fashioning Spaces*, 204–215.

78. "Bulletin," *Le Gaulois*, January 8, 1894, 2; "Les Dernieres modes," *La grande dame: Revue de l'élégance et des arts*, January 1896, 6; "Le Concours de coiffures," *Le Journal*, December 14, 1903, 4; "Echos de Paris," *Le Gaulois*, July 22, 1892, 1.

79. "Environs of Florence," *International Herald Tribune*, February 1, 1893, 5; Therese, "Paris à la mode," *Town Topics*, April 13, 1893, 28; "Millinery at the Paris Exhibition," *Millinery Trade Review* 14, no. 7 (July 1889): 16.

80. Theodore Child, "Along the Parisian Boulevards," *Harper's New Monthly Magazine* (1892): 866.

81. For Metternich as a client of Petit: *Annuaire-almanach du commerce, de l'industrie, de la magistrature et de l'administration* (Paris: Firmin Didot et Bottin, 1874), 826; Pauline Clementine Marie Walburgh Metternich-Winneburg, *My Years in Paris* (London: Nash, 1922), 58–60.

82. Mary Chamberlain to Ellen Endicott, March 18, 1902, Hotel Metropolitan, AC4/3/1078, University of Birmingham, Cadbury Research Library, Chamberlain Collection (hereafter

UBCRL-CC). All citations to Chamberlain-Endicott letters were graciously provided by Phillada Ballard.

83. Dana Cooper, "From New England to Old England: The Anglo-American Life of Mary Endicott Chamberlain Carnegie, 1864–1957," *Massachusetts Historical Review* 13 (January 2011): 105–106.

84. Phillada Ballard, email to the author, June 17, 2020; "To Be Married Thursday," *Boston Daily Globe*, November 14, 1888, 1 (attributes wedding outfit to Worth); "Gossip of the Capital," *Evening Journal*, November 16, 1888, 1.

85. Chamberlain to Endicott, December 5, 1888, Hotel des Heldes, AC3/4/42, UBCRL-CC.

86. Phillada Ballard, email to the author, June 17, 2020.

87. For the wedding: "Quiet and Simple," *Fort Worth Daily Gazette*, November 16, 1888, 5; Diana Whitehill Laing, *Mistress of Herself* (Barre, MA: Barre Publishers, 1965), 55; Ballard, "Mary Chamberlain and Fashion," Chamberlain Highbury Trust, July 2019, https://chamberlainhighburytrust.files.wordpress.com/2019/07/cht-mary-chamberlain-and-fashion.pdf; Donna Seger, "Puritan Princess," *Streets of Salem* (blog), February 21, 2017, streetsofsalem.com/tag/mary-endicott.

88. Chamberlain to Endicott, February 16, 1890, Hotel des Heldes, AC4/3/132, UBCRL-CC.

89. Chamberlain to Endicott, February 21, 1890, 40 Prince's Gardens, AC4/3/134, UBCRL-CC. Chamberlain later sent the gray dress back to Worth for cleaning and remodeling. Jeanne-Marie Roland (1754–1793) was a French revolutionary.

90. Chamberlain to Endicott, March 18, 1902, Hotel Metropolitan, AC4/3/1078, UBCRL-CC. Richard Ormond and Elaine Kilmurray, eds., *John Singer Sargent: Complete Paintings* (New Haven, CT: Yale University Press, 1998), 3:72–73.

91. Chamberlain to Endicott, March 22, 1902, Hotel Metropolitan, AC4/3/1079, UBCRL-CC.

92. Chamberlain to Endicott, November 4, 1902, 40 Prince's Gardens, AC4/3110, UBCRL-CC.

93. Chamberlain to Endicott, February 8, 1889, Highbury, AC3/4/57, UBCRL-CC. See Laing, *Mistress of Herself*, 68–69; Chamberlain to Endicott, April 22, 1903, 40 Prince's Gardens, AC3/4/1143 and October 30, 1903, Highbury, AC3/4/1158, UBCRL-CC.

94. Chamberlain to Endicott, March 18, 1902, Hotel Metropolitan, AC4/3/1078, UBCRL-CC.

95. G.P., "M. Auguste Petit," 2; "La Fête annuelle des ouvriers coiffeurs," *Le Petit Parisien*, February 8, 1909, 3.

96. For example, *Paris and Environs with Routes from London to Paris: Handbook for Travellers* (Paris: K. Baedeker, 1891), 11; *Tout-Paris: Annuaire de la société parisienne* (Paris: A. La Fare, 1899), 643.

97. *Annual Report, United States National Museum* (Washington, DC: Smithsonian Institution, 1913), 106.

98. Georges Avenel, *Le Mécanisme de la vie moderne* (Paris: Colin, 1902), 83, 103; Octave Uzanne, *The Modern Parisienne* (New York: G. P. Putnam's Sons, 1912), 38.

99. Mary Lynn Stewart, "Copying and Copyrighting Haute Couture: Democratizing Fashion, 1900–1930s," *French Historical Studies* 28, no. 1 (Winter 2005): 109.

100. Cole, *Colbert and a Century of French Mercantilism*, 2:190; Steele, *Paris Fashion*, 26; Michael Stephen Smith, *The Emergence of Modern Business Enterprise in France, 1800–1930* (Cambridge, MA: Harvard University Press, 2006), 45; Parmal, "La Mode," 19–25.

101. Smith, *The Emergence of Modern Business Enterprise in France*, 45.

102. Smith, *The Emergence of Modern Business Enterprise in France*, 45, 158.

103. Smith, *The Emergence of Modern Business Enterprise in France*, 153; De la Haye and Mendes, *The House of Worth*, 100–105.

104. Victoria Sherrow, *Encyclopedia of Hair: A Cultural History* (Westport, CT: Greenwood Press, 2006), 163.

105. Steve Zdatny, *Fashion, Work, and Politics in Modern France*, 1.

106. Léonard, *The Souvenirs of Léonard, Hairdresser to Queen Marie-Antoinette*, trans. A. Teixeira de Mattos (London: privately printed, 1897), 34–35.

107. "How to Wear Your Hair," *The Sun*, April 13, 1890, 16.

108. *Evening Star*, January 14, 1886, 4.

109. "Notes about Hair," *The Sun*, October 25, 1891, 24.

110. Sherrow, *Encyclopedia of Hair*, 39, 210–211, 332n20.

111. Arlene Alpert, Margrit Altenburg, and Diane Bailey, *Milady's Standard Cosmetology* (Clifton Park, NY: Cengage Learning, 2002), 9.

112. "Sanctum Chat," *Saturday Evening Post*, November 3, 1883, 8.

113. "Madish [*sic*] Hair Dressing," *Brooklyn Daily Eagle*, September 6, 1902, 10.

114. "French Ideas about Hairdressing," 4.

115. "Clever and Helpful Criticism," *New York Times*, October 7, 1894, 18.

116. Invoice from Émile Landry to Madame Goelet, 1892, Goelet Family Papers, Series 4: Personal expenses, Salve Regina University, Newport, RI.

117. "How to Wear Your Hair," *The Sun*, April 13, 1890, 16.

118. For example, "City Matters," *Milwaukee Daily Sentinel*, April 10, 1873, 8.

119. Jones, *Beauty Imagined*, 33; Vanessa R. Schwartz, *Modern France: A Very Short Introduction* (Oxford: Oxford University Press, 2011), 85.

120. Nancy L. Green, *The Pletzl of Paris: Jewish Immigrant Workers in the Belle Epoque* (New York: Holmes & Meier, 1986), 31.

121. Kjellberg and North, *Style and Splendour*, 80.

122. Kjellberg and North, *Style and Splendour*, 80; Kate Strasdin, *Inside the Royal Wardrobe: A Dress History of Queen Alexandra* (London: Bloomsbury Academic, 2017), 8.

123. For example, "Fashions from Paris," *New York Times*, November 25, 1888, 16; Violette, "Paris Fashions," *Woman's World* 2, no. 5 (April 1889): 249.

124. Fashion plates in *La Mode illustrée*, April 22, 1883, 121–128.

125. Violette, *L'Art de la toilette chez la femme* (Paris: Libraire de la Société des gens de lettres, 1885), 187. "Violette" was a pseudonym for an unidentified writer. Joseph Bristow, ed., *Wilde Discoveries: Traditions, Histories, Archives*, CCS 19 (Toronto: University of Toronto Press, 2013), n. 7; Musée de la mode et du costume and palais Galliera, *Femmes fin de siècle, 1885–1895* (Paris: Editions Paris-Musées, 1990), 101n30; Violette, "Paris Fashions," 2, no. 6 (May 1889): 23; Theodore Child, *The Praise of Paris* (New York: Harper and Brothers, 1893), 109–110.

126. Fashion plates in *Moniteur des dames et des demoiselles*, April 1883.

127. "Mouvement Féminin," *La Femme: Journal bi-mensuel*, April 1, 1892, 53.

128. Patricia Cunningham, "Healthful, Artistic, and Correct Dress," in Thieme, *With Grace & Favour*, 23.

129. Michelle Tolini Finamore, "Callot Sisters," in *The Berg Companion to Fashion,* ed. Valerie Steele (London: Bloomsbury Academic, 2010), 113–114.

130. "Small Talk of the Week," *Sketch: A Journal of Art and Actuality*, February 27, 1901, 217.

131. "Small Talk of the Week," 217.

132. "Dressmakers in Paris," *The Sun*, June 30, 1901, 5.

133. Daniel James Cole and Nancy Diehl, *History of Modern Fashion* (London: Laurence King, 2015), 66.

134. Metternich-Winneburg, *My Years in Paris*, 61. See "Renée Marie Jeanne Worth" at http://gw .geneanet.org.

135. In January 1945, the modern version of the Chambre syndicale de la couture was enacted, in which the use of the terms *couture* and *haute couture*, among others, was strictly regulated. Kurkdjian, "The Cultural Value of Parisian Couture," 148–149, 62.

136. Green, *The Pletzl of Paris*, 12.

137. Green, *The Pletzl of Paris*, 27–28.

138. Christopher R. Friedrichs, "From Rags to Riches–Jews as Producers and Consumers of Fashion," in *Broken Threads: The Destruction of the Jewish Fashion Industry in Germany and Austria*, ed. Roberta S. Kremer (Oxford: Berg, 2007), 20–23.

139. Christian Schramm, "Architecture of the German Department Store," trans. John Gort, in Kremer, *Broken Threads*, 31, 47.

140. Ingrid Loschek, "Contributions of Jewish Fashion Designers in Berlin," in Kremer, *Broken Threads*, 55; Mila Ganeva, "Elegance and Spectacle in Berlin: The *Gerson* Fashion Store and the Rise of the Modern Fashion Show," in Potvin, *The Places and Spaces of Fashion,* 122–124.

141. Claire Zalc, "Trading on Origins: Signs and Windows of Foreign Shopkeepers in Interwar Paris," *History Workshop Journal* 70 (Autumn 2010): 133.

142. Green, *The Pletzl of Paris*, 111.

143. "The Bradley Martin Fete," *New York Times*, February 10, 1897, 7.

144. Charles William Calhoun, *The Gilded Age: Perspectives on the Origins of Modern America* (Lanham, MD: Rowman & Littlefield, 2007), 76–79.

145. Mme D. Michaux (U.S.). Dress, 1885–1889. Green silk faille and velvet. Kent State University Museum, Silverman/Rodgers Collection, 1983.001.0165 ab.

146. Madame Victorine (U.S.). Two-piece dress, ca. 1889. Rose silk faille trimmed with rust velvet ribbon, white wool and bands of green wool cutwork. The Museum at FIT, New York, Gift of Edith Twining, 98.1.1.

147. *New York Tribune*, November 25, 1900, 15.

148. Amelia des Moulins, "The Dressmaker's Life Story," *Independent* 56 (1904): 941.

149. Des Moulins, "The Dressmaker's Life Story," 942.

150. See, for example, Green, *Ready-to-Wear and Ready-to-Work*, passim.

1. "Le Monde et la ville," *Le Figaro*, May 1, 1901, 2; "Échos," *Le Journal*, May 10, 1901, 1; "Felix, Noted French Dressmaker, Fails," *St. Louis Republic*, June 29, 1901, 1.

2. "Félix Retired Wealthy," *Evening Star*, June 29, 1901, 2.

3. Diana De Marly, *The History of Haute Couture, 1850–1950* (London: B. T. Batsford, 1980), 115.

4. For example, Alexander C. T. Geppert, *Fleeting Cities: Imperial Expositions in Fin-de-Siècle Europe* (New York: Palgrave Macmillan, 2010).

5. Françoise Tétart-Vittu, "Key Dates in Fashion and Commerce, 1851–89," in *Impressionism, Fashion, and Modernity*, ed. Gloria Groom (New Haven, CT: Yale University Press, 2012), 271; "Vanity Fair-Fads, Foibles, and Fashions," *Current Literature*, May 1889, 388–390; Chantal Trubert-Tollu et al., *The House of Worth 1858–1954: The Birth of Haute Couture* (London: Thames & Hudson, 2017), 20–21.

6. Parmal, "La Mode," 63–64; De la Haye and Mendes, *The House of Worth*, 13; Trubert-Tollu et al., *The House of Worth 1858–1954*, 21.

7. Charles Legrand, *Rapport général sur l'Exposition internationale de Bruxelles 1897* (Brussels, 1898), 104. The names of committee members in this report from 1897 are annotated with involvement in previous expositions.

8. Legrand, *Rapport général sur l'Exposition internationale de Bruxelles,* 104; Elizabeth A. Coleman. *The Opulent Era: Fashions of Worth, Doucet and Pingat* (New York: Thames and Hudson; Brooklyn Museum, 1989), 21–22; B.D.F., "Gowns at the Exposition," *New York Times*, July 22, 1900, 5.

9. Anne Dymond, "Embodying the Nation: Art, Fashion, and Allegorical Women at the 1900 Exposition Universelle," *RACAR: Revue d'art canadienne / Canadian Art Review* 36, no. 2 (2011): 1–6; Steele, *Paris Fashion*, 197.

10. Véronique Pouillard, "A Woman in International Entrepreneurship: The Case of Jeanne Paquin," in *Entreprenørskap i naeringsliv og politikk: Festsskrift til Even Lange*, ed. Knut Sogner, Einar Lie, and Håvard Brede Aven (Oslo: Novus Forlag, 2016), 191–193.

11. Pouillard, "A Woman in International Entrepreneurship," 192–193.

12. Pouillard, "A Woman in International Entrepreneurship," 203–204.

13. Sculptor Pierre Imans created some of the wax models for the display. Alison Matthews David, "Cutting a Figure: Tailoring, Technology and Social Identity in Nineteenth-Century Paris" (PhD diss., Stanford University, 2002), 97–98; Jean-Philippe Worth, *A Century of Fashion* (Boston: Little Brown, 1928), 186–188; De la Haye and Mendes, *The House of Worth*, 21.

14. "Collective Exhibition," *International Herald Tribune*, May 27, 1900, 2; B.D.F., "Gowns at the Exposition," 5.

15. *La Sylphide*, January 20, 1850, 32.

16. Ada Cone, "My Lady's Carriage," *Courier-Journal*, October 14, 1889, 3.

17. "The Paris Exhibition: The Opening," *Birmingham Daily Post*, May 10, 1889, 4.

18. Maude Bass-Krueger, "Fashion Collections, Collectors, and Exhibitions in France, 1874–1900: Historical Imagination, the Spectacular Past, and the Practice of Restoration," *Fashion Theory* 22, no. 4–5 (2018): 419–422.

19. *Exposition des arts de la femme: Palais de l'industrie: Guide-livret illustré* (Paris: A. Warmont, 1892), 20–21.

20. "La Belle France at the Fair," *Los Angeles Herald*, October 25, 1893, 6; *The Official Directory of the World's Columbian Exposition* (Chicago: W. B. Conkey, 1893), 117–118.

21. Legrand, *Rapport général sur l'Exposition internationale de Bruxelles 1897*, 104.

22. Geppert, *Fleeting Cities*, 62–63.

23. Bass-Kreuger, "Fashion Collections," 407.

24. The two displays are often conflated in the secondary literature. For clarification of the difference, see De la Haye and Mendes, *The House of Worth*, 21; and Bass-Kreuger, "Fashion Collections," 424, 426.

25. Philippe Jullian, *The Triumph of Art Nouveau: Paris Exhibition, 1900*, trans. Stephen Hardman (New York: Larousse, 1974), 21; Bass-Kreuger, "Fashion Collections," 425.

26. "Paris Costume Exhibition," *Pictorial Review* 1, no. 10 (June 1900): 3.

27. For images of the coiffures, see *Catalogue illustré des coiffures* (Paris: L'Academie de coiffure, 1900); *Palais du costume: Le Costume de la femme à travers les âges*, 61–64; "Les Attractions à l'Exposition," *The Nineteen Hundred* 9, no. 1 (July 15, 1899), 13.

28. "La glorification de la mode et l'apothéose de la femme," in *Palais du costume: Le Costume de la femme à travers les âges*, 2.

29. "Le Théâtre et les spectacles à l'Exposition universelle de 1900," *Le Mênestrel*, March 31, 1901, 98–99.

30. *Palais du costume: Le Costume de la femme à travers les âges*, 1–58.

31. *L'Exposition de Paris (1900)* (Paris: Librairie illustrée, Montgredien et cie, 1900), 215. For an example of a contemporary review, see "Exposition universelle," *Le Monde artiste: Théâtre, musique, beaux-arts, littérature*, May 20, 1900, 309.

32. *Harper's Guide to Paris and the Exposition of 1900* (London: Harper and Brothers, 1900), 181.

33. Katherine de Forest, "June Days in Paris," *Harper's Bazar*, June 16, 1900, 432.

34. *Palais du costume: Le costume de la femme à travers les âges*, 58.

35. Bass-Kreuger, "Fashion Collections," 422.

36. "The Paris Exhibition: A Feast of Fashion," *Irish Times*, May 8, 1900, 5.

37. Evans, *The Mechanical Smile*, 21.

38. Potvin, *The Places and Spaces of Fashion, 1800–2007*, 8; Entwistle and Wilson, *Body Dressing*, 1–10.

39. Ella de C. Bello, "Paris Exhibition," *The Queen*, March 10, 1900, 387.

40. Marie A. Belloc, "An Interview with M. Félix, the Great Parisian Dress Artist," *The Woman at Home*, September 1900: [3]. See also Emma Bullet, "The Paris Exposition," *Brooklyn Daily Eagle*, August 27, 1899, 19. Early documentation of Félix's engagement for the project is in "Exposition universelle de 1900," *Le Temps*, December 17, 1897, 2.

41. Bello, "Paris Exposition," 387; Emma Bullet, "How to See the Exposition," *Brooklyn Daily Eagle*, June 17, 1900, 23; "Paris Costume Exhibition," 3; "The Paris Exhibition: A Feast of Fashion," 5.

42. The quotation is from Theodore Bentzon, "Woman at the Paris Exhibition," *Outlook* 66, no. 5 (September 29, 1900): 259. See also "Les Attractions à l'Exposition," *The Nineteen Hundred* 9, no. 1 (July 15, 1899), 13.

43. "Au Palais du costume," *Le Matin: Derniers télégrammes de la nuit*, April 21, 1900, 1; "Dress of All Ages," *Evening Star*, June 16, 1900, 22; "Le Palais du costume," *Le Mois littéraire et pittoresque*, September 1900, 326; Albert Gayet, *Le Costume en Egypte: Du IIIe au XIIIe siècle* (Paris: Ernest Leroux, 1900).

44. De Forest, "June Days in Paris," 432.

45. "The Paris Exhibition: A Feast of Fashion," 5.

46. "At the Paris Expo," *Evening Times-Republican*, April 21, 1900, 2.

47. "At the Paris Expo," 2.

48. See Damien Delille, "Entre art et industrie: La réforme de la mode au passage du XXe siècle," *Regards croisés* 6 (2016): 66.

49. "At the Exhibition," *International Herald Tribune*, November 3, 1900, 6.

50. The board of directors is listed in *Palais du costume: Le costume de la femme à travers les âges*, 4.

51. See Félix (Émile Martin) Poussineau, *La Maternité chez ouvrière* (Paris: La Mutualité maternelle, 1910); and Lori R. Weintrob, "Mobilizing Mothers in the Nation's Service: Civic Culture in France's Familial Welfare State, 1890–1914," in *Maternalism Reconsidered: Motherhood, Welfare and Social Policy in the Twentieth Century*, ed. Marian van der Klein, Rebecca Jo Plant, Nichole Sanders, and Lori R. Weintrob (New York: Berghahn, 2015), 64–74.

52. Weintrob, *Maternalism Reconsidered*, 65–67.

53. Tiersten, *Marianne in the Market*, 21–22.

54. Jean Bennet, *Biographies de personnalités mutualistes, XIXe–XXe siècles* (Paris: Mutualité française, 1987), 361–364. The street is Allée Félix Poussineau in Talant, France.

55. Emma Bullet, "The Choice of Paris," *Brooklyn Daily Eagle*, October 3, 1897, 17; "Description of Gowns from Paris Exposition," *Pictorial Review* (November 1900), 4.

56. "Orpheum Has Another Good Bill," *San Francisco Call*, April 22, 1901, 7; "Francesca Redding and Her Parisian Gowns," *San Francisco Call*, May 5, 1901, 3.

57. Genevieve Green, "Around the Exposition," *San Francisco Call*, June 24, 1900, 2; Frederic Mayer, "Frederick [*sic*] Mayer's Letter on the Paris Exposition," *Butte Weekly Miner*, April 19, 1900, 11.

58. "The Great Paris Exposition," *Sunday World-Herald*, January 14, 1900, 21.

59. Weintrob, *Maternalism Reconsidered*, 68.

60. Sterling Heilig, "For Working Women," *Evening Star*, April 30, 1900, 15. For an image of the Palais de la femme, see René Baschet, *Le Panorama: Exposition universelle 1900* (Paris: Ludovic Baschet, 1900), unpaginated.

61. Tiersten, *Marianne in the Market*, 24.

62. Colin Jones, *Paris: The Biography of a City* (New York: Penguin, 2006), 335; Walter Benjamin, *The Arcades Project*, trans. Howard Eiland and Kevin McLaughlin (Cambridge, MA: Harvard University Press, 1999 [1927–1940]), 7.

63. "Letters to the Herald," *International Herald Tribune*, August 4, 1900, 6.

64. "Le Palais du costume à l'Exposition," *L'Art et la mode*, October 20, 1900, 829; "Le Théâtre et les spectacles," *Le Ménestrel: Journal de musique*, April 7, 1901, 106–107.

65. Jullian, *The Triumph of Art Nouveau*, 204; "Débris of the Exhibition," *International Herald Tribune*, December 9, 1900, 4.

66. "Sales at the Hotel Drouot," *International Herald Tribune*, January 20, 1901, 5; "Sales at the Hotel Drouot," *International Herald Tribune*, January 22, 1901, 5; Carol S. Porter, *Meeting Louis at the Fair: The Projects and Photographs of Louis Clemens Spiering, World's Fair Architect* (St. Louis, MO: Virginia Publishing, 2004), 101.

67. *Paris in London: 1902, Earl's Court: Official Guide and Catalogue* (London: Gale & Polden, 1902), 13, 50–53.

68. "Opening of Earl's Court," *The Gentlewoman and Modern Life* 24, no. 620 (May 24, 1902): 738.

69. "Felix, Noted French Dressmaker, Fails," 1.

70. "Felix, Noted French Dressmaker, Fails," 1.

71. "Social and Personal," *Washington Times*, June 30, 1901, 5.

72. "Le Monde et la ville," *Le Figaro*, May 1, 1901, 2; "Échos," *Le Journal*, May 10, 1901, 1.

73. "Félix Retired Wealthy," *Evening Star*, June 29, 1901, 2.

74. "Felix Closes His Doors," *New York Tribune*, June 30, 1901, 2; "Art News and Notes," *The Art Amateur* 45, no. 4 (September 1901): 108.

75. Tillie May Fornay, "Sing a Song of Seasons," *Table Talk* 16 (January 1901): 375.

76. Tiersten, *Marianne in the Market*, 25–33, 64–68.

77. See Rita Felski, *The Gender of Modernity* (Cambridge, MA: Harvard University Press, 1995), 66–74.

78. Judith G. Coffin, *The Politics of Women's Work: The Paris Garment Trades, 1750–1915* (Princeton, NJ: Princeton University Press, 1996), 177; Green, *The Pletzl of Paris*, 128.

79. Coffin, *The Politics of Women's Work*, 180–181; "Couturières et tailleurs pour dames," *La Fronde*, February 18, 1901, 1.

80. Porter, *Meeting Louis at the Fair*, 101.

81. "Exposition de St. Louis," *Le Panthéon de l'industrie*, November 1904, 7.

82. *World's Fair Bulletin* 5, no. 6 (April 1904), 76; Janet Gordon, "Early Fall Fashions," *Southern Woman's Magazine* 2, no. 2 (September 1904): 21.

83. "Contract for Palais du costume," *World's Fair Bulletin* 5, no. 1 (November 1903), 36; Porter, *Meeting Louis at the Fair*, 100.

84. "Ruins Gowns Worth $200,000," *New York Times*, August 21, 1904, 1.

85. Ida B. Cole, "Museums of Costumes and Material," *Woman's Magazine* 20, no. 6 (January 1910): 30–31.

86. Dean L. Merceron, *Lanvin* (New York: Rizzoli, 2016), 32, 366.

87. Jess Berry, *House of Fashion: Haute Couture and the Modern Interior* (London: Bloomsbury Visual Arts, 2018), 41, 62, 65.

88. Merceron, *Lanvin*, 18.

89. For Lanvin's men's department at 15, rue du Faubourg Saint-Honoré, see Merceron, *Lanvin*, 32, 366.

90. Pouillard, "A Woman in International Entrepreneurship," 193–198, 205.

91. Font, "International Couture," 30–47; Pouillard, "A Woman in International Entrepreneurship," 205–206.

92. "A Magnificent Exhibit," *World's Fair Bulletin* 5, no. 10 (August 1904), 57; Paul Dreyfus-Bing and G.-Roger Sandoz, *Exposition internationale de Milan, 1906: Rapport général de la section française* (Paris: Comité français des expositions à l'étranger, 1913), 452.

93. Troy, *Couture Culture*, 147–149.

94. De la Haye and Mendes, *The House of Worth*, 327.

CHAPTER 5

1. "Dressmakers in Paris," *The Sun*, June 30, 1901, 5.

2. Lenard R. Berlanstein, *Daughters of Eve: A Cultural History of French Theater Women from the Old Regime to the Fin de Siècle* (Cambridge, MA: Harvard University Press, 2001), 233–236; Troy, *Couture Culture*, 13. See also Felski, *The Gender of Modernity*, 63–66.

3. Charles Blanc, *Art in Ornament and Dress* (London: Chapman and Hall, 1877), 273.

4. Maureen E. Montgomery, *Displaying Women: Spectacles of Leisure in Edith Wharton's New York* (New York: Routledge, 1998), 135; Penny Sparke, "Interior Decoration and Haute Couture: Links between the Developments of the Two Professions in France and the USA in the Late Nineteenth and Early Twentieth Centuries: A Historiographical Analysis," *Journal of Design History* 21, no. 1 (Spring 2008): 105.

5. "Originating Fashions," *Good Housekeeping*, September 1, 1888, 214.

6. Bourdieu, *Distinction*, 6–7.

7. "Walks with Empress Elizabeth," *New York Tribune*, January 22, 1899, 3.

8. Redfern eagerly began putting out advertisements of the royal patronage in the mid-1870s. Strasdin, *Inside the Royal Wardrobe*, 103–108.

9. Strasdin, *Inside the Royal Wardrobe*, 8; "Social and Personal," *Washington Times*, June 30, 1901, 5.

10. Strasdin, *Inside the Royal Wardrobe*, 12–14, 143.

11. Strasdin, *Inside the Royal Wardrobe*, 129.

12. Strasdin, *Inside the Royal Wardrobe*, 85; Kjellberg and North, *Style and Splendor*, 10, 77; "A Félix Creation," *San Francisco Call*, July 26, 1896, 29.

13. Coryne Hall, *Little Mother of Russia: A Biography of the Empress Marie Feodorovna (1847–1928)* (Teaneck, NJ: Holmes & Meier, 2006), 121.

14. Miller, *The Bon Marché*, 37.

15. I thank Julie Stoner for this information. *Bradshaw's Illustrated Guide through Paris and Its Environs* (London: W. J. Adams, 1882), xiii–xiv; *Le Journal des transports*, December 27, 1889, 447.

16. Cole and Diehl, *History of Modern Fashion*, 89.

17. Rebecca N. Mitchell, ed., *Fashioning the Victorians: A Critical Sourcebook* (London: Bloomsbury Academic, 2018), 15.

18. Mitchell, *Fashioning the Victorians*, 15. See also de Young, "Not Just a Pretty Picture," 114.

19. For example, "Dress and Fashion," *Weekly Irish Times*, May 21, 1887, 2.

20. Elisabetta Merlo and Francesca Polese, "Accessorizing, Italian Style: Creating a Market for Milan's Fashion Merchandise," in *Producing Fashion: Commerce, Culture, and Consumers*, ed. Regina Lee Blaszczyk (Philadelphia: University of Pennsylvania Press, 2008), 53.

21. Christine Ruane, "Spreading the Word: The Development of the Russian Fashion Press," in Blaszczyk, *Producing Fashion*, 34–35.

22. Yuniya Kawamura. "Japanese Fashion," in Steele, *The Berg Companion to Fashion*, 435–440.

23. "Fashion," in "Adoration for the 'Sweet France,'" sec. 2, in Modern Japan and France: Adoration, Encounter and Interaction, National Diet Library, Tokyo, Japan, https://www.ndl.go.jp /france/en/column/s2_2.html.

24. Nancy Micklewright, "London, Paris, Istanbul, and Cairo: Fashion and International Trade in the Nineteenth Century," *New Perspectives on Turkey* 7 (Spring 1992): 130, 134.

25. Katharine de Forest, "Our Paris Letter," *Harper's Bazar*, November 3, 1894, 875.

26. Lilla Belle Viles-Wyman, Lilla Belle Viles-Wyman Journals, 1893, Schlesinger Library, Radcliffe College. I thank Hayley Mercer for drawing my attention to the journals.

27. Viles-Wyman, Lilla Belle Viles-Wyman Journals, 1893, entry prior to May 29, 1893.

28. Viles-Wyman, Lilla Belle Viles-Wyman Journals, 1893, entry prior to June 20, 1893.

29. For example, Viles-Wyman, Lilla Belle Viles-Wyman Journals, 1893, June 20, 1893.

30. Viles-Wyman, Lilla Belle Viles-Wyman Journals, 1893, June 3, 1893.

31. For example, advertisement for Wakelee's Camelline facial foundation, *Black and White*, April 27, 1895, 584.

32. Josie Hall as "Light and Shade," from the series Fancy Dress Ball Costumes (N73) for Duke brand cigarettes. Issued by W. Duke, Sons & Co. (New York and Durham, NC), 1889. The Metropolitan Museum of Art, New York, The Jefferson R. Burdick Collection, Gift of Jefferson R. Burdick, 63.350.204.73.23. Madge Bannister as "The Fisher Maiden," from the series Fancy Dress Ball Costumes (N73) for Duke brand cigarettes. Issued by W. Duke, Sons & Co. (New York and Durham, NC), 1889. The Metropolitan Museum of Art, New York, The Jefferson R. Burdick Collection, Gift of Jefferson R. Burdick, 63.350.204.73.21.

33. "The Cost of Clothes," *Washington Post*, February 23, 1882, 2; Berlanstein, *Daughters of Eve*, 233–236.

34. "What It Costs a Prima Donna to Dress," *San Francisco Call*, January 28, 1900, 5.

35. "The Cost of Clothes," 2.

36. "Dressmakers in Paris," *The Sun*, June 30, 1901, 5.

37. Katherine B. Child, "Dress," *American Kitchen* 15, no. 2 (May 1901): 48; Sharon Marcus, *The Drama of Celebrity* (Princeton, NJ: Princeton University Press, 2019), 155.

38. Eliza Davis Aria, *Costume* (London: Macmillan, 1906), 258.

39. Parisis, "Le Costume au théâtre," *Le Figaro*, September 27, 1886, 1.

40. "Mrs. Langtry," *Michigan Farmer*, November 28, 1882, 7; Advertisement for Langtry bustle, *Harper's Bazar*, December 4, 1886, 812; "The Shopper," *Godey's Lady's Book*, July 1887, 71; Mackenzie, "Mrs. Langtry's Paris Dresses," *Frank Leslie's Weekly*, March 8, 1890, 106.

41. "Fashion Notes," *Arthur's Home Magazine*, July 1883, 439.

42. Katherine Armstrong, "Studies in Dress," *Godey's Lady's Book*, April 1888, 321.

43. Worth, *A Century of Fashion*, 161.

44. Cole and Diehl, *History of Modern Fashion*, 37, 68; "Bernhardt's New Gowns," *The Theatre*, March 29, 1886, 52; "The Queen of Fashion," *Cincinnati Enquirer*, January 28, 1888, 13.

45. De Forest, "Our Paris Letter," June 27, 1896, 542.

46. Marni Kessler, "Dusting the Surface, or the Bourgeoise, the Veil, and Haussmann's Paris," in *The Invisible Flâneuse? Gender, Public Space and Visual Culture in Nineteenth Century Paris* (Manchester, UK: Manchester University Press, 2010), 52.

47. Kessler, "Dusting the Surface," 50–52.

48. Marni Kessler, *Sheer Presence: The Veil in Manet's Paris* (Minneapolis: University of Minnesota Press, 2006), 39–40.

49. Susan Hiner, *Accessories to Modernity: Fashion and the Feminine in Nineteenth-Century France* (Philadelphia: University of Pennsylvania Press, 2010), 77–106.

50. Susan Hiner, "The Modiste's Palette and the Artist's Hat," in *Degas, Impressionism, and the Millinery Trade*, ed. Simon Kelly and Esther Bell (San Francisco: Fine Arts Museums of San Francisco, 2017), 71–72.

51. F. Adolphus, *Some Memories of Paris* (Edinburgh: W. Blackwood, 1895), 188.

52. Adolphus, *Some Memories of Paris*, 194.

53. See S/S *Campania*, Cunard Line, ship record, Norway-Heritage: Hands across the Sea, http://www.norwayheritage.com/p_ship.asp?sh=campa.

54. Montgomery, *Displaying Women*, 27.

55. Robert Muccigrosso, "New York Has a Ball: The Bradley Martin Extravaganza," *New York History* 75, no. 3 (July 1994): 300–301.

56. Patricia Beard, *After the Ball: Gilded Age Secrets, Boardroom Betrayals, and the Party That Ignited the Great Wall Street Scandal of 1905* (New York: Harper Collins, 2003), 71; Advertisement for 144 et 146, Avenue des Champs-Élysées, *Le Figaro*, July 15, 1889, 4.

57. Pascal Payen-Appenzeller, Brice Payen, and Patrick Mazery, *Dictionnaire historique, architectural et culturel des Champs-Élysées* (Paris: Ledico éditions, 2013), 494–499.

58. Advertisement for 144 et 146, Avenue des Champs-Élysées, *Le Figaro*, July 15, 1889, 4.

59. Cécile Gastaldo, "Jules Février (1842–1937), architecte méconnu à l'origine de l'hôtel Gaillard," *Livraisons de l'histoire de l'architecture* 33 (2017): 97–109.

60. Thorstein Veblen, "The Theory of the Leisure Class," in *The Collected Works of Thorstein Veblen* (London: Routledge, 1994), 1:29.

61. Gail MacColl and Carol Wallace, *To Marry an English Lord* (New York: Workman, 1989), 140.

62. Invoices from Franck Trousseaux & Layettes, Monsieur Virot, and Madame Léoty Corsets to Madame Goelet, 1891, Goelet Family Papers, Series 4: Personal expenses, Salve Regina University, Newport, RI.

63. Goelet Family Papers, Series 4: Personal expenses, Salve Regina University, Newport, RI.

64. Montgomery, *Displaying Women*, 23; Chauncey Hotchkiss, "Mrs. Astor at Home," *New York World*, January 8, 1905, magazine section, 1.

65 Elizabeth Drexel Lehr (Lady Decies), *King Lehr and the Gilded Age: With Extracts from the Locked Diary of Harry Lehr* (Bedford, MA: Applewood Books, 2005), 85; "Mr. William Astor's Funeral," *International Herald Tribune*, April 29, 1892, 1.

66. "Astor Wedding," *Rutland Daily Globe*, March 28, 1876, 1.

67. The couple lived in England until her death from unknown causes in 1893.

68. "A Notable Social Event," *New York Times*, November 19, 1878, 1.

69. "Globelets," *Daily Globe* (St. Paul, MN), November 8, 1879, 2.

70. "Mrs. Drayton Married," *New York Times*, December 18, 1896, 8; "Married," *New York Times*, December 19, 1896, 8.

71. "Wilson-Astor Wedding," *News and Citizen*, December 18, 1884, 1.

72. "The Season's Fashions," *Brooklyn Daily Eagle,* October 26, 1884, 10; "Our Notebook," *Illustrated London News*, December 6, 1884, 547. The rest of the trousseau by Worth is described in "A Wedding amid Flowers," *New York Times*, November 19, 1884, 5.

73. "An Astor as a Bride," *Indianapolis Journal*, November 12, 1884, 5; "The Wilson-Astor Wedding," *Indianapolis Journal*, November 19, 1884, 5.

74. "The Wilson-Astor Wedding," *Indianapolis Journal*, November 19, 1884, 5.

75. "Wilson-Astor Wedding," *News and Citizen*, December 18, 1884, 1.

76. "A Magnificent Wedding," *New York Times*, February 18, 1891, 1; Harvey O'Connor, *The Astors* (New York: A. A. Knopf, 1941), 220.

77. Rebecca J. Kelly, "Fashion in the Gilded Age: A Profile of Newport's King Family," in *Twentieth-Century American Fashion*, ed. Linda Welters and Patricia A. Cunningham (Oxford: Berg, 2008), 9–32.

78. Kelly, "Fashion in the Gilded Age," 9–32.

79. Beard, *After the Ball*, 70.

80. Charles L. Robertson, *The International Herald Tribune: The First Hundred Years* (New York: Columbia University Press, 1987), 41.

81. Beard, *After the Ball*, 73; Elizabeth Otis Williams, *Sojourning, Shopping and Studying in Paris: A Handbook Particularly for Women* (Chicago: A. C. McClurg, 1907), 49.

82. Huybertie Pruyn Hamlin, *An Albany Girlhood* (Albany, NY: Washington Park Press, 1990), 299.

83. Hamlin, *An Albany Girlhood*, 315. The wedding dress was deaccessioned by the Albany Institute in the 1970s.

84. King, *A Season of Splendor*, 28; Sylvia D. Hoffert, *Alva Vanderbilt Belmont: Unlikely Champion of Women's Rights* (Bloomington: Indiana University Press, 2012), 11–14, 32; Stuart, *Consuelo and Alva Vanderbilt*, 31–33, 42.

85. George B. Watts, "The Teaching of French in the United States: A History," *French Review* (American Association of Teachers of French) 37, no. 1 (October 1963): 40.

86. Richard Harding Davis, *About Paris* (New York: Harper, 1895), 186, 190.

87. Green, *The Other Americans in Paris*, 6–7.

88. Green, *The Other Americans in Paris*, 7.

89. *Résultats statistiques dénombrement de 1896 pour la ville de Paris* (Paris: G. Masson, 1899), 35.

90. *Résultats statistiques dénombrement de 1896 pour la ville de Paris*, 35.

91. *Annuaire statistique de la ville de Paris, 1901* (Paris: Masson et cie, 1903), 142–143.

92. Green, *The Other Americans in Paris*, 17.

93. Green, *The Other Americans in Paris*, 7.

94. Albert Sutliffe, *The Americans in Paris* (Paris: Printed for the author and editor, 1887), 59–60.

95. Metternich-Winneburg, *My Years in Paris*, 134.

96. William Edward Johnston, *Memoirs of "Malakoff": Being Extracts from the Correspondence of the Late William Edward Johnson*, ed. Robert Matteson Johnston (London: Hutchinson, 1907), 2:451.

97. Johnston, *Memoirs of "Malakoff,"* 2:451.

98. Johnston, *Memoirs of "Malakoff,"* 2:452.

99. François Guillaume Dumas, ed., *Illustrated Biographies of Modern Artists* (Paris: Baschet, 1882), 260.

100. Leanne Zalewski, "Alexandre Cabanel's Portraits of the American 'Aristocracy' of the Early Gilded Age," *Nineteenth-Century Art Worldwide* 4, no. 1 (Spring 2005), http://www.19thc-artworldwide.org/spring05/300–alexandre-cabanels-portraits-of-the-american-aristocracy-of-the-early-gilded-age. Cabanel's painting of Leiter is at Kedleston Hall, Derbyshire, England.

101. "Will Wed Today," *Daily Globe*, April 22, 1895, 1; Nigel Nicolson, *Mary Curzon* (New York: Harper & Row, 1977), 78–79; Thomas, "Embodying Imperial Spectacle," 369–400.

102. Vincent Meylan, *The Secret Archives of Boucheron* (Woodbridge, Suffolk, UK: Antique Collectors Club, 2011), 59–60.

103. See Tiffany & Co. (U.S., 1837–present). Cup from the Mackay Service, 1878. Silver-gilt and enamel. The Metropolitan Museum of Art, New York, Purchase, Cranshaw Corporation Gift, 2017, 2017.196.3.

104. "Mrs. Mackay's Jewels," *New York Times*, January 14, 1884, 5; Meylan, *The Secret Archives of Boucheron*, 59–67.

105. For example, "Mrs. Mackay in Paris," *Eureka Daily Sentinel*, August 3, 1884, 3.

106. "Miss Mackay's Marriage," *New York Times*, February 25, 1885, 3.

107. "Mrs. Mackay's Portrait," *Daily Alta California*, March 17, 1884, 8; "Un Meissonier détruit," *Le Gaulois*, February 16, 1884, 1.

108. Laura Carter Holloway, *Famous American Fortunes and the Men Who Have Made Them* (Philadelphia: Garretson, 1885), 79.

109. "Palmer Honoré Brilliant Wedding in High Life," *Chicago Tribune*, July 29, 1870.

110. Jachimowicz, *Eight Chicago Women and Their Fashions, 1860–1929*, 19–23. Much of the Potter Palmers' paintings collection was acquired by the Art Institute of Chicago.

111. "Wedding Gifts for Miss Grant," *International Herald Tribune*, September 24, 1899, 1.

112. Ishbel Ross, *Silhouette in Diamonds: The Life of Mrs. Potter Palmer* (New York: Arno Press, 1975); Jachimowitz, *Eight Chicago Women and Their Fashions*, 20.

113. Jachimowitz, *Eight Chicago Women and Their Fashions*, 47. Pingat was sold to A. Wallès & cie in 1896. Lily Fehler, "1820–1901—Emile Pingat," Fashion History Timeline, Fashion Institute of Technology, State University of New York, last updated July 14, 2020, https://fashionhistory.fitnyc.edu/1820-1901-emile-pingat.

114. Jachimowitz, *Eight Chicago Women and Their Fashions*, 47; George Peter Alexander Healy (U.S., 1813–1894). *Abbie Louise Spencer Eddy*, 1878. Chicago History Museum, 1979.54.; Emile Pingat (French, ca. 1820–1901). Dinner dress, 1878. Silk brocade, lace, silk satin. Chicago History Museum, Gift of Mr. Albert J. Beveridge, III, 1976.270.1a-b. The travel logs and a photograph of Eddy in the dress were formerly in the Chicago History Museum. Their location is now unknown.

115. Elizabeth Jachimowicz, "Where to Shop in 1890: The European Addresses of a Chicago Lady," in *Aspects of Costume: The Nineteenth Century. Selected Papers*, ed. Mariliina Perkko (Alfabox, Finland: ICOM International Costume Committee, 1990), 12. The Glessner Family Papers are in the Chicago History Museum, Research Center.

116. Jachimowicz, "Where to Shop in 1890," 14.

117. Object record for Emile Pingat (French, ca. 1820–1901). Dinner dress, 1878. Silk brocade, lace, silk satin. Chicago History Museum, Gift of Mr. Albert J. Beveridge, III, 1976.270.1a-b.

118. Jachimowicz, "Where to Shop in 1890," 15–16.

119. Harriet S. Blaine, ed., *Letters of Mrs. James G. Blaine* (New York: Duffield, 1908), 297.

120. Blaine, *Letters of Mrs. James G. Blaine*, 120.

121. "Le mariage du président des États-Unis," *La Petite Presse*, May 8, 1886, 1; "Lectures étrangères," *Le Temps*, May 11, 1886, 3; Anna Dunlap, *Frank: The Story of Frances Folsom Cleveland, America's Youngest First Lady* (Albany, NY: Excelsior Editions, 2009), 3, 125; "Miss Folsom's Gowns," *New York Times*, May 30, 1886.

122. Skirt and bodices worn by Frances Folsom Cleveland. Original floral chine skirt and peach velvet bodice, probably ca. 1895 by the House of Doucet, Paris. Floral bodice created later from fabric taken out of the skirt. Green velvet bodice made by dressmaker Lottie M. Barton of Baltimore. National Museum of American History, Smithsonian Institution, Washington, DC, Gifts of Mr. and Mrs. Richard Cleveland and the Heirs of the Estates of Richard F. and Jessie B. Cleveland, 253358.

123. Cole and Diehl, *History of Modern Fashion*, 23; Frank G. Carpenter, *Carp's Washington* (New York: McGraw-Hill, 1960), 101.

124. Carpenter, *Carp's Washington*, 101.

125. Advertisement for J. Rochon, *Evening Star*, January 14, 1886, 4.

126. Marguerite Cassini, *Never a Dull Moment* (New York: Harper and Brothers, 1956), 144.

127. Cassini, *Never a Dull Moment*, 134.

128. Cassini, *Never a Dull Moment*, 134.

129. Cassini, *Never a Dull Moment*, 146–147.

130. Edwards, *New Spirits*, 98.

131. "Some Americans Who Have Married Titles," *Cosmopolitan*, July 1899, 227–237.

132. "Saunterings," *Town Topics*, November 14, 1895, 7. The column was overseen by editor-in-chief Colonel E. D. Mann. Other disdainful reporters expressed concern over the amount of millions the brides took out of circulation in the United States. For example, "Women Who Wedded Titles," *Salt Lake Herald*, March 24, 1895, 15.

133. "Joseph Chamberlain," *New York Graphic*, November 17, 1888, 3.

134. "Twenty Newport Girls Worth $200,000,000," *Saint Paul Globe*, June 14, 1896, 22.

135. "Racing for Titles," *Bottineau Courant*, May 27, 1899, 2.

136. William Dean Howells, *A Fearful Responsibility* and *Tonelli's Marriage* (Edinburgh: David Douglas, 1882), 97.

137. "Bloc-Notes Parisien," *Le Gaulois*, May 14, 1895, 1.

138. "Saunterings," *Town Topics*, November 14, 1895, 7.

139. MacColl and Wallace, *To Marry an English Lord*, 163.

140. "Causerie," *Journal du dimanche: Littérature, histoire, voyages, musique*, April 3, 1895, 1.

141. "The Gould Marriage," *The World*, February 24, 1895, 22.

142. Ella Star, "The Gould-Castellane Wedding," *Frank Leslie's Weekly*, March 14, 1895, 170–172.

143. Maurice M. Minton, "Now a French Countess," *New York Times*, March 5, 1895, 1.

144. Star, "The Gould-Castellane Wedding," 172.

145. Boniface de Castellane, *How I Discovered America: Confessions of the Marquis Boni de Castellane* (New York: Alfred A. Knopf, 1924), 157.

146. "The Chamberlain-Endicott Marriage," *Boston Weekly Globe*, November 14, 1888, 1.

147. Hoffert, *Alva Vanderbilt Belmont*, 42–49; "Saunterings," *Town Topics*, November 14, 1895, 2.

148. "Features: Miss Consuelo Vanderbilt's Trousseau," *Vogue*, November 14, 1895, 330–332; Cole and Diehl, *History of Modern Fashion*, 66.

149. "Fashion: Bridal Gown—Miss Consuelo Vanderbilt," *Vogue*, November 14, 1895, 315.

150. Consuelo Vanderbilt Balsan, *The Glitter and the Gold* (London: Heinemann, 1953), 41–42. For example, "Price Never Asked," *Richmond Dispatch*, October 20, 1895, 6.

151. For example, "She Has Landed Her Duke," *The Herald*, September 21, 1895, 1.

152. Hoffert, *Alva Vanderbilt Belmont*, 40–41.

153. Katherine Armstrong, [Untitled], *Godey's Lady's Book*, October 1887, 296.

154. Craig Clinton, *Cora Urquhart Potter: The Victorian Actress as Provocateur* (Jefferson, NC: McFarland, 2010), 3.

155. Clinton, *Cora Urquhart Potter*, 3.

156. Alan Dale, *Queens of the Stage* (New York: G. W. Dillingham, 1896), 57–58.

157. "Langtry and Brown Potter," *Hartford Courant*, September 18, 1888, 2.

158. Clinton, *Cora Urquhart Potter*, 35.

159. Cited in Clinton, *Cora Urquhart Potter*, 98–99.

160. For example, "A New Play in London," *New York Times*, April 13, 1899, 7.

161. Veblen, "The Theory of the Leisure Class," 29.

CHAPTER 6

1. "Masters of Fashion," *Brooklyn Daily Eagle*, January 31, 1897, 15.

2. "Description des coiffures," *Le Journal des coiffeurs: Publication des coiffeurs réunis*, January 1, 1843, 754. The present chapter updates some information on maison Félix in Elizabeth L. Block, "Maison Félix Couturier and the Body Types of Its Clients, 1875–1900," *West 86th: A Journal of Decorative Arts, Design History, and Material Culture* 26, no. 1 (Spring–Summer 2019): 80–103.

3. *Mémorial du commerce et de l'industrie: Répertoire universel, théorique et pratique, législatif et judiciaire de la science commerciale* (Paris, 1860), 476; L. Bourne, "M. Émile Félix," *Le Panthéon de l'industrie: Journal hebdomadaire illustré*, May 14, 1882, 145; "La Coiffure, c'est l'homme," *Le Moniteur de la coiffure: Journal mensuel de l'art du coiffeur*, June 10, 1864, 7; "Causerie," *Le Moniteur de la coiffure: Journal mensuel de l'art du coiffeur*, November 10, 1869, 4; Henry Poujol, "Women's Hair," *St. Louis Globe-Democrat*, June 5, 1881, 18.

4. John Maass, *The Glorious Enterprise: The Centennial Exhibition of 1876 and H. J. Schwarzmann, Architect-in-Chief* (Watkins Glen, NY: Institute for the Study of Universal History through Arts and Artifacts, 1973), 50, 105, fig. 14.

5. Bourne, "M. Émile Félix," 145; Bennet, *Biographies de personnalités mutualists*, 361–364.

6. Throughout this book, "Félix" is used interchangeably with "maison Félix." The owner of the maison is referred to as Émile Martin Poussineau. Émile Martin Poussineau married Marie-Rose Berthé Renault (1848–1924) in 1875, and they had four children together.

7. Bourne, "M. Émile Félix," 145–146.

8. "New French Gowns," *New York Times*, November 11, 1888, 2. By 1895, there was a full section for hats. "At the Costumers," *International Herald Tribune*, May 12, 1895, 8. The earliest mention of Félix at 15, rue du Faubourg Saint-Honoré is "Modes," *Le Journal des coiffeurs: Publication des coiffeurs réunis*, July 1, 1849, 55, where coiffures are featured, and it is also listed as a parfumerie at that location. The business appears in *Annuaire-almanach du commerce, de l'industrie, de la magistrature et de l'administration* as early as 1857 as "coiffeur" at 15, rue du Faubourg Saint-Honoré and continues almost yearly through 1901.

9. See *Annuaire-almanach du commerce, de l'industrie, de la magistrature et de l'administration*, 1857–1901; and Charles Dickens, *Dickens's Dictionary of Paris: An Unconventional Handbook* (London: Macmillan, 1882), 262.

10. Child, "Dress," 48–49; Véronique Pouillard, "Design Piracy in the Fashion Industries of Paris and New York in the Interwar Years," *Business History Review* 85 (Summer 2011): 322; De

la Haye and Mendes, *The House of Worth*, 52. The firm also seems to have tried out designing handbags. A prototype woolen bag with leather straps and metal buckles is in the Archives de Paris: Filing D6U10 558 T 6190 of December 31, 1870, by Auguste Poussineau. Greffe des Tissus du Conseil de Prud'hommes de Paris. I thank Jean-Charles Virmaux for providing this information.

11. Merceron, *Lanvin*, 32, 366; Tétart-Vittu, "Key Dates," 277. Poussineau's first name is erroneously given as Étienne.

12. Eric Poussineau, email to the author, March 17, 2017. There are no known archives for maison Félix.

13. M. Griffith, "Paris Dressmakers," *Strand Magazine: An Illustrated Monthly*, July–December 1894, 748–750; "Dressmakers of Paris," *Washington Post*, March 25, 1888, 10; Brevik-Zender, *Fashioning Spaces*, 209–212, 318n21; "Features: Paris," *Vogue*, January 18, 1894, S3.

14. For Félix's use of live models, see Emma Bullet, "Dress Show Exegesis," *Brooklyn Daily Eagle*, January 7, 1894, 5; Intime, "A Parisian Prince of Dress," *Lady's Realm: An Illustrated Monthly Magazine* 9 (November 1900–April 1901): 25.

15. Intime, "A Parisian Prince of Dress," 23; "La toilette féminine en 1897," *Le Figaro*, supplément exceptionnel, August 19, 1897, 1–3.

16. A. E. F. Eliot-James, "Shopping in London," *Woman's World*, 1889, 5.

17. Isabel Dundas, "Fashions' Mirror," *Godey's Lady's Book*, February 1895, 209. See Block, "Maison Félix Couturier and the Body Types of Its Clients, 1875–1900."

18. Block, "Maison Félix Couturier and the Body Types of Its Clients," 88.

19. Sarah Bernhardt, *My Double Life: The Memoirs of Sarah Bernhardt*, trans. Victoria Tietze Larson (Albany: State University of New York Press, 1999), 38, 152.

20. Mary Louise Roberts, *Disruptive Acts: The New Woman in Fin-de-Siècle France* (Chicago: University of Chicago Press, 2002), 124.

21. "Women's Department," *Morning Oregonian*, December 2, 1894, 13.

22. The only extant volume of *Félix-Mode* is from 1897 and is in the Bibliothèque nationale de France in Paris. Later mentions of the periodical are in A. Martinot, *Bulletin des nominations, informations, lois nouvelles et décrets* (Paris: Neuilly, July 7, 1900), 2 and (Paris: Neuilly, January 4, 1901), 2.

23. For example, *La Mode de style*, December 16, 1891, 402.

24. "Social and Personal," *Washington Times*, June 30, 1901, 5.

25. Richard Wagner and Cosima Wagner, *Lettres à Judith Gautier* (Paris: Gallimard, 1964), 177–182 (letters 35, 36, and 37, fols. 163–168), 321n2 (trans. Sarah McFadden).

26. Wagner and Wagner, *Lettres à Judith Gautier*, 177, fols. 163–168, March–April 1877 (trans. Sarah McFadden).

27. Wagner and Wagner, *Lettres à Judith Gautier*, 178, fols. 165–168, April 2, 1877 (trans. Sarah McFadden).

28. Wagner and Wagner, *Lettres à Judith Gautier*, 181, fol. 161–162, April 1877 (trans. Sarah McFadden).

29. "Tribunaux," *Le Temps*, February 11, 1884, 3.

30. Wagner and Wagner, *Lettres à Judith Gautier*, 177, fols. 163–164, March 1877.

31. "Visits to Dressmakers," *International Herald Tribune*, January 5, 1896, 2.

32. "Visits to Dressmakers," 2.

33. "Judgment against Mrs. Carter," *Evening Times*, February 6, 1901, 5; "Dressmakers in Paris," *The Sun*, June 30, 1901, 5.

34. Intime, "A Parisian Prince of Dress," 25. On Worth keeping measurements on file, see Marie Belloc, "La Maison Worth," *Lady's Realm* 1 (November 1896–April 1897): 144.

35. Intime, "A Parisian Prince of Dress," 22.

36. Émile Martin Poussineau, unpublished memoir, collection of Martin Chatillon, France. Client letters to Félix—from Isabelle d'Orléans, comtesse de Paris; la comtesse d'Eu; Louise Geyer (on behalf of the duchesse d'Aumale); la maréchale de Mac-Mahon; and Madame Carnot—were sold at auction by Rossini in 2006. *Lettres et manuscrits autographes, documents historiques salle des ventes Rossini, 7 avril 2006* (Paris: T. Bodin, 2006), lot 201. I thank Marie-France Faudi for this information. For Félix's designs for Maria Pia, see "Paris and Vienna Salons," *Le Follet*, November 1, 1896, 7–8.

37. Olivier Saillard, Valerie Steele, and Claude Arnaud, *La Mode retrouvée: Les robes trésors de la comtesse Greffulhe* (Paris: Palais Galliera, 2015), 16–17.

38. Constance de Castelbajac and Eric Mension-Rigau, *Journal de Constance de Castelbajac, marquise de Breteuil: 1885–1886* (Paris: Perrin, 2003), 209.

39. "A Gown of Lilac Silk and Diamonds," *San Francisco Call*, June 7, 1896, 26.

40. "Life in the French Chateaux," *International Herald Tribune*, November 19, 1899, 2.

41. Representative examples are provided here. For Bernhardt, see "Tribunaux," *Le Temps*, February 11, 1884, 3; for Bernhardt and several others, see "New Gowns in Paris," *Daily Evening Bulletin*, April 15, 1882, 7; for Croizette, see "Courrier des théatres," *Le Figaro*, February 15, 1876, 3; for Langtry, see Emma Bullet, "Her Toilets: Mrs. Langtry's Preparations in Paris for America," *Brooklyn Daily Eagle*, October 2, 1886, 4; for Réjane, see "Le Théatre et les spectacles," *Le Ménestrel: Journal de musique*, April 7, 1901, 107; for Hading, see "Les Toilettes de Félix," suppl. to *Le Gaulois*, March 1, 1885, 2; for Russell, see "Lillian Russell's Gowns," *Detroit Free Press*, December 2, 1894, 10; for Judic, see "Stage and Other Gowns," *New York Times*, April 27, 1890, 16; for Rehan, see Mrs. Fenwick-Miller, "The Ladies' Column," *Illustrated London News*, November 28, 1891, 712; for Tempest, Hector Bolitho, *Marie Tempest* (Philadelphia: J. B. Lippincott, 1937), 89.

42. See, for example, "Mlle Bernhardt Arrives," *New York Times*, October 28, 1880, 8. For Croizette, see "Courrier des théatres," *Le Figaro*, February 15, 1876, 3; "Sarah Bernhardt," *St. Louis Globe-Democrat*, April 25, 1880, 15. The article mistakenly identifies Émile Martin Poussineau as the son of Joseph-Augustin Escalier, the original founder of maison Félix.

43. Bullet, "Her Toilets," 4.

44. Elizabeth L. Block, "Virginie Amélie Avegno Gautreau: Living Statue," *Nineteenth-Century Art Worldwide* 17, no. 2 (Autumn 2018), https://doi.org/10.29411/ncaw.2018.17.2.4; "La Belle Americaine," *New York Herald*, March 30, 1880.

45. "Sarah Bernhardt," 15.

46. Bullet, "Her Toilets," 4.

47. "New Gowns in Paris," 7.

48. Sadie E. Martin, *The Life and Professional Career of Emma Abbott* (Minneapolis, MN: L. Kimball Printing Company, 1891), 43, 86.

49. Martin, *The Life and Professional Career of Emma Abbott*, 92–93.

50. "The Buskined Stage," *Los Angeles Herald*, December 22, 1890, 2; "Gorgeous Gowns," *Atlanta Constitution*, January 19, 1890, 12.

51. Griffith, "Paris Dressmakers," 746.

52. Quoted in "Masters of Fashion," 15. See also Baroness Alethea Salvador, "Paris Winter Fashions," *Washington Post*, October 23, 1887, 7.

53. "Social and Personal," *Washington Times*, June 30, 1901, 5.

54. Marian Adams and Ward Thoron, *The Letters of Mrs. Henry Adams, 1865–1883* (Boston: Little, Brown, 1936), 179–180.

55. Mark Twain and Charles Dudley Warner, *The Gilded Age: A Novel* (London: George Routledge and Sons, 1874), 169.

56. Henry Adams to Charles Milnes Gaskell, August 25, 1867, in Henry Adams, *The Letters of Henry Adams*, ed. J. C. Levenson et al. (Cambridge, MA: Harvard University Press, 1982), 1:546.

57. "Fashion Interviews," *International Herald Tribune*, September 4, 1892, 5.

58. Intime, "Parisian Prince of Dress," 24–25.

59. "Dressmakers of Paris," 10.

60. Block, "Maison Félix Couturier and the Body Types of Its Clients," 95–97; Object file for Fancy dress costume. French. Silk, metal. The Metropolitan Museum of Art, New York, Gift of Orme Wilson and R. Thornton Wilson, in memory of their mother, Mrs. Caroline Schermerhorn Astor Wilson, 1949, 49.3.1a–c.

61. It was exhibited as Félix in two exhibitions at the Metropolitan Museum of Art, New York: *Seeds of Fashion* (February–August 1951) and *Dance* (December 17, 1986–September 6, 1987).

62. I thank Anna Yanofsky and Elizabeth Randolph for these observations.

63. See Marie Simon, *Fashion in Art: The Second Empire and Impressionism* (London: Zwemmer, 1995), 102–103.

64. Franck Trousseaux & Layettes, "Invoice from Franck to Madame Goelet" (1891), Goelet Family Papers, Series 4: Personal expenses, Salve Regina University, Newport, RI, 196.

CHAPTER 7

1. Chauncey Hotchkiss, "Mrs. Astor at Home," *New York World*, January 8, 1905, magazine section, 1; "Mrs. Astor Quits as Society Head," *Los Angeles Herald*, October 21, 1906, 8; "Mrs. W. Astor, Society Leader, Dies in Old Age," *Los Angeles Herald*, October 31, 1908, 1.

2. The ball at which she first wore the outfit has not yet been determined, but a similar dress is described in "Mrs. Astor's Dresses," *Richmond Dispatch*, November 24, 1889, 7. For the painting, see Simon, *Fashion in Art*, 102–103.

3. Entwistle and Wilson, *Body Dressing*, 1–10; Joanne Entwistle, *The Fashioned Body: Fashion, Dress and Modern Social Theory* (Cambridge, UK: Polity, 2015), 5. See also Sophie Woodward, *Why Women Wear What They Wear* (Oxford: Berg Publishers, 2007), 1–8. For fashion and interior design, see Montgomery, *Displaying Women*, 65–72; Troy, *Couture Culture*, 336; John Potvin, "The Velvet Masquerade: Fashion, Interior Design and the Furnished Body," in *Fashion, Interior Design, and the Contours of Modern Identity*, ed. Alla Myzelev and John Potvin (Surrey, UK: Ashgate, 2010), 9; Joel Sanders, "The Future of Cross-Disciplinary Practice," in *Shaping the American Interior: Structures, Contexts and Practices*, ed. Paula Lupkin and Penny Sparke (New York: Routledge, 2018), 195–197.

4. Veblen, "The Theory of the Leisure Class," 85; Colin Campbell, *The Romantic Ethic and the Spirit of Modern Consumerism*, new extended ed. (Cham, Switzerland: Palgrave Macmillan, 2018), 95–96.

5. See Andrew B. Trigg, "Veblen, Bourdieu, and Conspicuous Consumption," *Journal of Economic Issues* 35, no. 1 (March 2001): 108–109.

6. Veblen, "The Theory of the Leisure Class," 29.

7. Pierre Bourdieu, "The Forms of Capital," in *Handbook of Theory and Research for the Sociology of Education*, ed. John Richardson, trans. Richard Nice (241–258) (New York: Greenwood, 1986).

8. "A Social Barrier Broken Down," *Daily Evening Bulletin*, April 2, 1883, n.p.

9. Robert A. M. Stern, Thomas Mellins, and David Fishman, *New York 1880: Architecture and Urbanism in the Gilded Age* (New York: Monacelli Press, 1999), 570–600; King, *A Season of Splendor*, 141–164.

10. Stern, Mellins, and Fishman, *New York 1880*, 578–600; Michael C. Kathrens, *Great Houses of New York, 1880–1930* (New York: Acanthus Press, 2005), 26–42; Wayne Craven, *Gilded Mansions: Grand Architecture and High Society* (New York: W. W. Norton, 2009), 81–149; King, *A Season of Splendor*, 142–151; Thomas Mellins, "Architecture in Gilded Age New York," in *Gilded New York: Design, Fashion, and Society*, ed. Donald Albrecht and Jeannine Falino (New York: Monacelli Press, 2013), 138–141. See also "The Architectural Progress of New York City," *Frank Leslie's Popular Monthly*, April 1883, 4–9.

11. Penny Sparke, "The Domestic Interior and the Construction of Self: The New York Homes of Elsie de Wolfe," in *Interior Design and Identity*, ed. Susie McKellar and Penny Sparke (Manchester, UK: Manchester University Press, 2004), 73; Penny Sparke, "Elsie de Wolfe: A Professional Interior Decorator," in Lupkin and Sparke, *Shaping the American Interior*, 47–58.

12. Sparke, "Elsie de Wolfe," 50.

13. "A Paris Mania," *Cottage Hearth*, June 1875, 161.

14. Bruno Pons, *French Period Rooms, 1650–1800: Rebuilt in England, France, and the Americas*, trans. Ann Sautier-Greening (Dijon, France: Faton éditions, 1995), 96, 158.

15. Virginia Brilliant, Paul F. Miller, and Françoise Barbe, *Gothic Art in the Gilded Age: Medieval and Renaissance Treasures in the Gavet-Vanderbilt-Ringling Collection* (Sarasota, FL: John and Mable Ringling Museum of Art, 2009), xiii; Henry Balch Ingram, "Mr. Vanderbilt's Marble Hall," *Frank Leslie's Weekly*, February 27, 1892, 65.

16. "Her Millions for a Coronet," *The Redwood Gazette*, November 7, 1895, 7; Hoffert, *Alva Vanderbilt Belmont*, 1.

17. Belmont, Alva E. Belmont Memoir, 6.

18. Belmont, Alva E. Belmont Memoir, 10.

19. Belmont, Alva E. Belmont Memoir, 33, 38.

20. Belmont, Alva E. Belmont Memoir, 29–30.

21. Belmont, Alva E. Belmont Memoir, 32.

22. Eric Homberger, *Mrs. Astor's New York: Money and Social Power in a Gilded Age* (New Haven, CT: Yale University Press, 2002), 10–11; Hoffert, *Alva Vanderbilt Belmont*, 27–28.

23. Paul F. Miller, "Alva Vanderbilt Belmont, Arbiter Elegantiarum, and Her Gothic Salon at Newport, Rhode Island," *Journal of the History of Collections* 27, no. 3 (2015): 349; Murphy, "The François Premier Style in New York," 42.

24. Belmont, Alva E. Belmont Memoir, 70.

25. Belmont, Alva E. Belmont Memoir, 70.

26. Anca I. Lasc, Georgina Downey, and Mark Taylor, eds., *Designing the French Interior: The Modern Home and Mass Media* (London: Bloomsbury, 2015), 1–3; Anca I. Lasc, *Interior Decorating in Nineteenth-Century France: The Visual Culture of a New Profession* (Manchester, UK: Manchester University Press, 2018), 16–21.

27. Belmont, Alva E. Belmont Memoir, 92.

28. Miller, "Alva Vanderbilt Belmont," 351–352.

29. Miller, "Alva Vanderbilt Belmont," 356. The Allard firm opened a New York branch in 1885.

30. John Foreman and Robbe Pierce Stimson, *The Vanderbilts and the Gilded Age: Architectural Aspirations, 1879–1901* (New York: St. Martin's Press, 1991), 38–39; Murphy, "The François Premier Style in New York," 48; "Gentlewoman at Home," *The Gentlewoman and Modern Life* 28 (April 9, 1904): 493; "New York's Great Dazzle," *St. Louis Globe-Democrat*, March 29, 1883, 2.

31. Craven, *Gilded Mansions*, 110–127; Edward Strahan (Earl Shinn), *Mr. Vanderbilt's House and Collection* (Boston: George Barrie, 1883–1884); Leanne Zalewski, "Art for the Public: William Henry Vanderbilt's Cultural Legacy," *Nineteenth-Century Art Worldwide* 11, no. 2 (Summer 2012), http://www.19thc-artworldwide.org/summer12/leanne-zalewski-william-henry-vanderbilts-cultural-legacy.

32. Belmont, Alva E. Belmont Memoir typescript, 105.

33. Susan Gail Johnson, "Like a Glimpse of Gay Old Versailles: Three Gilded Age Balls," in Albrecht and Falino, *Gilded New York*, 89. For the social mores of dress requirements and the extravagance of balls, see Diana De Marly, *Worth: Father of Haute Couture* (London: Elm Tree Books, 1980), 60–74; Sophia Murphy, *The Duchess of Devonshire's Ball* (London: Sidgwick & Jackson, 1984), passim; Homberger, *Mrs. Astor's New York*, 120–148.

34. "Festivity at Eastertide," *New York Times*, March 25, 1883, 14; "All Society in Costume," *New York Times*, March 27, 1883, 1; "The Vanderbilt Ball," *New York Tribune*, March 27, 1883, 5; Charles H. Crandall, *The Season: An Annual Record of Society in New York, Brooklyn, and Vicinity* (New York: White, Stokes, & Allen, 1883), 298–299; Ward McAllister, *Society as I Have Found It* (New York: Cassell, 1890), 354; Homberger, *Mrs. Astor's New York*, 14; Craven, *Gilded*

Mansions, 125–126; Susan Gail Johnson, "Like a Glimpse of Gay Old Versailles: Three Gilded Age Balls," in Albrecht and Falino, *Gilded New York*, 89.

35. "The Vanderbilt Fancy Ball," *Harper's Bazar*, April 21, 1883, 242; Susannah Broyles, "Vanderbilt Ball—How a Costume Ball Changed New York Elite Society," *New York Stories* (blog), Museum of the City New York, August 6, 2013, https://blog.mcny.org/2013/08/06/vanderbilt -ball-how-a-costume-ball-changed-new-york-elite-society/; King, *A Season of Splendor*, 361.

36. The *Brooklyn Daily Eagle* reported that a number of men continued the party at the newly built Union League Club on 5th Avenue at 39th Street, in "all stages of *deshabille* . . . the silk and satin shimmered in the rays of the ascending sun." "Life in New York City," *Brooklyn Daily Eagle*, April 1, 1883, 1.

37. For example, Abby Longstreet Buchanan, *Social Etiquette of New York* (New York: Appleton, 1888), 200–206.

38. "Amusements This Evening," *New York Times*, March 26, 1883; "Mme Patti in 'Rigoletto,'" *New York Times*, March 27, 1883, 5; Homberger, *Mrs. Astor's New York*, 226–237.

39. "All Society in Costume," 1. See also "Marvels of Fancy Dress," *The Sun*, March 27, 1883, 1; Magidson, "A Fashionable Equation," 112.

40. Johnson, "Like a Glimpse of Gay Old Versailles," 90. See also "Personal," *Harper's Bazar*, March 24, 1883, 179, which reported that the Star Quadrille at the Vanderbilt ball was expected to be "illustrated by the electric light if possible, and each lady will carry a small electric battery." A later article related that the electric light "had to be abandoned as a too uncertain guest." See also "The Vanderbilt Fancy Ball," *Harper's Bazar*, April 21, 1883, 242.

41. "All Society in Costume," 1. See also "Festivity at Eastertide," 14. Klunder designed the flowers for many of Astors' events. His shop was near 307 5th Avenue.

42. Crandall, *The Season*, 296; "The Vanderbilt Ball," *New York Tribune*, March 27, 1883, 5; "New York's Great Dazzle," 2.

43. "Festivity at Eastertide," 14. See also "Costumes of History and Romance," *Art Amateur*, May 1883, 142; "New York's Great Dazzle," 2.

44. Crandall, *The Season*, 300; "A Beautiful Ball," *The Milwaukee Sentinel*, March 27, 1883, 3.

45. Ardern Holt, *Fancy Dresses Described: Or, What to Wear at Fancy Balls* (London: Debenham and Freebody, 1879). Holt later published *Gentlemen's Fancy Dress: How to Choose It* (London: Wyman & Sons, 1882).

46. See Jose Maria Mora, *Mrs. William Seward Webb (neé Lila Osgood Vanderbilt) as Hornet*, 1883, Museum of the City of New York, 41.132.63. Holt's influence extended to Canada, where a certain Laura Smith wore a similar hornet outfit to the Ottawa Skating Carnival in 1889. See William James Topley (Canadian, 1845–1930), Miss L. Smith, April 1889. Photograph. National Archives of Canada, 1936-270 NPC. The concept also appealed to children. See plate 035, 1884–1887, Costume Institute Fashion Plates, The Metropolitan Museum of Art, New York.

47. "All Society in Costume," 1; Benjamin Linley Wild, *Carnival to Catwalk: Global Reflections on Fancy Dress Costume* (London: Bloomsbury Visual Arts, 2020), 37.

48. *Puck*, October 12, 1881, cover; *Puck*, April 18, 1883, centerfold.

49. *Puck*, December 10, 1879, 650–651; *Puck*, October 29, 1884, cover.

50. Belmont, Alva E. Belmont Memoir, 108. For a photograph of Yznaga at the ball, see Jose Maria Mora, *Lady Mandeville (née Consuelo Yznaga), William K. Vanderbilt ball, March 26, 1883*, Museum of the City of New York, X2012.96.2.31.

51. Holt, *Fancy Dresses Described*, vii.

52. Holt, *Fancy Dresses Described*, 4.

53. "Calico Party," *Los Angeles Herald*, May 6, 1881, 3.

54. Kawamura, *Fashion-ology*, chap. 3.

55. For example, "New York City Life," *Brooklyn Daily Eagle*, April 15, 1883, 1; "An Easter Ball," *Godey's Lady's Book*, May 1883, 458; Albrecht and Falino, *Gilded New York*, 45.

56. Mora's photographs of the Vanderbilt ball are held in the Museum of the City of New York, the New-York Historical Society, and the Preservation Society of Newport County.

57. Jose Maria Mora, photograph of Miss Olivia Murray (later Mrs. Bayard Cutting), Museum of the City of New York, F2012.58.1314 (attributed with earlier date).

58. I am grateful to Kevin Jones and Christina Johnson for sharing their knowledge and images of this ensemble.

59. Holt, *Fancy Dresses Described*, 27; Crandall, *The Season*, 299.

60. For the portrait by Porter, see Barbara Dayer Gallati and Ortrud Westhedier, eds., *High Society: American Portraits of the Gilded Age* (Munich: Hirmer Verlag, 2008), 96–97. The following miniature is thought to be based on the portrait by Porter: Fernand Paillet (French, 1850–1918). *Mrs. William Douglas Sloane (1852–1946)*, 1891. Watercolor on ivory. New-York Historical Society, Gift of the Estate of Peter Marié, 1905.231.

61. Crandall, *The Season*, 296–297.

62. "An Easter Ball," *Godey's Lady's Book*, May 1883, 458; McAllister, *Society as I Have Found It*, 353–354; Broyles, "Vanderbilt Ball."

63. "The Vanderbilt Ball," *Frank Leslie's Illustrated Newspaper*, April 7, 1883, 107; Foreman and Stimson, *The Vanderbilts and the Gilded Age*, 26.

64. "New York's Great Dazzle," *St. Louis Globe-Democrat*, March 29, 1883, 2.

65. Potvin, *The Places and Spaces of Fashion*, 1–14; Crewe, *The Geographies of Fashion*, 5–10; Brevik-Zender, *Fashioning Spaces*, 17, 129, 188. See also Sparke, "Interior Decoration and Haute Couture," 101–107.

66. Entwistle and Wilson, *Body Dressing*, 1–10.

67. "The Town Terrier," *Puck*, April 4, 1883, 69.

68. "Fitznoodle in America: No. CCLXXV The Vanderbilt Ball," *Puck*, April 4, 1883, 70.

69. "Wicked Extravagance," *Maine Farmer*, April 5, 1883, 2.

70. Patriarch, "Society," *New York Times*, January 12, 1896, 10; "The Social World," *New York Times*, January 28, 1896, 8; Kathrens, *Great Houses of New York*, 76. The salon and library are preserved in the John and Mable Ringling Museum of Art, Sarasota, Florida.

71. Albrecht and Falino, *Gilded New York*, 18. For a report on one of Astor's balls in Newport, see "Mrs. Astor's Grand Ball," *The Morning Call*, September 6, 1891, 16.

72. Kathrens, *Great Houses of New York*, 72–73; King, *A Season of Splendor*, 170.

73. King, *A Season of Splendor*, 175–177; Craven, *Gilded Mansions*, 219–221; Albrecht and Falino, *Gilded New York*, 19; Hotchkiss, "Mrs. Astor at Home," 1.

74. Kathrens, *Great Houses of New York*, 72–80; King, *A Season of Splendor*, 172–173; Craven, *Gilded Mansions*, 215–217.

75. "Society," *New York Times*, February 9, 1896, 20; "The Social World," *New York Times*, February 11, 1896, 8.

76. "Carmen at the Opera," *New York Times*, February 4, 1896.

77. "The Social World," *New York Times*, February 4, 1896, 8.

78. "Dancing in a Vast Bower," *New York Times*, January 3, 1890, 1. For the stomacher, see Hotchkiss, "Mrs. Astor at Home," 1.

79. Caroline Weber, *Queen of Fashion* (New York: Henry Holt, 2006), 99, 123; Chrisman-Campbell, *Fashion Victims*, 20–31.

80. "Carmen at the Opera," *New York Times*, February 4, 1896.

81. "Mrs. William Astor's Dance," *New York Times*, February 4, 1896.

82. Edith Wharton and Ogden Codman Jr., *The Decoration of Houses* (London: B. T. Batsford, 1898), 135.

83. "The Bradley Martin Ball," *New York Tribune*, February 11, 1897, 7.

84. "The Bradley-Martin Ball," *Los Angeles Herald*, February 11, 1897, 1. See King, *A Season of Splendor*, 370–376; Johnson, "Like a Glimpse of Gay Old Versailles," 93–98. The Waldorf Hotel and Astoria Hotel merged later in 1897. See Kathrens, *Great Houses of New York*, 73.

CHAPTER 8

1. Palmer, "New Directions," 305.

2. Ilya Parkins and Elizabeth M. Sheehan, eds., *Cultures of Femininity in Modern Fashion* (Hanover: University of New Hampshire Press, 2012), 12.

3. "Mrs. Astor's Seized Gowns," *Evening World*, July 21, 1891, 1. For conversion purposes, $100 (or 500 francs) in 1890 was equal to $2,541.10 in 2016.

4. "Two Famous Gowns," *Boston Daily Globe*, August 16, 1891, 12; "Mrs. Astor's Dresses," *International Herald*, August 17, 1891, 3.

5. "French Dressmakers, How They Cheat American Customers and the U.S. Treasury," *Watertown Times*, December 23, 1890, 7; "High Prices for Astor Dresses," *New York Times*, September 2, 1891, 8; "City and Suburban News," *New York Times*, August 15, 1891, 3; O'Connor, *The Astors*, 231.

6. Sven Beckert, *The Monied Metropolis: New York City and the Consolidation of the American Bourgeoisie, 1850–1896* (Cambridge, UK: Cambridge University Press, 2003), 305.

7. Tariff of 1890 (McKinley Tariff), 51st Cong., Sess. 1 (1890), chap. 1244, Schedule L, Silk and Silk Goods, sections 409–414, p. 598.

8. See an article by the foremost expert on United States tariff legislation at the time: "The McKinley Tariff Act," *Economic Journal* 1, no. 2 (June 1891): 337–338. I thank John R. Balow for this information.

9. "Up Go the Prices Now," *New York Times*, October 21, 1890, 12; Edwards, *New Spirits*, 30.

10. Andrew Wender Cohen, "Smuggling, Globalization, and America's Outward State, 1870–1909," *Journal of American History* 97, no. 2 (2010): 373.

11. Edwards, *New Spirits*, 30; Beckert, *The Monied Metropolis*, 305, 307.

12. Beckert, *The Monied Metropolis*, 305.

13. For example, "Dinner in Aid of the Reform of the Tariff [Held by] the Reform Club [at] Metropolitan Opera House," Menu, 1888, The Buttolph Collection of Menus, Rare Book Division, New York Public Library Digital Collections, New York.

14. *Reform Club; Officers and Committees, Members, Constitution, By-Laws, Rules* (New York, 1896), 117.

15. *Puck*, January 2, 1884, centerfold.

16. "Mrs. Astor and the Tariff," *Evening World*, December 23, 1890, 1.

17. "Against the Tariff," *Morning Call*, February 9, 1891, 4.

18. "Ex Parte Fassett," 142 U.S. 479 (1892).

19. [Untitled], *Evening Journal*, September 3, 1891, 2; [Untitled], *Town Topics*, September 10, 1891, 2.

20. "Daily Times," *Watertown Times*, September 5, 1891, 4.

21. "Mrs. Astor's New Gowns," *Morning Oregonian*, September 20, 1891, 15

22. Advertisement for Bloomingdale's, *Evening World*, January 4, 1892, 3.

23. "Quarantine and Conscience," *Evening World*, September 26, 1892, 4.

24. Cohen, "Smuggling, Globalization, and America's Outward State," 379.

25. Cohen, "Smuggling, Globalization, and America's Outward State," 380.

26 "Valuable Costumes Seized," *New York Times*, October 16, 1891, 8; "Dreams of Gowns from Paris," *New York Times*, December 29, 1893, 3.

27. "McKinley and the Fashions," *Puck*, September 23, 1891, 80.

28. "Saunterings," *Town Topics*, April 20, 1893, 1.

29. "Will Be Wed in Soiled Gown," *New York Times*, April 13, 1893, 1.

30. "Countess of Craven," *San Francisco Call*, April 19, 1893, 1.

31. Joanne Reitano, *The Tariff Question in the Gilded Age: The Great Debate of 1888* (University Park: Pennsylvania State University, 1994), 132.

32. See, for example, Sara B. Marketti and Jean L. Parsons, "American Fashions for American Women: Early Twentieth Century Efforts to Develop an American Fashion Identity," *Dress: The Journal of the Costume Society of America* 34, no. 1 (2007): 88.

33. *Report of the Industrial Commission on the Relations and Conditions of Capital and Labor Employed in Manufactures and General Business* (Washington, DC: Government Printing Office, 1901), 689.

34. Lewis L. Gould, "Diplomats in the Lobby: Franco-American Relations and the Dingley Tariff of 1897," *The Historian* 39, no. 4 (1977): 660–661.

35. "Godey's Fashions," *Godey's Magazine*, October 1897, 428.

36. "Women and the Tariff," *Godey's Magazine*, November 1897, 549.

37. "Our Washington Letter," *The Independent* 49 (February 11, 1897): 6.

38. Advertisement for Emery, Bird, Thayer, and Co., *Kansas City Journal*, September 13, 1897, 5.

39. Robert Muccigrosso, "New York Has a Ball: The Bradley Martin Extravaganza," *New York History* 75, no. 3 (July 1994): 299.

40. "A Fortune in a Ball," *Telegram-Herald*, January 25, 1890, 8; Johnson, "Like a Glimpse of Gay Old Versailles," 93. For the Bradley-Martins as *arrivistes*, see "What Society Talks Of," *Milwaukee Journal*, February 2, 1897, 5.

41. Wild, *Carnival to Catwalk*, 36–43; Kjellberg and North, *Style & Splendor*, 8.

42. Laing, *Mistress of Herself*, 112.

43. "Mrs. Bradley Martin's Costume," *New York Times*, February 11, 1897, 2.

44. Jean-Philippe Worth (French, 1856–1926) for the House of Worth. Fancy dress costume, 1897. Organza, metallic thread, rhinestone, silk (fiber), velvet (fabric weave), taffeta, lace, satin. Museum of the City of New York, Anonymous Gift, 1942, 42.146.8AB.

45. For Cornelia Martin's costume, see "The Bradley Martin Ball," *Evening Telegraph*, February 12, 1897, 4; E. S. Martin, "This Busy World," *Harper's Weekly*, February 20, 1897, 175, 180–181; "A Modern Masquerade," *Munsey's Magazine* 17 (May 1897): 192. Two ensembles in the Liberty Hall Museum, Union, New Jersey, are believed to have been worn at the Bradley-Martin ball by Elizabeth d'Hauteville Kean (as a maid of honor to Mary Queen of Scots) and Julian Halsted Kean (as a squire). I thank Kevin Jones and Nicholas Lambing for sharing this information.

46. "The Bradley-Martin Fancy Ball," *Harper's Bazar*, February 20, 1897, 150.

47. Holt, *Fancy Dresses Described*, 2; "The Bradley Martin Ball," *Morning Times*, February 11, 1897, 3; Johnson, "Like a Glimpse of Gay Old Versailles," 97; "She Will Go Barefoot," *News and Observer*, February 7, 1897, 9.

48. "The Bradley-Martin Fancy Ball," 150, 157.

49. "New York Society," *Daily Telegraph*, January 25, 1897, 7.

50. "Bradley-Martin's Ball," *Indiana State Journal*, January 27, 1897, 7.

51. "Talked on the Coming Ball," *New York Times*, February 4, 1897, 7; "Are Luxuries Wasted Wealth?," *Gunton's Magazine of American Economics and Political Science*, March 1897, 151.

52. "Readers Commend Mrs. Bradley Martin," *New York Journal*, January 30, 1897, 9; Henry Collins Brown, *In the Golden Nineties* (Hastings-on-Hudson, NY: Valentine's Manual, 1928), 330–334; Johnson, "Like a Glimpse of Gay Old Versailles," 94.

53. "Luxury," *Rocky Mountain Christian Advocate*, February 19, 1897, 1.

54. "Saunterings," *Town Topics*, January 28, 1897, 1; "Socialism and Private Rights," *Washington Post*, February 2, 1897, 6.

55. "Bradley-Martin Fancy Ball," *Harper's Bazar*, February 20, 1897, 150.

56. "A Modern Masquerade," 192.

57. "These Were Not There," *The World*, February 14, 1897, 9.

58. Martin, "This Busy World," 175, 180–181.

59. "Travesty at Olympia," *New York Times*, March 23, 1897, 6.

60. Gracchus, "Our Gilded Youth," *Reynolds's Newspaper*, February 21, 1897, 2.

61. "The Work Side of a Large Ball," *Vogue*, February 18, 1897, vi; *The Standard Designer*, April 1897, 106. Frederick Townsend Martin, Bradley's brother, recalled, "owing to the short notice, many New York shops sold out brocades and silks which been lying in their stockrooms for years." Frederick Townsend Martin, *Things I Remember* (London: E. Nash, 1913), 240.

62. "The Bradley Martin Ball," *New York Times*, February 9, 1897, 3.

63. "The Bradley Martin Fete," 7.

64. Ellen D. Bacon, "Hair," *World's Columbian Exposition, Chicago, Ill., 1893* (Washington, DC: Government Printing Office, 1901), 740.

65. Helen Sheumaker, *Love Entwined: The Curious History of Hairwork in America* (Philadelphia: University of Pennsylvania Press, 2007), 41–43; Tariff Act of 1890 (McKinley Tariff), 51st Cong., Sess. 1 (1890), chap. 1244, Schedule N, Sundries, section 461 (manufactured human hair), p. 602, and Free list, section 604 (raw human hair), p. 606.

66. Tariff of 1897 (Dingley Tariff), 51st Cong., Sess. 1 (1897), chap 11, Schedule N, Sundries, section 429 (human hair, clean or drawn but not manufactured), p. 191, and section 450 (manufactured hair), p. 193.

67. "Saunterings," *Town Topics*, February 11, 1897, 1.

68. "The Bradley Martin Fete," 7.

69. "Personal," *Harper's Bazar*, March 6, 1897, 191.

70. For example, "Saunterings," *Town Topics*, November 14, 1895, 6; Veblen, "The Theory of the Leisure Class," 85.

71. Phelps, "Are We on the Brink of a Revolution?"

72. "Is Wealth a Possession or a Trust?," *Our Day* 17, no. 107 (March 1897): 72. The caricature is credited to the *Chicago Inter-Ocean*.

73. Muccigrasso, "New York Has a Ball," 318–319.

74. Gould, "Diplomats in the Lobby," 661.

75. Emma Bullet, "The Fashions in Paris," *Brooklyn Daily Eagle*, August 22, 1897, 22.

76. Emma Bullet, "The Newest Styles," *Brooklyn Daily Eagle*, September 19, 1897, 10.

77. For example, "Saint-Étienne," *Journal des chambres de commerce*, September 10, 1898, 266–267.

78. Marketti and Parsons, "American Fashions for American Women," 88.

79. "Small Talk," *Sketch*, September 1, 1897, 212. The piece cites the McKinley Tariff but may have meant to refer to the Dingley Tariff, which had passed two months before.

80. Belloc, "An Interview with M. Félix, the Great Parisian Dress Artist," [9].

81. "Latest Customs Rulings," *New York Times*, February 26, 1908, 9.

82. "Latest Customs Rulings," *New York Times*, May 20, 1909, 11.

83. "Tax on Wearing Apparel," *New York Times*, July 27, 1897, 1.

84. "Society Women Boycotters," *Milwaukee Journal*, September 13, 1897, 5.

85. Invoice from E. Deraisme to Ogden Goelet, 1893 and invoice from Bigot to Madame Goelet, 1892, Goelet Family Papers, Series 4: Personal expenses, Salve Regina University, Newport.

CHAPTER 9

1. Cohen, "Smuggling, Globalization, and America's Outward State," 390.

2. Troy, *Couture Culture*, 17.

3. Troy, *Couture Culture*, 9, 196, 233, 239.

4. Strasdin, *Inside the Royal Wardrobe*, 29–31.

5. Strasdin, *Inside the Royal Wardrobe*, 83–86.

6. House of Worth (French, 1858–1956). Dress, 1893. Silk. Peabody Essex Museum, Salem, Mass., Gift of Mrs. Joseph Chamberlain, 1912, 103495.1. Unknown photographer (Britain). Mrs. Joseph Chamberlain, 1893. Albumen print. Peabody Essex Museum, Salem, Mass., Gift of Mr. George Peabody Gardner, 1958, 129162.

7. Jean-Philippe Worth (French, 1856–1926). Afternoon dress, ca. 1902. Silk satin five-panel trained skirt; bodice with handmade bobbin lace collar. National Gallery of Australia, 1981.1040.1–3.

8. Virginia Tatnall Peacock, *Famous American Belles of the Nineteenth Century* (Philadelphia: J. P. Lippincott, 1901), 46.

9. Jachinowitz, "Where to Shop in 1890," 11.

10. Jachinowitz, "Where to Shop in 1890," 13.

11. "Woman of Fashion," *Seattle Post-Intelligencer*, February 22, 1891, 11.

12. I thank Michael J. Shepherd for this information.

13. Belmont, Alva E. Belmont Memoir, 7.

14. Nancy Camilla Carlisle, *Cherished Possessions: A New England Legacy* (Boston: Society for the Preservation of New England Antiquities, 2003), 86–87; invoice from Mlle. Lipman, Paris, to Miss. French, Boston, 1883. Historic New England. Information about French's will is in a letter of March 8, 2004, from David H. Wood in the object file for the ensemble by maison Lipman (fig. 9.5 in the present book). Maison Lipman (French, late 19th century). Blue velvet ensemble, 1883. Courtesy of Historic New England. Gift of Nancy Olive Morison Allis, 1990.507A-G.

15. "Danced Assembly Ball as in Days of 1840," *New York Times*, April 19, 1906, 13.

16. For example: Cap crown, 2nd quarter of the 18th century. Bobbin lace, point d'Angleterre. The Metropolitan Museum of Art, New York, Gift of Mrs. John Jacob Astor, 1888, 88.1.68. See also Elena Kanagy–Loux, "Addicted to Frills: The Fervour for Antique Lace in New York High Society, 1840–1900," *Journal of Dress History* 4, no. 2 (Summer 2020): 42–74.

17. "A Notable Social Event," *New York Times*, November 19, 1878, 1.

18. "Cast-off Finery," *Rocky Mountain News*, July 20, 1883, 6.

19. De Marly, *The History of Haute Couture*, 123; Strasdin, *Inside the Royal Wardrobe*, 138, 143.

20. Philippe Perrot, *Fashioning the Bourgeoisie: A History of Clothing in the Nineteenth Century*, trans. Richard Bienvenu (Princeton, NJ: Princeton University Press, 1994), 42; Strasdin, *Inside the Royal Wardrobe*, 139.

21. Strasdin, *Inside the Royal Wardrobe*, 137–139; Jennifer Le Zotte, *From Goodwill to Grunge: A History of Secondhand Styles and Alternative Economies* (Chapel Hill: University of North Carolina Press, 2017), 28; Madeleine Ginsburg, "Rags to Riches: The Second-hand Clothes Trade," *Costume: The Journal of the Costume Society* 14, no. 1 (1980): 121, 124.

22. Strasdin, *Inside the Royal Wardrobe*, 137.

23. Ginsburg, *"Rags to Riches,"* 125; Le Zotte, *From Goodwill to Grunge*, 29.

24. For example, "Wanted, Cast Off Clothing," *Brooklyn Daily Eagle*, June 12, 1896, 10.

25. "Rummage Sale Workers Reply to Mr. Nichols," *Brooklyn Daily Eagle*, February 5, 1901, 3.

26. Le Zotte, *From Goodwill to Grunge*, 28.

27. "Personal and Other Jottings," *San Francisco Call*, May 24, 1891, 11.

28. "Orpheum Has Another Good Bill," *San Francisco Call*, April 22, 1901, 7; "Francesca Redding and Her Parisian Gowns," *San Francisco Call*, May 5, 1901, 3.

29. For the secondhand dealer for actresses' gowns, see "Heaps of Cast-off Finery," *The Sun* (New York), December 18, 1892, 3. For the Martinot auction, see "Thousands in the Trinkets," *New York Times*, May 15, 1901, 8.

30. "Heaps of Cast-Off Finery," 2.

31. Michelle Oberly, "The Fabric Scrapbooks of Hannah Ditzler Alspaugh," in Thieme, *With Grace & Favour*, 11.

32. Walkley and Foster, *Crinolines and Crimping Irons*, 30, 162.

33. The dress bears a sewn-in Worth label with the number 80719. Family descendants have also preserved a cream-colored lace, long-sleeved stage blouse worn by Gould.

34. "Many Valuable Gowns Stolen," *New York Times*, January 21, 1893, 2.

35. "Mrs. Gould Robbed," *Hartford Courant*, November 26, 1894, 2.

36. "Marks of Distinction," *Life*, August 15, 1895, 26.

37. "The Montauk Reception," *Brooklyn Daily Eagle*, January 27, 1893, 5.

38. Kathryn Allamong Jacob, *Capital Elites: High Society in Washington, D.C., after the Civil War* (Washington, DC: Smithsonian Institution Press, 1995), 91, 178.

39. Carpenter, *Carp's Washington*, 300.

40. "The Inaugural Ball," *Washington Post*, March 5, 1889, 5.

41. Carpenter, *Carp's Washington*, 91.

42. William Eleroy Curtis, "Wealthy Women of America," *Cosmopolitan*, October 1889, 593.

43. "Some Astor Diamonds," *San Francisco Call*, October 11, 1891, 14; "Une première," *Le Parti ouvrier*, January 28, 1899, 1.

44. "Gossip of the Capital," *Evening Journal*, November 16, 1888, 1.

45. *Titled Americans: A List of American Ladies Who Have Married Foreigners of Rank* (New York: Street and Smith, 1890), 215–252.

46. *Titled Americans*, 204.

47. "Mrs. George Gould Left $1,000,000 Gems," *New York Times*, February 10, 1923, 2.

48. Cohen, "Smuggling, Globalization, and America's Outward State," 374.

49. "Successful Smuggling," *Los Angeles Herald*, June 12, 1888, 5.

50. "Quarantine and Conscience," 4; Cohen, "Smuggling, Globalization, and America's Outward State," 389.

51. Véronique Pouillard, "The Milton Case (1955–1962). Defending the Intellectual Property Rights of Haute Couture in the United States," *Journal of Design History* 30, no. 4 (November 2017): 356–357; Stewart, "Copying and Copyrighting Haute Couture: Democratizing Fashion, 1900–1930s," 120.

52. Véronique Pouillard and Tereza Kuldova, "Interrogating Intellectual Property Rights in Post-War Fashion and Design," *Journal of Design History* 30, no. 4 (November 2017): 348; Pouillard, "The Milton Case," 358.

53. Pouillard and Kuldova, "Interrogating Intellectual Property Rights," 345–346; Pouillard, "Design Piracy," 329; Stewart, "Copying and Copyrighting Haute Couture," 22.

54. De la Haye and Mendes, *The House of Worth*, 18. For Madame Worth et cie, see *Ladies Gazette of Fashion*, August 1882, 183.

55. Troy, *Couture Culture*, 22–25; Tétart-Vittu, "Key Dates," 272.

56. "400's Dressmaker Dead," *New York Times*, April 18, 1906, 11. Dresses by Catharine Donovan (b. Ireland, ca. 1826–1906) are preserved in the Metropolitan Museum of Art, New York; Historic New England; Philadelphia Museum of Art; Fashion Institute of Design and Merchandising Museum, Los Angeles; Fashion Museum, Bath; and other collections. Her husband, Charles Donovan, died about 1854.

57. Belmont, Alva E. Belmont Memoir, 87.

58. "400's Dressmaker Dead," 11.

59. "Festivity at Eastertide," *New York Times*, March 25, 1883, 14.

60. Phillada Ballard, email to the author, June 17, 2020.

61. Chamberlain to Endicott, February 8, 1889, Highbury, AC3/4/57, UBCRL-CC.

62. "Woman Confesses Smuggling Plot," *New York Times*, March 28, 1913, 24. Catharine Donovan had been involved in a smuggling case in 1893. "Dreams of Gowns from Paris," *New York Times*, December 29, 1893, 3.

63. De Marly, *The History of Haute Couture*, 115; Stewart, "Copying and Copyrighting Haute Couture," 110.

64. Stewart, "Copying and Copyrighting Haute Couture," 109; Troy, *Couture Culture*, 240.

65. For example, "An Attractive Display," *New York Times*, September 22, 1889, 12.

66. For designs made expressly for the U.S. trade, see Parisiana, "The Glass of Fashion," *The Nineteen Hundred* 2, no. 2 (February 1896): 11; and "Mandel Brothers' Grand Display," *Chicago Daily Tribune*, October 9, 1890, 8.

67. "The Great World's Fair Just Opened at Paris," *Frank Leslie's Weekly*, May 12, 1900, 370.

68. "Fashions and Fabrics," *Le Follet*, February 1, 1886, n.p.

69. Samuel Hopkins Adams, "The Dishonest Paris Label," *Ladies Home Journal*, March 1913, 7–8; "Minneapolis Club Fighting Fake Paris Label," *Marketing Communications* 83 (1913): 80–81.

70. "La Mode et les modes," *Les Modes: Revue mensuelle illustrée des arts décoratifs appliqués à la femme*, November 1908, 25; "La Mode et les modes," *Les Modes: Revue mensuelle illustrée des arts décoratifs appliqués à la femme*, December 1915, 31.

71. "They Are Just Lovely," *Detroit Free Press*, September 27, 1891, 8.

72. Parisiana, "The Glass of Fashion," 11.

73. Belloc, "An Interview with M. Félix, the Great Parisian Dress Artist," [9].

74. Best, *The History of Fashion Journalism*, 16.

75. Best, *The History of Fashion Journalism*, 40.

76. For example, "Worth Basque and Full-Trained Trimmed Skirt," *Harper's Bazar*, December 19, 1874, cover and 830; Emery, *A History of the Paper Pattern Industry*, 40–48. Demorest's also published the magazine *Mrs. Demorest's What to Wear and How to Make It*.

77. "Exhibition of Costumes," *New York Times*, March 10, 1895, 8; "Displays at the Garden," *New York Times*, March 12, 1895, 3.

78. Strasdin, *Inside the Royal Wardrobe*, 143.

79. Richmond Brooks Barrett, *Good Old Summer Days* (New York: D. Appleton-Century, 1941), 29.

CHAPTER 10

1. "Marriage Announcement," *New York Times*, September 3, 1903, 7; "Miss Goelet's Trousseau," *Rosebud County News*, November 5, 1903, 4; Leila "Belle" Wilson to her parents, August 14, 1886, Sir Michael Herbert Papers, Wilton House, Wiltshire, cited in Maureen E. Montgomery, *"Gilded Prostitution": Status, Money and Transatlantic Marriages, 1870–1914* (London: Routledge, 2013), 141–142.

BIBLIOGRAPHY

Adams, Henry. *The Letters of Henry Adams*. Edited by J. C. Levenson, Ernest Samuels, Charles Vandersee, and Viola Hopkins Winner. 3 vols. Cambridge, MA: Harvard University Press, 1982.

Adams, Marian, and Ward Thoron. *The Letters of Mrs. Henry Adams, 1865–1883*. Boston: Little, Brown, 1936.

Adams, Samuel Hopkins. "The Dishonest Paris Label." *Ladies Home Journal*, March 1913, 7–8.

Adolphus, F. *Some Memories of Paris*. Edinburgh: W. Blackwood, 1895.

Albrecht, Donald, and Jeannine Falino, eds. *Gilded New York: Design, Fashion, and Society*. New York: Monacelli Press, 2013.

Alpert, Arlene, Margrit Altenburg, and Diane Bailey. *Milady's Standard Cosmetology*. Clifton Park, NY: Cengage Learning, 2002.

Amnéus, Cynthia. *A Separate Sphere: Dressmakers in Cincinnati's Golden Age*. Lubbock: Texas Tech University Press, 2003.

Annuaire-almanach du commerce, de l'industrie, de la magistrature et de l'administration. Paris: Firmin Didot et Bottin, 1870–1907.

Annuaire des coiffeurs. Paris: Bureau central de placement, 1895.

Annuaire statistique de la ville de Paris, 1901. Paris: Masson et cie, 1903.

Annual Report, United States National Museum. Washington, DC: Smithsonian Institution, 1913.

Aria, Eliza Davis. *Costume*. London: Macmillan, 1906.

Armstrong, Katherine. [Untitled]. *Godey's*, October 1887, 296.

Armstrong, Katherine. "Studies in Dress." *Godey's Lady's Book*, April 1888, 321.

Avenel, Georges. *Le Mécanisme de la vie moderne*. Paris: Colin, 1902.

Bacon, Ellen D. "Hair." *World's Columbian Exposition, Chicago, Ill., 1893*. Washington, DC: Government Printing Office, 1901.

Ballard, Phillada. "Mary Chamberlain and Fashion." The Chamberlain Highbury Trust, July 2019, https://chamberlainhighburytrust.files.wordpress.com/2019/07/cht-mary-chamberlain-and-fashion.pdf.

Balsan, Consuelo Vanderbilt. *The Glitter and the Gold*. London: Heinemann, 1953.

Barberet, Joseph. *Le Travail en France: Monographies professionnelles*. Paris: Berger-Levrault, 1887.

Barrett, Richmond Brooks. *Good Old Summer Days*. New York: D. Appleton-Century, 1941.

Baschet, René. *Le Panorama: Exposition universelle 1900*. Paris: Ludovic Baschet, 1900.

Bass-Krueger, Maude. "Fashion Collections, Collectors, and Exhibitions in France, 1874–1900: Historical Imagination, the Spectacular Past, and the Practice of Restoration." *Fashion Theory* 22, no. 4–5 (2018): 405–433.

Baumgarten, Linda. *What Clothes Reveal: The Language of Clothing in Colonial and Federal America: The Colonial Williamsburg Collection*. Williamsburg, VA: Colonial Williamsburg Foundation, 2002.

B.D.F. "Gowns at the Exposition." *New York Times*, July 22, 1900, 5.

Beard, Patricia. *After the Ball: Gilded Age Secrets, Boardroom Betrayals, and the Party That Ignited the Great Wall Street Scandal of 1905*. New York: Harper Collins, 2003.

Beckert, Sven. *The Monied Metropolis: New York City and the Consolidation of the American Bourgeoisie, 1850–1896*. Cambridge, UK: Cambridge University Press, 2003.

Bello, Ella de C. "Paris Exposition." *The Queen*, March 10, 1900, 387.

Belloc, Marie A. "An Interview with M. Félix, the Great Parisian Dress Artist." *The Woman at Home*, September 1900, [9].

Belloc, Marie A. "La Maison Worth." *Lady's Realm* 1 (November 1896–April 1897): 144.

Belmont, Alva. Alva E. Belmont Memoir. Matilda Young Papers, Rare Book Manuscript and Special Collections Library, Duke University, Durham, NC.

Benjamin, Walter. *The Arcades Project*. Translated by Howard Eiland and Kevin McLaughlin. Cambridge, MA: Harvard University Press, 1999 (1927–1940).

Bennet, Jean. *Biographies de personnalités mutualistes, XIXe–XXe siècles*. Paris: Mutualité française, 1987.

Bentzon, Theodore. "Woman at the Paris Exhibition." *Outlook* 66, no. 5 (September 29, 1900): 259.

Berlanstein, Lenard R. *Daughters of Eve: A Cultural History of French Theater Women from the Old Regime to the Fin de Siècle*. Cambridge, MA: Harvard University Press, 2001.

Bernhardt, Sarah. *My Double Life: The Memoirs of Sarah Bernhardt*. Translated by Victoria Tietze Larson. Albany: State University of New York Press, 1999.

Berry, Jess. *House of Fashion: Haute Couture and the Modern Interior*. London: Bloomsbury Visual Arts, 2018.

Best, Kate. *The History of Fashion Journalism*. London: Bloomsbury Academic, 2017.

Blaine, Harriet S., ed. *Letters of Mrs. James G. Blaine*. New York: Duffield, 1908.

Blanc, Charles. *Art in Ornament and Dress*. London: Chapman and Hall, 1877.

Blaszczyk, Regina Lee, ed. *Producing Fashion: Commerce, Culture, and Consumers.* Philadelphia: University of Pennsylvania Press, 2008.

Block, Elizabeth L. "Maison Félix and the Body Types of Its Clients, 1875–1900." *West 86th: A Journal of Decorative Arts, Design History, and Material Culture* 26, no. 1 (Spring-Summer 2019): 80–103.

Block, Elizabeth L. "Virginie Amélie Avegno Gautreau: Living Statue." *Nineteenth-Century Art Worldwide* 17, no. 2 (Autumn 2018). https://doi.org/10.29411/ncaw.2018.17.2.4.

Bolitho, Hector. *Marie Tempest*. Philadelphia: J. B. Lippincott, 1937.

Bourdieu, Pierre. *Distinction: A Social Critique of the Judgement of Taste*. Translated by Richard Nice. Cambridge, MA: Harvard University Press, 1984.

Bourdieu, Pierre. "The Forms of Capital." In *Handbook of Theory and Research for the Sociology of Education*, edited by John Richardson. Translated by Richard Nice (241–258). New York: Greenwood, 1986.

Bourdieu, Pierre, and Yvette Delsaut. "Le Couturier et sa griffe: Contribution à une théorie de la magie." *Actes de la recherche en sciences sociales* 1, no. 1 (1975): 7–36.

Bourne, L. "M. Émile Félix." *Le Panthéon de l'industrie: Journal hebdomadaire illustré*, May 14, 1882, 145.

Brackman, Barbara. "M. T. Hollander and the Abolitionist Baby Quilt." *Civil War Quilts: Quilts & Women's History Focusing on the American Civil War* (blog), November 8, 2014, http://civilwarquilts .blogspot.com/2014/11/mt-hollander-and-abolitionist-baby-quilt.html.

Bradshaw's Illustrated Guide through Paris and Its Environs. London: W. J. Adams, 1882.

Brevik-Zender, Heidi. *Fashioning Spaces: Mode and Modernity in Late Nineteenth-Century Paris*. Toronto: University of Toronto Press, 2015.

Brilliant, Virginia, Paul F. Miller, and Françoise Barbe. *Gothic Art in the Gilded Age: Medieval and Renaissance Treasures in the Gavet-Vanderbilt-Ringling Collection*. Sarasota, FL: John and Mable Ringling Museum of Art, 2009.

Bristow, Joseph, ed. *Wilde Discoveries: Traditions, Histories, Archives*. CCS 19. Toronto: University of Toronto Press, 2013.

Brown, Henry Collins. *In the Golden Nineties*. Hastings-on-Hudson, NY: Valentine's Manual, 1928.

Broyles, Susannah. "Vanderbilt Ball—How a Costume Ball Changed New York Elite Society." *New York Stories* (blog), Museum of the City New York, August 6, 2013, https://blog.mcny.org/2013/08/06 /vanderbilt-ball-how-a-costume-ball-changed-new-york-elite-society.

Buchanan, Abby Longstreet. *Social Etiquette of New York*. New York: Appleton, 1888.

Bullet, Emma. "The Choice of Paris." *Brooklyn Daily Eagle*, October 3, 1897, 17.

Bullet, Emma. "Dress Show Exegesis." *Brooklyn Daily Eagle*, January 7, 1894, 5.

Bullet, Emma. "The Fashions in Paris." *Brooklyn Daily Eagle*, August 22, 1897, 22.

Bullet, Emma. "Her Toilets: Mrs. Langtry's Preparations in Paris for America." *Brooklyn Daily Eagle*, October 2, 1886, 4.

Bullet, Emma. "How to See the Exposition." *Brooklyn Daily Eagle*, June 17, 1900, 23.

Bullet, Emma. "The Newest Styles." *Brooklyn Daily Eagle*, September 19, 1897, 10.

Bullet, Emma. "The Paris Exposition." *Brooklyn Daily Eagle*, August 27, 1899, 19.

Calhoun, Charles William. *The Gilded Age: Perspectives on the Origins of Modern America*. Lanham, MD: Rowman & Littlefield, 2007.

Campbell, Colin. *The Romantic Ethic and the Spirit of Modern Consumerism*. New extended ed. Cham, Switzerland: Palgrave Macmillan, 2018.

Carlisle, Nancy Camilla. *Cherished Possessions: A New England Legacy*. Boston: Society for the Preservation of New England Antiquities, 2003.

Carpenter, Frank G. *Carp's Washington*. New York: McGraw-Hill, 1960.

Cassini, Marguerite. *Never a Dull Moment*. New York: Harper and Brothers, 1956. *Catalogue illustré des coiffures*. Paris: L'Académie de coiffure, 1900.

Child, Katherine B. "Dress." *American Kitchen Magazine* 15, no. 2 (May 1901): 48–49.

Child, Theodore. "Along the Parisian Boulevards." *Harper's New Monthly Magazine*, 1892, 866.

Child, Theodore. *The Praise of Paris*. New York: Harper and Brothers, 1893.

Chrisman-Campbell, Kimberly. *Fashion Victims: Dress at the Court of Louis XVI and Marie-Antoinette*. New Haven, CT: Yale University Press, 2015.

Clark, Jessica P. *The Business of Beauty: Gender and the Body in Modern London*. London: Bloomsbury Visual Arts, 2020.

Clinton, Craig. *Cora Urquhart Potter: The Victorian Actress as Provocateur*. Jefferson, NC: McFarland, 2010.

Coffin, Judith G. *The Politics of Women's Work: The Paris Garment Trades, 1750–1915*. Princeton, NJ: Princeton University Press, 1996.

Cohen, Andrew Wender. "Smuggling, Globalization, and America's Outward State, 1870–1909." *Journal of American History* 97, no. 2 (2010): 373.

Cole, Charles Woolsey. *Colbert and a Century of French Mercantilism*. Hamden, CT: Archon Books, 1964.

Cole, Daniel James, and Nancy Diehl. *History of Modern Fashion*. London: Laurence King Publishing, 2015.

Cole, Ida B. "Museums of Costumes and Material." *Woman's Magazine* 20, no. 6 (January 1910): 29–30

Coleman, Elizabeth A. *The Opulent Era: Fashions of Worth, Doucet and Pingat* (New York: Thames and Hudson; Brooklyn Museum, 1989).

Cone, Ada. "My Lady's Carriage." *Courier-Journal*, October 14, 1889, 3.

Cooper, Dana. "From New England to Old England: The Anglo-American Life of Mary Endicott Chamberlain Carnegie, 1864–1957." *Massachusetts Historical Review* 13 (2011): 105–106.

Crandall, Charles H. *The Season: An Annual Record of Society in New York, Brooklyn, and Vicinity*. New York: White, Stokes, & Allen, 1883.

Craven, Wayne. *Gilded Mansions: Grand Architecture and High Society*. New York: W. W. Norton, 2009.

Crewe, Louise. *The Geographies of Fashion: Consumption, Space, and Value*. London: Bloomsbury Academic, 2017.

Cunningham, Patricia. "Healthful, Artistic and Correct Dress." In *With Grace & Favour: Victorian & Edwardian Fashion in America*, edited by Otto Charles Thieme (14–25). Cincinnati, OH: Cincinnati Art Museum, 1993.

Curtis, William Eleroy. "Wealthy Women of America." *Cosmopolitan*, October 1889, 593.

Dale, Alan. *Queens of the Stage*. New York: G. W. Dillingham, 1896.

David, Alison Mathews. "Cutting a Figure: Tailoring, Technology and Social Identity in Nineteenth-Century Paris." PhD diss., Stanford University, 2002.

Davidson, Hilary. *Dress in the Age of Jane Austen*. New Haven, CT: Yale University Press, 2019.

Davis, Mary E. *Classic Chic: Music, Fashion, and Modernism*. Berkeley: University of California Press, 2006.

Davis, Richard Harding. *About Paris*. New York: Harper, 1895.

De Castelbajac, Constance, and Eric Mension-Rigau. *Journal de Constance de Castelbajac, marquise de Breteuil: 1885–1886*. Paris: Perrin, 2003.

De Castellane, Boniface. *How I Discovered America: Confessions of the Marquis Boni de Castellane*. New York: Alfred A. Knopf, 1924.

De Fontenoy, Marquise. *Eve's Glossary: The Guidebook of a Mondaine*. Chicago: Herbert S. Stone, 1897.

De Forest, Katherine. "June Days in Paris." *Harper's Bazar*, June 16, 1900, 432.

De Forest, Katherine. "Our Paris Letter." *Harper's Bazar*, November 3, 1894, 875.

De Forest, Katherine. "Our Paris Letter." *Harper's Bazar*, June 27, 1896, 542.

De la Haye, Amy, and Valerie D. Mendes. *The House of Worth: Portrait of an Archive*. London: V&A Publishing, 2014.

Delille, Damien. "Entre art et industrie: La Réforme de la mode au passage du XXe siècle." *Regards croisés* 6 (2016): 61–84.

De Marly, Diana *The History of Haute Couture, 1850–1950*. London: B. T. Batsford, 1980.

De Marly, Diana. *Worth: Father of Haute Couture, 1980*. London: Elm Tree Books, 1980.

Demornex, Jacqueline. *Lucien Lelong*. London: Thames & Hudson, 2008.

Des Moulins, Amelia. "The Dressmaker's Life Story." *Independent* 56 (1904): 941–942.

De Spare, Baronne. "Carnet parisien." *La Grande Revue*, 1889, 215.

De Young, Justine. "Not Just a Pretty Picture: Fashion as News." In *Getting the Picture: The Visual Culture of the News*, edited by Jason Hill and Vanessa R. Schwartz (109–115). London: Bloomsbury, 2015.

De Young, Justine. "Representing the Modern Woman: The Fashion Plate Reconsidered (1865–75)." In *Women, Femininity, and Public Space in European Visual Culture, 1789–1914*, edited by Temma Balducci and Heather Belnap Jensen (97–114). Farnham, UK: Ashgate, 2014.

Dickens, Charles. *Dickens's Dictionary of Paris: An Unconventional Handbook*. New York: Macmillan, 1882.

Doggett's New-York City Directory. New York: J. Doggett, Jr., 1845.

Dreyfus-Bing, Paul, and G.-Roger Sandoz. *Exposition internationale de Milan, 1906: Rapport général de la section française*. Paris: Comité français des expositions à l'étranger, 1913.

Dumas, François Guillaume, ed. *Illustrated Biographies of Modern Artists*. Paris: Baschet, 1882.

Dundas, Isabel. "Fashions' Mirror." *Godey's Lady's Book*, February 1895, 209.

Dunlap, Anna. *Frank: The Story of Frances Folsom Cleveland, America's Youngest First Lady*. Albany, NY: Excelsior Editions, 2009.

Dymond, Anne. "Embodying the Nation: Art, Fashion, and Allegorical Women at the 1900 Exposition Universelle." *RACAR: Revue d'art canadienne / Canadian Art Review* 36, no. 2 (2011): 1–14.

Edwards, Rebecca. *New Spirits: Americans in the "Gilded Age," 1865–1905*. New York: Oxford University Press, 2011.

Elliam. "Interview Chez Lenthéric." *La Revue mondaine illustrée*, November 25, 1892, 3.

Eliot-James, A. E. F. "Shopping in London." *Woman's World*, 1889, 5.

Emery, Joy Spanabel. *A History of the Paper Pattern Industry: The Home Dressmaking Fashion Revolution*. London: Bloomsbury Academic, 2014.

Entwistle, Joanne. *The Fashioned Body: Fashion, Dress and Modern Social Theory*. Cambridge, UK: Polity, 2015.

Entwistle, Joanne, and Elizabeth Wilson, eds. *Body Dressing*. Oxford: Berg, 2001.

Evans, Caroline. *The Mechanical Smile: Modernism and the First Fashion Shows in France and America, 1900–1929*. New Haven, CT: Yale University Press, 2013.

Exposition des arts de la femme: Palais de l'industrie: Guide-livret illustré. Paris: A. Warmont, 1892.

"Fashion." In "Adoration for the 'Sweet France,'" sec. 2, in Modern Japan and France: Adoration, Encounter and Interaction, National Diet Library Tokyo, https://www.ndl.go.jp/france/en/column/s2_2.html.

Fehler, Lily. "1820–1901—Emile Pingat." Fashion History Timeline. Fashion Institute of Technology, State University of New York, last updated July 14, 2020, https:fashionhistory.fitnyc.edu/1820-1901-emile-pingat.

Felski, Rita. *The Gender of Modernity*. London: Harvard University Press, 1995.

Fenwick-Miller, Mrs. "The Ladies' Column." *Illustrated London News*, November 28, 1891, 712. Finamore, Michelle Tolini. "Callot Sisters." In *The Berg Companion to Fashion*, edited by Valerie Steele (113–114). London: Bloomsbury Academic 2010.

Fletcher, Ella Adelia. *The Woman Beautiful*. New York: Brentano's, 1901.

Font, Lourdes M. "International Couture: The Opportunities and Challenges of Expansion, 1880–1920." *Business History* 54, no. 1 (February 2012): 30–47.

Foreman, John, and Robbe Pierce Stimson. *The Vanderbilts and the Gilded Age: Architectural Aspirations, 1879–1901*. New York: St. Martin's Press, 1991.

Fornay, Tillie May. "Sing a Song of Seasons." *Table Talk* 16 (January 1901): 375.

Frank Leslie's Illustrated Historical Register of the Centennial Exposition 1876. New York: Frank Leslie's Publishing House, 1877.

Friedrichs, Christopher R. "From Rags to Riches–Jews as Producers and Consumers of Fashion." In *Broken Threads: The Destruction of the Jewish Fashion Industry in Germany and Austria*, edited by Roberta S. Kremer (18–27). Oxford: Berg, 2007.

Gallati, Barbara Dayer, and Ortrud Westheidier. *High Society: American Portraits of the Gilded Age*. Munich: Hirmer Verlag, 2008.

Ganeva, Mila. "Elegance and Spectacle in Berlin: The Gerson Fashion Store and the Rise of the Modern Fashion Show. In *The Places and Spaces of Fashion, 1800–2007*, edited by John Potvin (121–138). New York: Routledge 2009.

Gardner, Deborah S. "'A Paradise of Fashion': A. T. Stewart's Department Store, 1862–1875." In *A Needle, a Bobbin, a Strike: Women Needleworkers in America*, edited by Joan M. Jensen and Sue Davidson (60–80). Philadelphia: Temple University Press, 1984.

Gastaldo, Cécile. "Jules Février (1842–1937), architecte méconnu à l'origine de l'hôtel Gaillard." *Livraisons de l'histoire de l'architecture* 33 (2017): 97–109.

Gayet, Albert. *Le Costume en Egypte: Du IIIe au XIIIe siècle*. Paris: Ernest Leroux, 1900.

Geppert, Alexander C. T. *Fleeting Cities: Imperial Expositions in Fin-de-Siècle Europe*. New York: Palgrave Macmillan, 2010.

Ginsburg, Madeleine. "Rags to Riches: The Second-Hand Clothes Trade." *Costume: The Journal of the Costume Society* 14, no. 1 (January 1980): 121–135.

Goelet Family Papers. Series 4: Personal expenses. Salve Regina University, Newport.

Gordon, Janet. "Early Fall Fashions." *Southern Woman's Magazine* 2, no. 2 (September 1904): 21.

Gould, Lewis L. "Diplomats in the Lobby: Franco-American Relations and the Dingley Tariff of 1897." *The Historian* 39, no. 4 (1977): 660–661.

G.P. "M. Auguste Petit." *Le Panthéon de l'industrie*, September 5, 1886, 1.

Gracchus. "Our Gilded Youth." *Reynolds's Newspaper*, February 21, 1897, 2.

Green, Genevieve. "Around the Exposition." *San Francisco Call*, June 24, 1900, 2.

Green, Nancy L. *The Other Americans in Paris: Businessmen, Countesses, Wayward Youth, 1880–1941*. Chicago: University of Chicago Press, 2014.

Green, Nancy L. *The Pletzl of Paris: Jewish Immigrant Workers in the Belle Epoque*. New York: Holmes & Meier, 1986.

Green, Nancy L. *Ready-to-Wear and Ready-to-Work: A Century of Industry and Immigrants in Paris and New York*. Durham, NC: Duke University Press, 1997.

Griffith, M. "Paris Dressmakers." *Strand Magazine: An Illustrated Monthly*, July–December 1894, 748–750.

Groom, Gloria, ed. *Impressionism, Fashion, and Modernity*. New Haven, CT: Yale University Press, 2012.

Hahn, Hazel H. *Scenes of Parisian Modernity: Culture and Consumption in the Nineteenth Century*. New York: Palgrave, 2009.

Hale, Sarah Josepha Buell. *Manners: Happy Homes and Good Society All the Year Round*. Boston: Lee and Shepard, 1889.

Hall, Coryne. *Little Mother of Russia: A Biography of the Empress Marie Feodorovna (1847–1928)*. Teaneck, NJ: Holmes & Meier, 2006.

Hamlin, Huybertie Pruyn. *An Albany Girlhood*. Albany, NY: Washington Park Press, 1990.

Harper's Guide to Paris and the Exposition of 1900. London: Harper and Brothers, 1900.

Hathaway, Anne. "Scent and Scent Bottles." *Woman's World* 2, no. 6 (May 1889): 321–325.

Haulman, Kate. *The Politics of Fashion in Eighteenth-Century America*. Chapel Hill: University of North Carolina Press, 2011.

Heilig, Sterling. "For Working Women." *Evening Star*, April 30, 1900, 15.

Hiner, Susan. *Accessories to Modernity: Fashion and the Feminine in Nineteenth-Century France*. Philadelphia: University of Pennsylvania Press, 2010.

Hiner, Susan. "The Modiste's Palette and the Artist's Hat." In *Degas, Impressionism, and the Millinery Trade*, edited by Simon Kelly and Esther Bell (66–81). San Francisco: Fine Arts Museums of San Francisco, 2017.

Hoffert, Sylvia D. *Alva Vanderbilt Belmont: Unlikely Champion of Women's Rights*. Bloomington: Indiana University Press, 2012.

Holloway, Laura Carter. *Famous American Fortunes and the Men Who Have Made Them*. Philadelphia: Garretson, 1885.

Holt, Ardern. *Fancy Dresses Described: Or, What to Wear at Fancy Balls*. London: Debenham and Freebody, 1880.

Holt, Ardern. *Gentlemen's Fancy Dress: How to Choose It*. London: Wyman & Sons, 1882.

Homberger, Eric. *Mrs. Astor's New York: Money and Social Power in a Gilded Age*. New Haven, CT: Yale University Press, 2002.

Hotchkiss, Chauncey. "Mrs. Astor at Home." *New York World*, January 8, 1905, magazine section, 1.

House of Worth. *A History of Feminine Fashion*. London: Ed. J. Burrow, 1928.

Howells, William Dean. *A Fearful Responsibility* and *Tonelli's Marriage*. Edinburgh: David Douglas, 1882.

Iarocci, Louisa. *The Urban Department Store in America, 1850–1930*. Burlington, VT: Ashgate, 2014.

Ignota. "A Chat with the Leading Paris Hairdresser." *Hearth and Home*, August 6, 1896, 491.

Ingram, Henry Balch. "Mr. Vanderbilt's Marble Hall." *Frank Leslie's Weekly*, February 27, 1892, 65.

Intime. "A Parisian Prince of Dress." *Lady's Realm: An Illustrated Monthly Magazine* 9 (November 1900–April 1901): 23–25.

Jachimowicz, Elizabeth. *Eight Chicago Women and Their Fashions, 1860–1929*. Chicago: Chicago Historical Society, 1978.

Jachimowicz, Elizabeth. "Where to Shop in 1890: The European Addresses of a Chicago Lady." In *Aspects of Costume: The Nineteenth Century. Selected Papers*, edited by Mariliina Perkko (10–16). Alfabox, Finland: ICOM International Costume Committee, 1990.

Jacob, Kathryn Allamong. *Capital Elites: High Society in Washington, D.C., after the Civil War*. Washington, DC: Smithsonian Institution Press, 1995.

Jensen, Joan M., and Sue Davidson, eds. *A Needle, a Bobbin, a Strike: Women Needleworkers in America*. Philadelphia: Temple University Press, 1984.

Johnson, Susan Gail. "Like a Glimpse of Gay Old Versailles: Three Gilded Age Balls." In *Gilded New York: Design, Fashion, and Society*, edited by Donald Albrecht and Jeannine Falino (83–106). New York: Monacelli Press, 2013.

Johnston, William Edward. *Memoirs of "Malakoff": Being Extracts from the Correspondence and Papers of the Late William Edward Johnston*. 2 vols. Edited by Robert Matteson Johnston. London: Hutchinson, 1907.

Jones, Colin. *Paris: The Biography of a City*. New York: Penguin, 2006.

Jones, Geoffrey. *Beauty Imagined: A History of the Global Beauty Industry*. Oxford: Oxford University Press, 2010.

Jullian, Philippe. *The Triumph of Art Nouveau: Paris Exhibition, 1900*. Translated by Stephen Hardman. New York: Larousse, 1974.

Kanagy–Loux, Elena. "Addicted to Frills: The Fervour for Antique Lace in New York High Society, 1840–1900." *Journal of Dress History* 4, no. 2 (Summer 2020): 42–74.

Kaplan, Joel H., and Sheila Stowell. *Theatre and Fashion: Oscar Wilde to the Suffragettes*. Cambridge, UK: Cambridge University Press, 1995.

Kathrens, Michael C. *Great Houses of New York, 1880–1930*. New York: Acanthus Press, 2005.

Kawamura, Yuniya. *Fashion-ology: An Introduction to Fashion Studies*. London: Bloomsbury Academic, 2018.

Kawamura, Yuniya. "Japanese Fashion." In *The Berg Companion to Fashion*, edited by Valerie Steele (435–440). Oxford: Bloomsbury Academic, 2010.

Kelly, Rebecca J. "Fashion in the Gilded Age: A Profile of Newport's King Family." In *Twentieth-Century American Fashion*, edited by Linda Welters and Patricia A. Cunningham (9–32). Oxford: Berg, 2008.

Kelly, Simon, and Esther Bell, eds. *Degas, Impressionism, and the Millinery Trade*. San Francisco: Fine Arts Museums of San Francisco, 2017.

Kessler, Marni. "Dusting the Surface, or the Bourgeoise, the Veil, and Haussmann's Paris." In *The Invisible Flâneuse? Gender, Public Space and Visual Culture in Nineteenth Century Paris* (49–64). Manchester, UK: Manchester University Press, 2010.

Kessler, Marni. *Sheer Presence: The Veil in Manet's Paris*. Minneapolis: University of Minnesota Press, 2006.

Kindleberger, Charles P. "Origins of United States Direct Investment in France." *Business History Review* 48, no. 3 (Autumn 1974): 382–413.

King, Greg. *A Season of Splendor: The Court of Mrs. Astor in Gilded Age New York*. Hoboken, NJ: John Wiley, 2009.

Kjellberg, Anne, and Susan North. *Style and Splendour: The Wardrobe of Queen Maud of Norway*. London: Victoria & Albert Museum, 2005.

Kremer, Roberta S., ed. *Broken Threads: The Destruction of the Jewish Fashion Industry in Germany and Austria*. Oxford: Berg, 2007.

Kurkdjian, Sophie. "The Cultural Value of Parisian Couture." In *Paris: Capital of Fashion*, edited by Valerie Steele (140–163). London: Bloomsbury Visual Arts, 2019.

Laing, Diana Whitehill. *Mistress of Herself*. Barre, MA: Barre Publishers, 1965.

Lasc, Anca I. *Interior Decorating in Nineteenth-Century France: The Visual Culture of a New Profession*. Manchester, UK: Manchester University Press, 2018.

Lasc, Anca I., Georgina Downey, and Mark Taylor, eds. *Designing the French Interior: The Modern Home and Mass Media*. London: Bloomsbury, 2015.

Laster, Margaret R., and Chelsea Bruner, eds. *New York: Art and Cultural Capital of the Gilded Age*. New York: Routledge, 2019.Leach, William. *Land of Desire: Merchants, Power, and the Rise of a New American Culture*. New York: Pantheon Books, 1993.

Legrand, Charles. *Rapport général sur l'Exposition internationale de Bruxelles 1897*. Brussels, 1898.

Lehmann, Ulrich. *Fashion and Materialism*. Edinburgh: University of Edinburgh Press, 2019.

Lehr, Elizabeth Drexel. *King Lehr and the Gilded Age: With Extracts from the Locked Diary of Harry Lehr*. Bedford, MA: Applewood Books [1935], 2005.

Léonard. *The Souvenirs of Léonard, Hairdresser to Queen Marie-Antoinette*. Translated by A. Teixeira de Mattos. London: privately printed, 1897.

Lettres et manuscrits autographes, documents historiques salle des ventes Rossini, 7 avril 2006, Paris: T. Bodin, 2006.

L'Exposition de Paris (1900). Paris: Librairie illustrée, Montgredien et cie, 1900.

Le Zotte, Jennifer. *From Goodwill to Grunge: A History of Secondhand Styles and Alternative Economies*. Chapel Hill: University of North Carolina Press, 2017.

Loschek, Ingrid. "Contributions of Jewish Fashion Designers in Berlin." In *Broken Threads: The Destruction of the Jewish Fashion Industry in Germany and Austria*, edited by Roberta S. Kremer (48–75). Oxford: Berg, 2007.

Lupkin, Paula, and Penny Sparke, eds. *Shaping the American Interior: Structures, Contexts and Practices*. New York: Routledge, 2018.

Maass, John. *The Glorious Enterprise: The Centennial Exhibition of 1876 and H. J. Schwarzmann, Architect-in-Chief*. Watkins Glen, NY: Institute for the Study of Universal History through Arts and Artifacts, 1973.

MacColl, Gail, and Carol Wallace. *To Marry an English Lord*. New York: Workman, 1989.

Mackenzie. "Mrs. Langtry's Paris Dresses." *Frank Leslie's Weekly*, March 8, 1890, 106.

Magidson, Phyllis. "A Fashionable Equation: Maison Worth and the Clothes of the Gilded Age." In *Gilded New York: Design, Fashion, and Society*, edited by Donald Albrecht and Jeannine Falino (107–130). New York: Monacelli Press, 2013.

Majer, Michele, ed. *Staging Fashion, 1880–1920: Jane Hading, Lily Elsie, Billie Burke*. New York: Bard Graduate Center, 2012.

Marcus, Sharon. *The Drama of Celebrity*. Princeton, NJ: Princeton University Press, 2019.

Marketti, Sara B., and Jean L. Parsons. "American Fashions for American Women: Early Twentieth Century Efforts to Develop an American Fashion Identity." *Dress: The Journal of the Costume Society of America* 34, no. 1 (2007): 79–95.

Martin, Frederick Townsend. *Things I Remember*. London: E. Nash, 1913.

Martin, Morag. *Selling Beauty: Cosmetics, Commerce, and French Society, 1750–1830*. Baltimore, MD: Johns Hopkins University Press, 2009.

Martin, E. S. "This Busy World." *Harper's Weekly*, February 20, 1897, 175.

Martin, Sadie E. *The Life and Professional Career of Emma Abbott*. Minneapolis, MN: L. Kimball, 1891.

Martinot, A. *Bulletin des nominations, informations, lois nouvelles et décrets*. Paris: Neuilly, July 7, 1900.

Martinot, A. *Bulletin des nominations, informations, lois nouvelles et décrets*. Paris: Neuilly, January 4, 1901.

Mayer, Frederic. "Frederick [*sic*] Mayer's Letter on the Paris Exposition." *Butte Weekly Miner*, April 19, 1900, 11.

McAllister, Ward. *Society as I Have Found It*. New York: Cassell, 1890.

McKellar, Susie, and Penny Sparke, eds. *Interior Design and Identity*. Manchester, UK: Manchester University Press, 2004.

Mellins, Thomas. "Architecture in Gilded Age New York." In *Gilded New York: Design, Fahsion, and Society*, edited by Donald Albrecht and Jeannine Falino (131–160). New York: Monacelli Press.

Mémorial du commerce et de l'industrie: Répertoire universel, théorique et pratique, législatif et judiciaire de la science commerciale. Paris, 1860.

Merceron, Dean L. *Lanvin*. New York: Rizzoli, 2016.

Merlo, Elisabetta, and Francesca Polese. "Accessorizing, Italian Style: Creating a Market for Milan's Fashion Merchandise." In *Producing Fashion: Commerce, Culture, and Consumers*, edited by Regina Lee Blaszczyk (42–61). Philadelphia: University of Pennsylvania Press, 2008.

Metternich-Winneburg, Pauline Clementine Marie Walburga. *My Years in Paris*. London: Nash, 1922.

Meylan, Vincent. *The Secret Archives of Boucheron*. Woodbridge, Suffolk, UK: Antique Collectors Club, 2011.

Micklewright, Nancy. "London, Paris, Istanbul, and Cairo: Fashion and International Trade in the Nineteenth Century." *New Perspectives on Turkey*, no. 7 (Spring 1992): 125–136.

Miller, Michael B. *The Bon Marché: Bourgeois Culture and the Department Store, 1869–1920*. Princeton, NJ: Princeton University Press, 1981.

Miller, Paul F. "Alva Vanderbilt Belmont, Arbiter Elegantiarum, and Her Gothic Salon at Newport, Rhode Island." *Journal of the History of Collections* 27, no. 3 (2015): 347–362.

Mitchell, Rebecca N., ed. *Fashioning the Victorians: A Critical Sourcebook*. London: Bloomsbury Academic, 2018.

Montgomery, Maureen E. *Displaying Women: Spectacles of Leisure in Edith Wharton's New York*. New York: Routledge, 1998.

Montgomery, Maureen E. *"Gilded Prostitution": Status, Money and Transatlantic Marriages, 1870–1914*. London: Routledge, 1989.

Moore, Claire Jessup. *Sensible Etiquette of the Best Society, Customs, Manners, Morals, and Home Culture*. Philadelphia: Porter and Coates, 1878.

Muccigrosso, Robert. "New York Has a Ball: The Bradley Martin Extravaganza." *New York History* 75, no. 3 (July 1994): 297–320.

Murphy, Kevin D. "The François Premier Style in New York: The William K. and Alva Vanderbilt House." In *New York: Art and Cultural Capital of the Gilded Age*, edited by Margaret R. Laster and Chelsea Bruner (41–65). New York: Routledge, 2019.

Murphy, Sophia. *The Duchess of Devonshire's Ball*. London: Sidgwick & Jackson, 1984.

Musée de la mode et du costume and palais Galliéra. *Femmes fin de siècle, 1885–1895*. Paris: Éditions Paris-Musées, 1990.

Myzelev, Alla, and John Potvin, eds. *Fashion, Interior Design, and the Contours of Modern Identity*. Surrey, UK: Ashgate, 2010.

Nicolson, Nigel. *Mary Curzon*. New York: Harper & Row, 1977.

North, Susan. "John Redfern and Sons, 1847 to 1892." *Costume* 42, no. 1 (2008): 145–168.

Nystrom, Paul H. *Economics of Fashion*. New York: Ronald Press, 1928.

Oberly, Michelle. "The Fabric Scrapbooks of Hannah Ditzler Alspaugh." In *With Grace & Favour: Victorian & Edwardian Fashion in America*, edited by Otto Charles Thieme (4–13). Cincinnati, OH: Cincinnati Art Museum, 1993.

O'Connor, Harvey. *The Astors*. New York: A. A. Knopf, 1941.

Official Catalogue of the New-York Exhibition of the Industry of All Nations. New York: G. P. Putnam, 1853.

Official Directory of the World's Columbian Exposition, The. Chicago: W. B. Conkey, 1893.

Ormond, Richard, and Elaine Kilmurray, eds., *John Singer Sargent: Complete Paintings*. New Haven, CT: Yale University Press, 1998.

Ossoli, Margaret Fuller. *At Home and Abroad*. Edited by Arthur B. Fuller. Boston: Crosby, Nichols, 1856.

Palais du costume: Le Costume de la femme à travers les âges. Project Félix. Exposition universelle de Paris 1900. Paris: Lemercier, 1900.

Palmer, Alexandra. "New Directions: Fashion History Studies and Research in North America and England." *Fashion Theory* 1, no. 3 (August 1997): 297–312.

Paris and Environs with Routes from London to Paris: Handbook for Travellers. Paris: K. Baedeker, 1891 and 1910 editions.

Paris and Its Environs, with Routes from London to Paris, Paris to the Rhine and Switzerland: Handbook for Travellers. Leipsic: K. Baedeker, 1874.

Parisiana. "The Glass of Fashion." *The Nineteen Hundred* 2, no. 2 (February 1896): 11.

Paris in London: 1902, Earl's Court: Official Guide and Catalogue. London: Gale & Polden, 1902.

Parisis. "Le Costume au theatre." *Le Figaro*, September 27, 1886, 1.

Parkins, Ilya, and Elizabeth M. Sheehan, eds. *Cultures of Femininity in Modern Fashion*. Hanover: University of New Hampshire Press, 2012.

Parmal, Pamela A. "La Mode: Paris and the Development of the French Fashion Industry." In *Fashion Show: Paris Style*, edited by Pamela A. Parmal and Didier Grumbach (13–25). Boston: MFA Publications, 2006.

Parsons, Jean L. "No Longer a 'Frowsy Drudge': Women's Wardrobe Management: 1880–1930." *Clothing and Textiles Research Journal* 20, no. 1 (January 2002): 33–44.

Payen-Appenzeller, Pascal, Brice Payen, and Patrick Mazery. *Dictionnaire historique, architectural et culturel des Champs-Élysées*. Paris: Ledico éditions, 2013.

Peacock, Virginia Tatnall. *Famous American Belles of the Nineteenth Century*. Philadelphia: J. P. Lippincott, 1901.

Perkko, Mariliina Perkko, ed. *Aspects of Costume: The Nineteenth Century. Selected Papers*. Alfabox, Finland: ICOM International Costume Committee, 1990.

Perrot, Philippe. *Fashioning the Bourgeoisie: A History of Clothing in the Nineteenth Century*. Translated by Richard Bienvenu. Princeton, NJ: Princeton University Press, 1994.

Phelps, H. F. "Are We on the Brink of a Social Revolution?" *Woman's Voice*, March 20, 1897, n.p.

Pons, Bruno. *French Period Rooms, 1650–1800: Rebuilt in England, France, and the Americas*. Translated by Ann Sautier-Greening. Dijon, France: Éditions Faton, 1995.

Porter, Carol S. *Meeting Louis at the Fair: The Projects and Photographs of Louis Clemens Spiering, World's Fair Architect.* St. Louis, MO: Virginia Publishing, 2004.

Potvin, John, ed. *The Places and Spaces of Fashion, 1800–2007.* New York: Routledge, 2009.

Potvin, John. "The Velvet Masquerade: Fashion, Interior Design and the Furnished Body." In *Fashion, Interior Design, and the Contours of Modern Identity*, edited by Alla Myzelev and John Potvin (1–18). Surrey, UK: Ashgate, 2010.

Pouillard, Véronique. "Design Piracy in the Fashion Industries of Paris and New York in the Interwar Years." *Business History Review* 85 (Summer 2011): 319–344.

Pouillard, Véronique. "Managing Fashion Creativity: The History of the Chambre Syndicale de la Couture Parisienne during the Interwar Period." *Economic History Research* 12 (2016): 76–89.

Pouillard, Véronique. "The Milton Case (1955–1962): Defending the Intellectual Property Rights of Haute Couture in the United States." *Journal of Design History* 30, no. 4 (November 2017): 356–370.

Pouillard, Véronique. "A Woman in International Entrepreneurship: The Case of Jeanne Paquin." In *Entreprenørskap i næringsliv og politikk: Festsskrift till Even Lange*, edited by Knut Sogner, Einar Lie, and Håvard Brede Aven (189–210). Oslo: Novus Forlag, 2016.

Pouillard, Véronique, and Waleria Dorogova, "Couture Ltd: French Fashion's Debut in London's West End." *Business History* (February 2020): 1–23.

Pouillard, Véronique, and Tereza Kuldova. "Interrogating Intellectual Property Rights in Post-War Fashion and Design." *Journal of Design History* 30, no. 4 (November 2017): 343–355.

Poujol, Henry. "Women's Hair." *St. Louis Globe-Democrat*, June 5, 1881, 18.

Poussineau, Félix (Émile Martin). *La Maternité chez ouvrière.* Paris: La Mutualité maternelle, 1910.

Reform Club: Officers and Committees, Members, Constitution, By-Laws, Rules. New York, 1896.

Reitano, Joanne. *The Tariff Question in the Gilded Age: The Great Debate of 1888.* University Park: Pennsylvania State University, 1994.

Remus, Emily. *A Shoppers' Paradise: How the Ladies of Chicago Claimed Power and Pleasure in the New Downtown.* Cambridge, MA: Harvard University Press, 2019.

Report of the Committee on Awards of the World's Columbian Commission. Washington, DC: Government Printing Office, 1901.

Report of the Industrial Commission on the Relations and Conditions of Capital and Labor Employed in Manufactures and General Business. Washington, DC: Government Printing Office, 1901.

Résultats statistiques dénombrement de 1896 pour la ville de Paris. Paris: G. Masson, 1899.

Reynolds, Anna. "John Singer Sargent Painting Fashion." *Metropolitan Museum Journal* 54 (2019): 106–124.

Ribeiro, Aileen. *Clothing Art: The Visual Culture of Fashion, 1600–1914.* New Haven, CT: Yale University Press, 2016.

Riello, Giorgio. *A Foot in the Past: Consumers, Producers and Footwear in the Long Eighteenth Century*. New York: Oxford University Press, 2006.

Rifelj, Carol de Dobay. *Coiffures: Hair in Nineteenth-Century French Literature and Culture*. Newark: University of Delaware Press, 2010.

Roberts, Mary Louise. *Disruptive Acts: The New Woman in Fin-de-Siècle France*. Chicago: University of Chicago Press, 2002.

Robertson, Charles L. *The International Herald Tribune: The First Hundred Years*. New York: Columbia University Press, 1987.

Rocamora, Agnès. *Fashioning the City: Paris, Fashion and the Media*. London: I. B. Tauris, 2009.

Rocamora, Agnès. "Pierre Bourdieu: The Field of Fashion." In *Thinking through Fashion: A Guide to Key Theorists*, edited by Agnès Rocamora and Anneke Smelik (233–250). London: I. B. Tauris, 2016.

Ross, Ishbel. *Silhouette in Diamonds: The Life of Mrs. Potter Palmer*. New York: Arno Press, 1975.

Ruane, Christine. "Spreading the Word: The Development of the Russian Fashion Press." In *Producing Fashion: Commerce, Culture, and Consumers*, edited by Regina Lee Blaszczyk (21–41). Philadelphia: University of Pennsylvania Press, 2008.

Saillard, Olivier, Valerie Steele, and Claude Arnaud. *La Mode retrouvée: Les Robes trésors de la comtesse Greffulhe*. Paris: Palais Galliera, 2015.

Sanders, Joel. "The Future of Cross-Disciplinary Practice." In *Shaping the American Interior: Structures, Contexts and Practices*, edited by Paula Lupkin and Penny Sparke (195–204). New York: Routledge, 2018.

Salvador, Baroness Alethea. "Paris Winter Fashions." *Washington Post*, October 23, 1887, 7.

Schramm, Christian. "Architecture of the German Department Store." Translated by John Gort. In *Broken Threads: The Destruction of the Jewish Fashion Industry in Germany and Austria*, edited by Roberta S. Kremer (28–47). Oxford: Berg.

Schwartz, Vanessa R. *Modern France: A Very Short Introduction*. Oxford: Oxford University Press, 2011.

Seger, Donna. "Puritan Princess." *Streets of Salem* (blog), February 21, 2017, streetsofsalem.com /tag/mary-endicott/.

Sherrow, Victoria. *Encyclopedia of Hair: A Cultural History*. Westport, CT: Greenwood Press, 2006.

Sheumaker, Helen. *Love Entwined: The Curious History of Hairwork in America*. Philadelphia: University of Pennsylvania Press, 2007.

Shilliam, Nicola. "The Sartorial Autobiography: Bostonians' Private Writings about Fashionable Dress, 1760s–1860s." *Textile and Text* 13, no. 3 (1991): 4–22.

Simon, Marie. *Fashion in Art: The Second Empire and Impressionism*. London: Zwemmer, 1995.

Smith, Kate. "Sensing Design and Workmanship: The Haptic Skills of Shoppers in Eighteenth-Century London." *Journal of Design History* 25, no. 1 (March 2012): 1–10.

Smith, Michael Stephen. *The Emergence of Modern Business Enterprise in France, 1800–1930*. Cambridge, MA: Harvard University Press, 2006.

Sparke, Penny. "The Domestic Interior and the Construction of Self: The New York Homes of Elsie de Wolfe." In *Interior Design and Identity*, edited by Susie McKellar and Penny Sparke (72–91). Manchester, UK: Manchester University Press, 2004).

Sparke, Penny. "Elsie de Wolfe: A Professional Interior Decorator." In *Shaping the American Interior: Structures, Contexts and Practices*, edited by Paula Lupkin and Penny Sparke (47–58). New York: Routledge, 2018.

Sparke, Penny. "Interior Decoration and Haute Couture: Links between the Developments of the Two Professions in France and the USA in the Late Nineteenth and Early Twentieth Centuries: A Historiographical Analysis." *Journal of Design History* 21, no. 1 (Spring 2008): 101–107.

Stamper, Anita A. *Clothing through American History. The Civil War through the Gilded Age, 1861–1899*. Santa Barbara, CA: Greenwood, 2011.

Star, Ella. "The Gould-Castellane Wedding." *Frank Leslie's Weekly*, March 14,1895, 170–172.

Steele, Valerie. *Paris Fashion: A Cultural History*. New York: Bloomsbury USA, 2017.

Steele, Valerie, ed. *The Berg Companion to Fashion*. Oxford: Bloomsbury Academic, 2010.

Steele, Valerie. "Paris, Capital of Fashion." In *Paris: Capital of Fashion*, edited by Valerie Steele (11–15) London: Bloomsbury Visual Arts, 2019.

Stern, Robert A. M., Thomas Mellins, and David Fishman. *New York 1880: Architecture and Urbanism in the Gilded Age*. New York: Monacelli Press, 1999.

Stewart, Mary Lynn. "Copying and Copyrighting Haute Couture: Democratizing Fashion, 1900–1930s." *French Historical Studies* 28, no. 1 (Winter 2005): 103–130.

Strahan, Edward (Earl Shinn). *Mr. Vanderbilt's House and Collection*. Boston: George Barrie, 1883–1884.

Strasdin, Kate. *Inside the Royal Wardrobe: A Dress History of Queen Alexandra*. London: Bloomsbury Academic, 2017.

Stuart, Amanda Mackenzie. *Consuelo and Alva Vanderbilt: The Story of a Daughter and a Mother in the Gilded Age*. New York: Harper Perennial, 2007.

Sumner, Charles. *Memoir and Letters of Charles Sumner*. Edited by Edward Lillie Pierce. 3 vols. London: Sampson Low, Marston, Searle, and Rivington, 1878.

Sutliffe, Albert. *The Americans in Paris*. Paris: Printed for the author and editor, 1887.

Tétart-Vittu, Françoise. "Who Creates Fashion?" In *Impressionism, Fashion, and Modernity*, edited by Gloria Groom (63–77). New Haven, CT: Yale University Press, 2012.

Tétart-Vittu, Françoise. "Key Dates in Fashion and Commerce, 1851–89." In *Impressionism, Fashion, and Modernity*, edited by Gloria Groom (270–279). New Haven, CT: Yale University Press, 2012.

Therese."Paris à la mode." *Town Topics*, April 13, 1893, 28.

Thieme, Otto Charles. "With Grace & Favour: Victorian & Edwardian Fashion in America." In *With Grace & Favour: Victorian & Edwardian Fashion in America*, edited by Otto Charles Thieme (26–86). Cincinnati, OH: Cincinnati Art Museum, 1993.

Thomas, Nicola J. "Embodying Imperial Spectacle: Dressing Lady Curzon, Vicereine of India 1899–1905." *Cultural Geographies* 14, no. 3 (July 2007): 369–400.

Tiersten, Lisa. *Marianne in the Market: Envisioning Consumer Society in Fin-de-Siècle France*. Berkeley, CA: University of California Press, 2002.

Titled Americans: A List of American Ladies Who Have Married Foreigners of Rank. New York: Street and Smith, 1890.

Tout-Paris: Annuaire de la société parisienne. Paris: A. La Fare, 1899.

Trigg, Andrew B. "Veblen, Bourdieu, and Conspicuous Consumption." *Journal of Economic Issues* 35, no. 1 (March 2001): 108–109.

Trow's New York City Directory. New York: J. F. Trow, 1878–1879.

Troy, Nancy J. *Couture Culture: A Study in Modern Art and Fashion*. Cambridge, MA: MIT Press, 2003.

Trubert-Tollu, Chantal, Françoise Tétart-Vittu, Jean-Marie Martin-Hattemberg, and Fabrice Olivieri. *The House of Worth 1858–1954: The Birth of Haute Couture*. London: Thames & Hudson, 2017.

Twain, Mark, and Charles Dudley Warner. *The Gilded Age: A Novel*. London: George Routledge and Sons, 1874.

Uzanne, Octave. *The Modern Parisienne*. New York: G. P. Putnam's Sons, 1912.

Van der Klein, Marian, Rebecca Jo Plant, Nichole Sanders, and Lori R. Weintrob, eds. *Maternalism Reconsidered: Motherhood, Welfare, and Social Policy in the Twentieth Century*. New York: Berghahn, 2015.

Veblen, Thorstein. "The Theory of the Leisure Class." In *The Collected Works of Thorstein Veblen*. Vol. 1. London: Routledge, 1994.

Viles-Wyman, Lilla Belle. Lilla Belle Viles-Wyman Journals, 1893. Schlesinger Library, Radcliffe College, Cambridge, MA.

Violette. *L'Art de la toilette chez la femme*. Paris: Libraire de la Société des gens de lettres, 1885.

Violette. "Paris Fashions." *Woman's World* 2, no. 5 (April 1889): 249.

Violette. "Paris Fashions." *Woman's World* 2, no. 6 (May 1889): 304–305.

Wagner, Richard, and Cosima Wagner. *Lettres à Judith Gautier*. Paris: Gallimard, 1964.

Walkley, Christina, and Vanda Foster. *Crinolines and Crimping Irons: Victorian Clothes: How They Were Cleaned and Cared For*. London: Owen, 1978.

Watts, George B. "The Teaching of French in the United States: A History." *French Review* (American Association of Teachers of French) 37, no. 1 (October 1963): 11–165.

Weber, Caroline. *Queen of Fashion*. New York: Henry Holt, 2006.

Weintrob, Lori R. "Mobilizing Mothers in the Nation's Service: Civic Culture in France's Familial Welfare State, 1890–1914." In *Maternalism Reconsidered: Motherhood, Welfare, and Social Policy in the*

Twentieth Century, edited by Marian van der Klein, Rebecca Jo Plant, Nichole Sanders, and Lori R. Weintrob (64–74). New York: Berghahn, 2015.

Welters, Linda, and Patricia A. Cunningham, eds. *Twentieth-Century American Fashion*. Oxford: Berg, 2008.

Wharton, Edith, and Ogden Codman Jr. *The Decoration of Houses*. London: B. T. Batsford, 1898.

Wild, Benjamin Linley. *Carnival to Catwalk: Global Reflections on Fancy Dress Costume*. London: Bloomsbury Visual Arts, 2020.

Willard, Emma. *Journal and Letters from France and Great-Britain*. Troy, NY: N. Tuttle, 1833.

Willard, Frances. Frances Willard Journals, February 24, 1869. Frances Willard Historical Association, Evanston, IL.

Williams, Elizabeth Otis. *Sojourning, Shopping and Studying in Paris: A Handbook Particularly for Women*. Chicago: A. C. McClurg and Co., 1907.

Woodward, Sophie. *Why Women Wear What They Wear*. Oxford: Berg, 2007.

Worth, Jean-Philippe. *A Century of Fashion*. Boston: Little Brown, 1928.

Young, John H. *Our Deportment, or, The Manners, Conduct and Dress of the Most Refined Society*. Detroit: F. B. Dickerson, 1882.

Zalc, Claire. "Trading on Origins: Signs and Windows of Foreign Shopkeepers in Interwar Paris." *History Workshop Journal* 70 (Autumn 2010): 133–151.

Zalewski, Leanne. "Alexandre Cabanel's Portraits of the American 'Aristocracy' of the Early Gilded Age." *Nineteenth-Century Art Worldwide* 4, no. 1 (Spring 2005), http://www.19thc-artworldwide.org/spring05/300--alexandre-cabanels-portraits-of-the-american-aristocracy-of-the-early-gilded-age.

Zalewski, Leanne. "Art for the Public: William Henry Vanderbilt's Cultural Legacy." *Nineteenth-Century Art Worldwide* 11, no. 2 (Summer 2012), http://www.19thc-artworldwide.org/summer12/leanne-zalewski-william-henry-vanderbilts-cultural-legacy.

Zdatny, Steve. *Fashion, Work, and Politics in Modern France*. London: Palgrave Macmillan, 2006.

Zdatny, Steve, ed. *Hairstyles and Fashion: A Hairdresser's History of Paris, 1910–1920*. Oxford: Oxford International, 1999.

INDEX